At Hard Labor

American University Studies

Series IX
History
Vol. 137

PETER LANG
New York • San Francisco • Bern • Baltimore
Frankfurt am Main • Berlin • Wien • Paris

Elinor Myers McGinn

At Hard Labor

Inmate Labor at the Colorado State Penitentiary, 1871–1940

PETER LANG
New York • San Francisco • Bern • Baltimore
Frankfurt am Main • Berlin • Wien • Paris

Library of Congress Cataloging-in-Publication Data

McGinn, Elinor Myers.
 At hard labor: inmate labor at the Colorado State Penitentiary,
1871–1940 / Elinor Myers McGinn.
   p.   cm. — (American university studies. Series IX, History; vol.
137)
 Includes bibliographical references.
   1. Convict labor—Colorado—History.   2. Prison industries—
Colorado—History.   3. Colorado State Penitentiary—History.
4. Prisons—Colorado—History.   I. Title.   II. Series.
 HV8929.C62M37   1993   365'.65—dc20   92-34581
 ISBN 0-8204-2097-2   CIP
 ISSN 0740-0462

Die Deutsche Bibliothek-CIP-Einheitsaufnahme

McGinn, Elinor Myers:
At hard labor: inmate labor at the Colorado State penitentiary, 1871–1940 /
Elinor Myers McGinn. - New York; Berlin; Bern; Frankfurt/M.; Paris; Wien:
Lang, 1993
 (American university studies : Ser. 9, History ; Vol. 137)
 ISBN 0-8204-2097-2
NE: American university studies / 09

The paper in this book meets the guidelines for permanence and durability of
the Committee on Production Guidelines for Book Longevity of the
Council on Library Resources.

Printed in the United States of America.

TABLE OF CONTENTS

ACKNOWLEDGMENTS

Interest in this research began during my residence in Cañon City, Colorado's foremost prison town - home to eight state prisons and planning for more.

Many people have aided in bringing to fruition the first comprehensive study of Colorado's early prison and inmate labor. My first appreciation goes to my friends in Cañon City who aided and encouraged the endeavor: Cara Fisher who has overseen the local history archives since their establishment in 1981, Superintendent Mark McGoff of the Women's Correctional Facility who has a mutual interest in the humanities and has critiqued my manuscript, and Donnie Smith who aided me with her word processing skills.

The next group to whom I am indebted includes the University of Colorado History Department. More specifically, I am grateful to Social Historian Ralph Mann and Western Historian Patti Limerick. Encouraging me with critiques and friendship were my colleagues - Joan Coffey, Ruth Helm, Anna Marie Pois and Leanne Sander.

The grant from the Colorado Endowment for the Humanities has made it possible to publish this early history of our incarcerated society. I also appreciate the personnel at the Colorado State Archives. Thanks to Shirley Jorgensen for her comments along the way.

Last, but not least, I wish to dedicate my work to my children - John, Judy, Janet and Jim and their most supportive father, John, whose interest in local history emanates from his pioneer forebears who were in Southern Colorado before the prison closed its doors on the first inmate.

INTRODUCTION

Fremont Welcomes Prison Expansion.
Prisons Become Plums in Job Creation Drive.
Colorado the Fastest Growing Prison in Nation.
Prison Overcrowded.
More Money Needed for Expansion of Prison.
Twenty-four Cities Submit Bids for New Prison.

For years, similar newspaper headlines have called attention not only to prison problems but also to the economic boost given to an area where a new prison is located. Indeed, the dominant theme in Colorado prison history has been the demand for more cells and new prisons because of overcrowding. Along with reluctant but "bite the bullet" legislative plans for new construction came the inevitable competition among cities to acquire that "plum" of economic opportunity.

In the mid 1980's, twenty-four Colorado cities submitted bids for the prize - another prison - to the state legislative prison committee. Since 1871, Cañon City had almost monopolized the prison industry, so once again it entered the race to add to the six prisons already within its environs and thus further stabilize its economy. Neither the lawmakers nor the citizenry considered any approach to its burgeoning prison population other than continual expansion of incarceration facilities. In the final analysis, a political and economic decision placed the two new 1985 prisons in remote rural eastern Colorado towns (Ordway in the district of a member of the Joint Budget Committee and Limon in the district of the House Speaker).

Although the politicians bypassed Cañon City at that time, a group of community boosters were deriving profit from the circumstance of living in a "prison town." To finance an archive for the Fremont-Custer Historical Society, they wrote historical vignettes and hosted local sight-seeing drives and walks for tourists. By far the most popular were the prison stories and inspections of the burials of over 400 inmates in Cañon City's historic Greenwood Cemetery on a hill overlooking the Territorial Prison across the Arkansas River. The next step to nurture the economy was to convert the old women's prison - located outside the main wall - to a museum depicting a bygone era of convict experience. After all, until only recently when prison authorities banned visitors, tourists paid twenty-five cents for an "inside look" that had generated thousands of dollars for the library and chapel funds.

Many questions sparked my interest in prison history. Since most convicts arrive from the populous Denver metropolitan area, why do politicians build prisons in rural areas far from the inmates' families and from specialized medical care? Was this in the best interest of the inmates or the taxpayers? Has this always been the situation? If a community desires a prison, is there actual profit from it? Certainly profit does not stem from cheap labor because prisoners no longer work outside the prison nor sell products on the open market. Historically, was that the case? How can Colorado afford to continue paying the cost of building and maintenance for the fastest growing prison population in the nation while the nation itself possesses the dubious record of the third largest percentage of incarcerated population in the world? And the questions continued.

Provoking further questions was the scar on the side of the limestone formation delineating the western boundary of the old prison caused by years of convict quarry work. Long ago, society had initiated a system of "hard labor" as punishment, and in the nineteenth century, had embraced a penitentiary as the mode for administering that prescription. What was that system and how did Colorado conform to it? Could, or did, the prisoners ever support themselves while incarcerated? Where did the prisoners work in earlier times before "Prison Industries"? If they once built roads and made bricks to sell, why are they not so engaged presently? What were the legal parameters for convict labor? Finding answers evoked more questions.

Unlike most state prisons, little researched history of Colorado's penitentiary existed. Dissertations abounded on other state prisons, but most dealt with sociological issues. Seemingly, even social historians avoided this part of society. There are a few pamphlets and newspaper accounts relating to inmate escapes, riots and unusual convicts such as Colorado's cannibal, Alfred Packer. Other published material dealt with political investigations of wardens. To answer these questions, I have focused on the economic aspects of the first Colorado prison - the complex that establishes the western periphery of Cañon City and today is designated as the Territorial Correctional Facility to differentiate it from the other seven prisons on the eastern outskirts of the city.

The time frame of this study, 1871-1940, was less than arbitrary because of certain phenomena. First, World War II brought vital changes to Colorado's population and its economy which affected the prison's population. A coincidental reason to conclude the study on the eve of World War II was that the inmates at that time razed the original cellhouse, the only one of the entire complex which they had not built themselves. But a third and most important consideration for this time period was that most of the wardens' biennium reports to the governor are unavailable after that time, and the minutes of the Board meetings had become nothing more than a listing of the bills paid. Obtaining good primary sources after 1940, therefore, would be difficult.

Germane to the understanding of the Colorado State Penitentiary would be an investigation of the philosophy of incarceration. Since I agree with the historical school which argues that institution building was a phase of western "conquest,"[1] my research had to delve into the traditions of incarceration which the pioneers had experienced before they migrated to Colorado.

Perhaps, more than any other institution, the prison is a captive of its social milieu just as the inmates are captive. Another perspective of research, therefore, required an analysis of that milieu. With a sparse and scattered population, why did early Coloradans request a prison when it could count only 27,909 scattered residents in a special 1867 census?[2] After all, had not the West developed instant justice with its miners' courts and people's courts? Were not county jails adequate? Colorado historian Duane Smith wrote that "everything in the West is done with a rush."[3] Was this the reason for the early establishment of a prison? Knowledge of the formative years of this institution, therefore, became crucial to this study.

Clearly, historiography indicated that nineteenth century Americans believed in prison building. Led by groups such as the Quakers, Americans based their theories and reforms on the framework of humanitarian incarceration and rehabilitation through religion and work. These became such appealing goals that their prospect, even with rare success, sustained the legitimacy of prisons. Among other historians, David Rothman, in both *Conscience and Convenience* and *The Discovery of the Asylum*, presented useful well-founded explanations of the proclivity for incarceration in America. His eminent studies place institutionalism in the social context of the Jacksonian period, i.e., deviants were victims of social disorder, and incarceration would rehabituate the criminal and promote the stability of society. Prisons and other asylums, he argued, served as places of unity and regimentation. While the pendulum swings between extremes of opinion, Rothman concluded that society has continued incarceration even when it is failing.

Explaining that labor and incarceration went hand-in-hand, Georg Rusche and Otto Kirchheimer in *Punishment and Social Structure* argued that changing economic and social structures altered ways of thinking about punishment as they related to convict labor throughout time, i.e., sometimes, as in the ancient world, the attitude had been to preserve the lives of criminals when they were needed for labor. When demand for labor diminished during the Middle Ages, society invoked fines, penance (the origin of the name of the penitentiary) and physical punishment. But with a new need for cheap labor after the rise of capitalism and mercantilism, society once again exploited criminals for galley labor and with penal servitude in workhouses. When religious and humanitarian leaders planned prisons for the rehabilitation of society's miscreants, Rusche claimed that industrialism led to prison factories and a renewed exploitation of labor.

Several other ideas relating to the reasons for imprisonment add to the historiography. Joan Smith and William Fried posited that incarceration is political in the sense that it is the end product of decisions to treat some and not other social harms as deserving of penal sanction regardless of the actual extent of social damage; therefore, all inmates are political prisoners.[4] To be sure, some prohibition and abortion offenders fit this category. Another idea from the theorist, Michel Foucault, *Discipline and Punish: The Birth of the Prison*, is that prison is society's way of mastering unreason - misfits must conform to middle class rules. Whether prison served social, economic, political or intellectual ends, it became America's heritage for punishment and Colorado's as well.

But the burden of analysis in this study is to place Colorado's prison history in a national context and study its management of inmate labor. In presenting a state prison history from its inception, Harry Elmer Barnes' comprehensive *Evolution of Penology in Pennsylvania, a Study in American Social History* provides a standard form. He traced the history of Pennsylvania's prisons in the context of interaction with the western world and with contemporary social and intellectual ideas, and he analyzed the innovations which emerged in that state's institutions as well. This study is similar in that it attempts to trace the heritage of a much newer western institution following established incarceration philosophy. An important finding will be the extent to which Coloradans followed precedent or innovated in response to their own environment and circumstances.

The primary sources of Colorado's prison history include the reports of the Board of Penitentiary Commissioners, the wardens, the Board of Charities and Corrections as well as the General Assembly statutes, the reports of various legislative and gubernatorial investigative committees, the reports of the Colorado and United States Bureaus of Labor Statistics, the state highway reports, the proceedings of prison societies and wardens' associations, the *Congressional Record* and the Territorial Records. To discern the prison's relation to the public and community, the newspapers of Cañon City, Denver and Pueblo provide a contemporary approach.

Much material admittedly is distorted or biased because the reports often try to impress, to accuse or to blame. Rothman, and many other historians, explain that wardens exaggerated their reports because the lawmakers looked only at the numbers of working inmates and the money saved or received from inmate labor. Of course, that situation described Colorado's posture. Sifting and weighing, nevertheless, are the historian's work from which a perception of the past evolves. Hopefully, this study will not only remove some rust of history but will illustrate that when past efforts of punishment prove ineffectual, when incarceration becomes so expensive that other ends of government are sacrificed or when prison building is viewed only as an opportunity to boost a town's economy, it is time for the public and lawmakers to seek new solutions and cast off the yoke of the past.

The organization of this study is both topical and chronological. The first chapter presents the historical ideas of incarceration and inmate labor which had developed by 1868 when Colorado Territory won its request for a prison. By then, the concept of making a prison pay had emerged along with objections to competitive inmate labor. The second chapter reconstructs the social milieu in which the Centennial State's prison emerged and the politics of locating it in southern Colorado - the same type of decision prevailing today. Complaints of violence and lawlessness went to Washington to support Colorado's prison bid, but, ironically, those did not end with the prison opening. Instead, crime and lynchings continued, some in front of the prison, and the number of convicts regularly increases along with a high rate of recidivism.

Trying to profit from inmate labor during the nineteenth century is the focus of the third chapter. While Colorado learned that it could not adopt the contract industrial labor system employed in eastern penitentiaries, it, nevertheless, utilized its natural resources to accommodate the demands of the mining and building industries and to return some cash earnings to the state treasury. To illustrate why

Colorado finally discontinued the sales of inmate products on the open market, the fourth chapter explains the opposition to inmate competition which led to an unlikely alliance between free labor and private enterprise.

The fifth chapter details Colorado's experience with road building and its honor camps which received national attention for their success in the early decades of the twentieth century. The sixth chapter discusses agriculture, building and new industries as ways to employ the inmates, maintain discipline, provide for prison expansion and add to prison support. The last chapter is an analysis of the research. Throughout, many exact quotations appear to recapture the original views and attitudes of early Coloradans.

NOTES - INTRODUCTION

[1]Robert G. Athearn, *Coloradans* (Albuquerque: University of New Mexico, 1976),p. 26. For a complete argument on this see Patricia N. Limerick, *Legacy of Conquest, The Unbroken Past of the American West* (New York: W.W. Norton, 1987).

[2]Schulze, Suzanne, comp., *A Century of the Colorado Census* (**Greeley**: Mitchener Library, 1976), Report for 1867, p. 4.

[3]Duane A. Smith, *The Birth of Colorado* (Norman, Okla.: University of Oklahoma, 1989), p. 36.

[4]Joan Smith and William Fried, *The Uses of the American Prison* (Lexington, Mass.: D.C. Heath, 1974), p. 140.

At Hard Labor

CHAPTER I

COLORADO'S PRISON HERITAGE

*No piece of history is true when set
apart to itself, divorced and isolated.
It is part of an intricately pieced whole,
and must needs be put in its place in the
netted scheme of events, to receive its
true color and estimation.*
Woodrow Wilson, 1904[1]

Historians argue that we can not understand any institution - social, political or economic - apart from the milieu in which it flourished; likewise we can not comprehend Colorado's prison without delving into its heritage or its *raison d'etre*. It is, therefore, particularly informative to reflect on the body of penal experience and philosophy available to those fewer than 30,000 new residents of the Colorado Territory when they began asking Congress for a prison in the 1860's. Although Colorado's early prospectors and entrepreneurs forged a unique institution dependent upon their particular resources, population characteristics and the contemporary economic and political forces of the territory, state, and nation, basically they relied on the system of incarceration and inmate labor which had moved westward with them. Defying Frederick Jackson Turner's thesis which implied that frontier conditions caused humanity to begin anew on the ladder of civilization, Colorado's pioneers modeled not only their structure but also their ideology and motivation for an institution on their heritage. In time, they molded this legacy to their resources and avoided some of the pitfalls which the earlier prisons experienced, but they seldom deviated from the established and evolving concepts of incarceration and inmate labor.

Incarceration as Punishment

From an historical perspective, wholesale imprisonment as a means of punishment is a relatively recent episode. Before the nineteenth century, offenders faced a variety of sanctions such as the lash, the pillory, the gallows and even exile. The convicted often served their victims rather than "time" in prison. That is not to say that incarceration did not exist, but it served different purposes. In colonial times, gaols or jails functioned chiefly as detention or custodial centers for debtors, prisoners of war, political prisoners or for pre-trial suspects.[2] Many early colonists preferred to punish by public humiliation for, in their way of thinking, crimes were violations of God's laws demanding severe retribution and expiation. Naturally depraved man, according to Calvinist thinking, left little optimism for reforming the criminal within a workhouse or prison.[3]

Apparently, one of the earliest responsible American leaders to prescribe imprisonment as a corrective treatment was the Quaker William Penn who had endured six months of horrors in London's Newgate prison for refusing to take an oath contrary to his religious beliefs. Having toured the Dutch workhouses, Proprietor Penn devised similar penal procedures for his Pennsylvania colony and substituted incarceration for the gallows, labor for bloody punishments, and workshops for the idleness and debauchery of the jailyard.[4] In 1682, the first assembly of Penn's colony enacted a legal code specifying hard labor in a "house of correction" for most criminals and retained the death penalty only for first-degree murder. Contrary to Calvinist practice, the Quakers emphasized personal reformation and prevention of crime as the sole end of punishment. But when Penn died in 1718, royal authority re-established a long list of capital crimes, and that aspect of his "noble experiment" ended. While a precedent for mild punishment carried out with incarceration and labor had emerged, renewed efforts of experimentation awaited the coming of American independence.

After the colonists had cast off the British yoke, they eagerly developed new laws and new institutions for implementing them. Indeed the birth of the American republic and the birth of an organized prison system seemed to occur almost simultaneously. As Blake McKelvey concurred in his appropriately entitled *History of American Prisons - a History of Good Intentions*, the penitentiary was one of the by-products of the intellectual and humanitarian movements of the eighteenth century that contributed so generously to the founding of the American nation.[5]

In David J. Rothman's seminal work, *The Discovery of the Asylum*, he traced criminal incarceration to the social optimism of European Enlightenment which found a receptive audience in the new American republic, steeped as it was in revolutionary activism.[6] Concepts recognizing humanity's basic dignity as well as its imperfections overpowered the "grim determinism" of Calvinist thought. In turn, Rothman credited the Italian theorist, Cesare Beccaria, for the enlightened thinking which encouraged Americans to reduce the capital crimes but adopt a definite and certain punishment. Beccaria's famous tract, *On Crimes and Punishment*, had pointed to the severity of laws often "a mere tool of the passions of some" and the self-defeating punishment which did not deter crime.[7] "Americans fully appreciated that the laws could be a tool of the passions of a handful of men," Rothman asserted. Prevailing public revulsion at cruel punishments had caused juries to let a prisoner go free rather than condemn him to the gallows for a petty theft. In a burst of enthusiasm, then, Americans located the roots of deviancy in the legal system, changed their laws to make punishment certain but humane, and prisons became the necessary adjuncts to reform and substitutes for capital and humiliating punishment. Whether or not Rothman's thesis is totally accurate, the fact remains that imprisonment came to be the organizational framework for post-Revolutionary punishment in America.

Early Prison Experiences - Pennsylvania and New York

Chiefly, it had been a repugnance of the gallows rather than any faith in the penitentiary that had spurred late eighteenth-century prison construction. Although few people had any clear idea what these structures should look like, they certainly should not resemble the jails which had become centers of promiscuous herding together all types of of prisoners. Jailers often locked up both sexes together at night, sold liquor to their charges and collected fees even from the acquitted while inmates begged alms at their cell windows. Consider the severe example of Simsburg, Connecticut, where an abandoned mine housed prisoners-of-war during the Revolution and until 1829 served as a state prison. There the officials attached wrongdoers at night by neck chains to an overhead beam — an action more akin to ancient Rome's sulphur pits than to a nineteenth-century American prison. In Maine, pits served as cells until 1828. Fortunately, those evils did not go unnoticed by a few reform-minded thinkers who suggested new prison systems applicable to goals far advanced of their times — actually goals still being sought today.

As the most important city in the world and the focal point for liberal European influences, Philadelphia set the appropriate stage for a new incarceration system. Once again, Penn's Quaker descendants inspired the experiment for the genesis of the American penitentiary model. The 1786 legislature reduced the number of capital crimes and substituted sentences of punishment at hard labor to reform the muiscreant. Accordingly, local sheriffs sent convict gangs to work on public roads and in the city streets. Insensitive officials chained the gangs to each other or attached heavy cannon balls to their legs while they worked under armed guards. To display their identity, the convicts wore pantaloons and exposed shaven bare heads. Quite naturally, the spectacle created by the interchange of obscenities between the convicts and the public fired indignation.[8]

Suggesting an alternative, Dr. Benjamin Rush, a concerned physician and signer of the Declaration of Independence, presented a paper entitled "An Inquiry into the Effect of Public Punishments upon Criminals and upon Society" at Benjamin Franklin's house in March, 1787. Punishment, he said, had three purposes: to reform the miscreant, to prevent further crimes, and to remove from society those who are "unfit to live in it." In tones of the enlightened writings, Rush stressed that public punishment caused men to lose their sense of shame and commit more crimes, and that the loss of liberty itself was "a punishment so severe, that death has often been preferred to it."[9] Concurrently, a group of Quakers reactivated the Society for Alleviating the Miseries of Public Prisons and reported on the evils in the Walnut Street Jail; their memorials propelled the legislature to adopt a new system of imprisonment affording private and solitary labor.[10] As a result, Pennsylvania appropriated funds in 1790 to renovate the old Walnut Street jail which became the model of prison reform for thirty years.

For a time, this renovated jail on Walnut Street worked quite well. Its widely imitated and innovative features included separation of classes of convicts, separate cells at night, private work within the prison to learn a trade, credits for work, debits for the inmates' care, rewards for cooperative behavior, exercise yards, gardens for work, solitary cells for the dangerous convicts, an unpaid board of managers, wardens, no corporal punishment, no weapons for guards, attention to the spiritual reform of the inmates and inmate silence except for certain periods. More than eighty years later, the first National Prison Association (the first "trade congress") endorsed most of those early principles of penology.[11]

With the basic principles of inmate labor and humane treatment in place, Walnut Street Jail experienced no escapes for four years while crime temporarily decreased in Philadelphia. Other states (New York, Virginia, Massachusetts, Vermont, Maryland, New Hamphshire) followed the lead of Pennsylvania and built similar prisons. Even visitors from the other side of the Atlantic proclaimed its excellence especially the workshops where men were busy at nail-manufacturing, marble-sawing and stone-cutting. In their own apartments, the women engaged in spinning cotton, carding wool, sewing, preparing flax and hemp, washing and mending.[12]

But like many idealistic prison experiments, Walnut Street Prison deteriorated in the face of overcrowding, eventual abandonment of the single cells by 1820, abuse of the pardoning power, party politics, relaxed discipline and inmate idleness. Through the vigilance of the *Philadelphia Society for Alleviating the Miseries of Public Prisons*, agitation arose for new state prisons based on the principle of solitary cells. In timely response, the legislature appropriated funds for two — one in Western Pennsylvania in 1818 and another one in Eastern Pennsylvania in 1821.[13]

Pennyslvania carefully designed its new fortress-like western edifice at Pittsburgh in a large semicircle with 190 small, dark individual cells. To understand why the Keystone State retained the extreme tendency for inmate separation and expended more than a million dollars in the necessary physical equipment to implement this system, consider the prevailing concept of "penitentiary." In the true sense of the word, the penitentiary should produce penitence, not retribution. There the wrongdoer could meditate in solitude with only the Bible.[14] But an intrusion on this ideal emerged when Pennsylvania's 1829 legislature, in coping with its mandate for "punishment at hard labor," ordered the introduction of individual labor into the prison. Almost immediately, it became apparent that the cells at the Pittsburgh institution were too small for work within. Other problems in the new edifice included the absence of exercise yards and the lack of soundproof walls. Again prisoners found ways to communicate, and an observer recorded that the "sole occupation of the convicts consisted in mutual corruption."[15] In reality, the Western Penitentiary, as originally built, fulfilled almost none of the hoped-for requirements until an expensive remodeling in 1833.

Pennsylvania's second prison differed markedly both in experience and architecture. Located in a cherry orchard in Eastern Pennsylvania, it opened in 1829 in Philadelphia's outskirts. Designed by one of the most noted prison architects, English-born John Haviland, the plan embraced the radiating wings or cell-blocks of the Ghent Prison and the central corridor and outside cells of the San Michele papal prison in Rome — certainly not entirely original.[16] Seven long wings of outside cells radiated from a central office and observation building. Arranged for strict solitary confinement, each cell was twelve by eight and ten feet high with an unroofed private exercise yard eighteen feet long. A key feature was that the prisoner never left the cell unless sick. In 1828, the Philadelphia Prison Society described the Eastern Penitentiary (called Cherry Hill) as ". . . the most extensive building in the United States," which suggested one of ". . . those magnificent and picturesque castles of the Middle Ages."[17] That hardly describes something totally American, but it illustrates the borrowing, interchange and adaptation of ideas. Henry Barnes praised Haviland's endeavors to eliminate the demoralizing congregate rooms utilized before 1820, but chastised the architect for ". . . fixing the gloomy castle architecture with its massive, dark and unhealthy construction upon the prison systems of the United States and Europe."[18] Cherry Hill's excessive expense engendered bitter criticism. When finished, it cost $2000 per prisoner. In comparison, a Connecticut prison under construction at the same time cost $258 per capita. Nevertheless the overpriced structure filled the architectural needs for Pennsylvania's prison discipline and excited the admiration and imitation of visitors from all parts of the United States and Europe.

Among the curious inspectors at Philadelphia's Walnut Street institution in its successful early years before the nineteenth century was Thomas Eddy, a New York business man and philanthropist. In 1796 he convinced New York to adopt the Philadelphia system and, for the first time, actually design a prison "to order" to accommodate New York's new prison discipline.[19] Inevitably, Eddy became the first warden of the Newgate Prison located on Greenwich Street near the Hudson's east bank about two miles from the New York City Hall. Although New York erected a large structure to house workshops, unfortunately, the planners omitted single cells because of the cost. With congregate housing in the Newgate prison, eight inmates shared a room with four mattresses. In addition to that unsavory situation, overcrowding and politics in the form of insecure administrations and graft doomed the experiment.[20]

Nevertheless, the New York prison contributed to the body of important prison traditions which became stock and trade in America. Throughout the entire nineteenth century nearly all American prisons observed the mealtime silence installed at Newgate. Other customs which Newgate pioneered included a resident warden, a chapel, hospital wards, a classification system to separate inmates according to their degree of criminality, family visitations and a distinct striped uniform. Probably most important to this study is Newgate's introduction of industries. When the state of New York entered the business of manufacturing for the "open market" (a system in later years called the "State Account System"), the first feeble protests of free labor and artisans in 1801 resulted in a New York law requiring the labeling of convict-made boots and shoes.[21] The struggle against inmate labor in New York set precedents for many other states and spread nationwide whenever any group perceived competition from convict labor.

Although Newgate's founder had prophesied that the structure would become a monument to wisdom, justice and humanity of its builders, ironically, in less than a generation it became the object of derision. Clearly the perennial overcrowding at Newgate led to mutual corruption and excessive pardoning. When the New York legislature chose to build another prison, they mandated solitary confinement and no industries. Many would-be criminal reformers at that time sought chiefly a spiritual conversion through solitary meditation and Bible reading.

For the short-lived experiment of solitary confinement, New York selected Auburn. Here the method of site selection became a familiar pattern in prison history when Auburn offered political and economic payments for the opportunity to host an institution. Its "frontier" residents switched parties from Federalist to Jeffersonian and extended free land with available water.[22] When completed, this imposing edifice became one of the most widely copied structures in the world. The five-tiers of cells measured seven feet long and three and one-half feet wide and were placed back to back. For four years they tried solitary idleness until the situation seemed to cause insanity and suicides. Consequently, prison leaders compromised with a creative plan consisting of daytime congregate but silent work and separate cells for sleeping. Soon, this became the model of so-called factory prisons where private companies contracted for inmate labor and returned some profit to the state. To control the discipline of congregating inmates and the forced factory work, however, Auburn's officials had to stray far from humanitarian ideals of reform and humane treatment. In reality and pragmatically, this "frontier" prison embraced a severe plan of discipline characterized by total silence and cruel physical punishment.[23]

Proudly for the new nation, a stream of foreigners visited, studied and critiqued America's eastern prisons. Endless debates arose on both sides of the Atlantic concerning the merits of the two pioneer systems — Auburn with its factory system versus Eastern Pennsylvania with its solitary workshops. Perhaps the greatest publicity accorded to American penology transpired when two distinguished French citizens — the publicist, Gustave Auguste de Beaumont and the Versailles judge, Alexis de Tocqueville — conducted and publicized their extensive studies.[24] Tocqueville accurately understood that, "In the United States, the execution of a fine prison seems as important as the pyramid of Cheops." In a long question and answer period with Auburn's stern warden, Elam Lynds, the French aristocrats learned that convict obedience stemmed from "bending them" with the whip and vigilance. The French commentators opined that the Auburn system was less costly to introduce and easily adapted to productive labor but less successfully administered by the generally mediocre type of officials in New York. If the choice were only between these two, Tocqueville and Beaumont agreed that they would choose Auburn.

They wrote that the Pennsylvania plan produced "more honest men" while the Auburn system developed "more obedient citizens." Tocqueville logically asked why the Pennsylvania prison needed a wall when the inmates never left their cells. After interviewing several inmates, he praised the avoidance of vice through inmate separation. In sum, they found both systems too severe, and noted, "While society in the United States gives the example of the most extended liberty, the prisons of the same country offer the spectacle of the most complete despotism."[25] Curiously,

French officialdom, apparently dissatisfied with their report, sent two more inspectors who preferred the Pennyslvania system. In time, England, Belgium, Sweden, Hungary, France, Prussia, Denmark, Norway and Holland adopted the main features of the Quaker-inspired systems.

While the supporters of separate work and confinement depended mainly upon foreign observers to champion their cause, Louis Dwight, founder of the Boston Prison Discipline Society, touted the superiority of the Auburn prison.[26] Thwarted by poor health in his ambition to become a minister, Dwight pursued another ministry of advocacy for prison reform. Inspired by both religious convictions and faith in institutional means for obtaining personal reforms, Dwight prepared twenty-nine excellent reports which propagandized Auburn and vigorously opposed the Pennyslvania system.[27] By 1833, Dwight's group "could point with satisfaction to the establishment of Auburn-style prisons in Maine, New Hampshire, Vermont, Massachusetts, Connecticut, New York, Virginia, Tennessee, District of Columbia, Louisiana, Missouri, Illinois, Ohio, and Upper Canada." Outside of Europe, only Pennsylvania, New Jersey, and Maryland adopted the expensive method of complete solitude.[28]

Although both systems of punishment were initially oriented around reformation, both soon revolved around economic concerns. From the first, Auburn played its trump card with lower construction cost for the smaller night cells and the daytime congregate workshops. Economy pleased all of history's taxpayers, and Auburn became a prison factory pattern. Establishing the concept that a prison could pay for itself crystallized another penological tradition — convict labor.

Development of Inmate Labor before 1860

Early historical records attest to labor as a means of punishment. When man disobeyed and was driven from the Garden of Eden for his sins, his punishment mandated that "in the sweat of thy face shalt thou eat bread."[29] From the beginning omniscient wisdom chose labor as the first means to restore fallen man. Centuries passed while the less fortunate, the condemned or the captured built Pharaoh's pyramids, Rome's roads and China's Great Wall or pulled oars on galleys, worked in salt mines or served an indenture of labor in America, but incarcerated labor chiefly began with the rise of the workhouses. Having studied Dutch workhouses, Penn advocated a similar system of labor for punishment which he hoped would lead to reformation of the criminal; a century later "a progressive system of contract labor was installed" in the renovated Walnut Street Jail in 1790.[30] For the first time in history, according to Barnes and Teeter, convicted felons worked at dignified productive tasks and earned wages.

Having established that labor could serve as punishment and reform, how did the new American prison system adapt it? Without a doubt, the issue of inmate labor soon related to more than teaching a trade, inculcating habits of discipline or rehabilitating the convict; it concerned economics — how to pay for the structures and the maintenance of the inmates, or even profit. Prison administrators who managed the labor quickly opened the door for favoritism, fraud and politics in the attempt to please the legislators and the public.

Overall, five different systems categorized the ways in which inmate labor operated in the nineteenth and twentieth centuries. Various procedures attempting to solve the difficult prison labor problem entered the arena according to the contemporary social, political and economic needs. The categories were the *contract*, the *lease*, the *public account*, the *state-use* and the *public works and ways*.

The most prevalent system was the *contract* procedure which involved the letting-out or selling of prison labor to an outside contractor who usually furnished the raw materials and machinery and then supervised the work. Guarding was usually the prison's only responsibility. For the prison, the chief advantage was that the capital outlay came from the private contractor, not the state. Generally, the contract guaranteed constant employment of the convicts, the best remunerative results and the avoidance of business risk on the part of the state. But the contractors who did not gain the cheap labor of the inmates could not compete with prison contractors who also received free utility power and work space from the prison. For the free worker, cheap labor lowered his wages. Other side effects of the contract system included exploitation of the inmate, graft, corruption and political manipulation.

In order to avoid the cost and maintenance of prisons, some states relinquished all supervision of felons to a *lease* agent who employed them in such outdoor labor as quarrying, agriculture, mining, bridge and road construction, in turpentine camps or on sugar cane plantations. Often, the *lease* form of labor approached peonage if not slavery, and the death and injury rates of prisoners were high. After the Civil War, the most notorious abuses of this system and its chain gangs appeared in the South. Not until 1936 did the last state abolish the lease system.[31] Historically and realistically, the thousands of indentured servants transported to the colonies by England foreshadowed the lease system in that the leaseholder often exploited and elongated their terms of labor.[32]

Another system, the *public* or *state account* system, allowed the prison to control its own production and sale of goods on the open market. As technology advanced, the prison faced an expensive outlay of state expenditures for materials and equipment. Thus, not only was this expense unpopular with taxpayers, but, like the other systems, it also stirred controversy *vis a vis* direct competition with free labor. Generally by 1936, protests from free labor, unions and manufacturers led to the more acceptable plan of *state-use* whereby production occurring under total prison auspices was sold only to state and local institutions.

When the average layman discussed convict labor, he recommended the system of *public works and ways* wherein the inmates built and repaired public roads and buildings. Citizens recognized the advantages when prisoners constructed public facilities such as roads, ditches and parks; they saw the inmates learning some skills and fulfilling their sentences to "hard work"; they saw the miscreants returning some value to the society which they had offended. On the other hand, this employment ended because of private competition for jobs and the difficulty of guarding the inmates away from the institution. Later, technology's advance complicated the inmate's contribution. Overall, lack of vision, inefficient administrators and politics hindered the public works system.

Specifically, how and why did the growing prisons develop various systems of inmate labor? The answer stemmed from the philosophy of the Boston Prison Discipline Society whose dictum that the prisoner should defray, by the fruits of his labor, his own expenses, and that became the general consensus. But then the consideration turns to the paradox of executing that dictum — the urgency of inmates for profitable work versus the inability of private enterprise to compete with low prison prices versus the demand for cheap raw materials for industry to stay in business versus resistance by taxpayers to incarceration costs. Those are the conflicts which shaped convict labor.

The battle between those opposing needs began at the beginning of the nineteenth century in New York's Newgate Prison which had been so carefully designed for inside labor. Challenged first by the shoemakers, New York's lawmakers required that convict-made boots and shoes be branded "State Prison." Pushed further by the free shoemakers, the legislature restricted the employment to only one-eighth of the convicts in shoe and boot production.[33] In an effort to overcome the continuing prison deficits of about $17,000 annually, New York added a statute in 1817 requiring that convicts work only on raw materials furnished and brought into the prison by an entrepreneur. In essence this was the *contract* system replacing the *public-account* method. At the same time, legislation allowed prisoners to work on public roads in nearby counties and the city as well as under the canal commissions.[34]

In the quest for more earnings, New York legalized the contract system in 1821 so that "the prisoners might be leased to outside firms or contractors at a daily rate per capita, specified in the contract." Furthermore in 1828, New York dictated that "... it shall be the duty of the agents to use their best efforts to defray all the expenses of the said prisons by the labor of the prisoners."[35] And so it came to pass that the criterion for judging a prison administration lay in its abiliity to be self-supporting. Some wardens or keepers actually turned a profit. Prison critic Jessica Mitford wrote: "The prisons for a while prospered and grew rich; that crime could be made to pay was proved by the Auburn prison, which from 1828 to 1833 netted over $25,000 in profits."[36]

The profits from inmate labor, according to labor historian, John R. Commons, increased from widening markets and the rise of the merchant-capitalist class who bought and sold in large quantities to distant markets.[37] Before market expansion, a large prison output lacked a market. Annually, the Philadelphia prison had been losing about $30,000 and the New York institution approximately $17,000 between 1797 and 1821.[38] During the 1820's, the newly-erected workrooms in the prison yards made it feasible for a single overseer to supervise and maintain silent discipline. The prison could also bid out inmates to contractors who competed for cheap labor. With those varied options, Auburn consummated almost a dozen contracts with such crafts as coopering, tailoring, shoemaking, weaving, toolmaking, and rifle-manufacturing.[39]

So what were the results of the prevalent contract system which became part of the heritage for Colorado's penitentiary? For all the interested parties — inmates, entrepreneurs, the prison administration, the taxpayers and free labor — the workings of the contract system generated mixed blessings if not harm.

For the inmate, a seemingly humane plan to reform him through industry turned him into a living machine. His task was to produce or he would receive behind prison walls the harsh physical punishment which had once been public. As New York's prison historian, W. D. Lewis, reflected: " . . . If he learned habits of industry and obedience, he secured such lessons at the cost of becoming a robot and a slave."[40] In most prisons under the contract system, financial considerations dominated, not rehabilitation. The exception was Pennsylvania where the solitary inmates never felt the sting of the contract system at its worst. Unlike Auburn's congregate system, Pennsylvania's penal leaders perceived the value of industry from their goal of convict reformation — to keep the mind occupied and away from "evil" thoughts and to prepare him for a self-supporting trade when his prison doors opened. Weaving, shoemaking, oakum-picking, cane-seating, chair-making and cigar-making rated among the skills nurtured in Pennsylvania throughout the nineteenth century.[41]

In considering the prison entrepreneur or contractor, there is no doubt that he often profited. Called in by the state of New York to investigate the prison conditions, lawyers and penologists, E.C. Wines and Theodore Dwight, labeled most of the contractors' prison transactions as "Napoleonic achievements in the science of public plunder."[42] One of many similar examples in Wines' investigative report illustrates how the state lost and the contractor gained by a system which allowed a contractor almost absolute monopoly. One Auburn official sold the inmate labor for forty cents a day, charged the contractor only $240 for $1500 worth of utility power, and assessed no rent for $2000 worth of yard and shop room. At the end of the second year, the contractor sold the balance of the contract to another party for a bonus of $30,000.[43] Yet far worse than the contract system was the *lease* system in which Wines and Dwight saw nothing but a money transaction while the leasee shorted the inmate on food, clothing, shelter and safety for the sake of profits. Kentucky and Illinois illustrate the blatant antebellum examples, but the harshest application of the lease system occurred in nearly all of the southern states after the Civil War.[44]

Inmate labor seemed a blessing to the taxpayers when the prisons paid their own way or placed profits into the general fund. Society banned the inmate, he was irreclaimable, and the public gave little thought to the fact that the inmate "was thrown to the mercy of men often more wicked than he."[45] As usual, the prevalent attitude emerged from economic motives and the idea that the disorderly classes were better "out of sight, out of mind."

Not so simple was the labor problem for the prison administrators (keepers, wardens, legislators) who answered to the political, social and economic demands of the public. If their prison work programs produced less profit than others, administrators felt the political pressure. Contact with the inmates from the factory supervisors caused breakdowns in the silent discipline while favoritism and smuggling of contraband created continual strife between the contractors and inmates. When contractors intervened, they hampered authority and discipline; the Wines report referred to this as "a power behind the throne greater than the throne."[46] Despite emphasis on the prison as a profitable factory, a fundamental principle of incarceration called for reformation of the wrongdoer, but contractors collided with prison goals. Wines and Dwight concluded from their investigation of eighteen state prisons that the contract labor system added to the turmoil of political appointments and produced a low grade of personnel and constant changes in the prison staff.[47]

Lastly and most vocally, free laborers perceived the potential of serious inmate labor competition. From the first protests of the shoemakers through the long (one and one-half centuries) drive against inmate labor, competition emerged as an extra impetus for the growth of solidarity and unions, according to Commons.[48] Assembling in New York City in 1823, the journeymen cabinetmakers (small independent producers) discussed the threat of convict labor. In that same year the mechanics (wage earners and forerunners of organized labor) petitioned the legislature with the following grievances:

> Your memorialists have seen the convicts imperfectly
> educated in various trades, hired out to individuals, in
> some instances at reduced compensation, and in others
> employed for the benefit of the state, and the products of
> their labour thrown into market and disposed of at a price
> very little above the cost of materials of which they were
> manufactured, to the ruin of . . . free mechanics.[49]

In an effort to reduce the competition of inmate labor, the mechanics proposed that the convicts work in a state marble quarry. Heeding their suggestion, New York selected the site for the new prison called Sing Sing "on account of its marble-beds, its accessibility by water and its salubrity."[50] Ironically, by 1831 the mechanics criticized the inmate operation because it sold marble to a museum for $500 which would have cost $7,000 on the open market. While the New York legislature hailed the self-support of the prisons in 1833, stone-cutters, coopers, and weavers condemned prison industry as a "tyrannical State monopoly." [51]

In a drive to establish a role for unions, the newly formed National Trades Union induced the state legislature in 1834 to appoint a commission to investigate prison labor; the union president, printer Ely Moore, won a place on the board. Unfortunately for Moore, the commission's report disappointed the union when it approved the prison labor system as a whole and recommended only minor changes. The mechanics continued to complain that contract labor lowered prices, established unfair competition, created an oversupply in certain industries such as shirts, shoes and furniture and crowded free labor out of those occupations. Furthermore, they claimed that prison administrators favored certain contractors who then taught trades to the inmates and developed apprentices out of the criminal classes.[52] So many petitions opposing prison labor appeared in the Assembly documents that prison historian Orlando Lewis discovered that "more petitions to the Legislature on the subject of contract labor had been presented than had ever before been presented on any subject."[53]

In the course of its 1835 convention, the National Trade Union condemned not only prison labor but also woman and child labor in the cotton factories as "destructive competition with the male labourer."[54] Certainly, this indicates that cheap labor of any kind was the crux of their complaint. Accelerated by some 200,000 signatures decrying the "war of the State upon the property and the rights of the honest and industrious mechanics," the New York legislature enacted a law in 1835 providing some alleviation for the free workers. Thereafter, the prison could teach no mechanical trade except to make goods usually imported, could issue no contracts for longer than five years and only after public bidding and could work only convicts who had learned the specific trade in domestic industries before incarceration.[55] However, despite several petitions against convicts, "of all people", making locks in prison, the legislature did not prohibit that trade.[56] During the next half decade, the prison authorities and contractors found the "joker" in the law to be *any trade*. Instead of limiting the trade to those with the acquired skill, they easily circumvented the law by interpreting it to mean an inmate with "any trade at all" before imprisonment.[57]

Following a lull in the controversy from 1835 to 1840, protests resumed when investigators uncovered violations of the 1835 law. Indeed, contractors had evaded the law, for, while the contractors had not taught the novice the *entire* trade, they had taught partial skills. For instance, they divided barrel making into twelve different processes, and a different convict learned each process. Following threats by the mechanics to use their votes (representing one-fourth of the total electorate) against the legislature, a new investigating committee condemned the contract system as "benefitting the few by the plunder and deprivations of the many."[58] Spurred by agitation of the mechanics, the legislature in 1842 clarified that convicts should work in prison only at specific trades previously learned. Despite the mechanics' struggle, they had not abolished prison labor, but they had restricted it to the point where the prison administrators found it more difficult to be self-supporting. And for the free laborer, the problem remained in special areas of overproduction where competition forced his wages down and compelled him to develop strength through unions to influence legislation.[59] Thus, on the eve of Colorado's prison development, the problem of inmate labor had not been resolved. Attempts to solve this problem became central to the history of inmate labor in Colorado.

Traditions for Female Incarceration and Labor

Like men, women could become elgible for both incarceration and labor, but their fewer numbers have merited little historical attention. European writers such as Crawford, Tocqueville and Beaumont noted that France incarcerated "five times" as many females as did the United States because of the tendency of American courts not to prosecute women.[60] A partial explanation for that trend derives from American social values which elevated virtuous women to a pedestal while offering no hope for the "fallen" women.[61] Popular attitudes relegated reason to men but feeling to women; hence men could be led back to righteousness but not women. A clear example of this appeared in the New York Assembly proceedings: "Staff members at Sing Sing agreed that when a woman stooped to crime her degradation was greater than that of vicious male offenders and especially so if she had been led into delinquency by prostitution."[62]

Appropriately described as the "ordeal of the unredeemables" by W. D. Lewis, their incarceration existence relegated them to limbo by confining them to cramped and unsanitary spaces in men's prisons where they sewed, mended and washed for the male department. Words from a chaplain at Auburn quoted in the New York legislative session records attest to this situation: "To be a male convict in this prison would be quite tolerable; but to be a female convict . . . would be worse than death."[63] In some areas they worked in the fields under the contract or lease system. In reality, most of the wayward women spent their incarceration in unsanitary, less protective and more crowded jails.

As their numbers increased, New York determined to build the first separate women's facility. As an attitudinal example, the arguments appearing in the legislative sessions regarding that new prison illustrate much of the public's sentiment toward the "unredeemables." First the concern was that both Auburn and Sing Sing should build separate women's prisons so that " . . . no single city or village would be forced to bear the entire brunt of the moral iniquity which the discharged women would bring back into society after they were released."[64] By contrast, communities lobbied for men's prisons. In addition, the senate prison committee suggested that the females be housed near Troy where a company offered to contract for the services of female convicts for one dollar a week.

In the end, the prison inspectors decided that inmate labor could build a woman's prison on their grounds where the male officers could efficiently supervise them, and the "women could actually provide a service for the men's prison by making, mending, and washing inmate clothing."[65] After all, economy proved the decisive factor in the ultimate choice of Sing Sing where male inmates built what was called "an imposing marble structure, after the model of a Greek temple, with massive columns."[66] But this location soon proved defective because it lay in the men's path to the quarry allowing unrestrained communication between the sexes. Poor ventilation and overcrowding caused illness and deaths as well as a high infant mortality rate.[67] So the "ordeal of the unredeemables" continued, and the poorly designed "temple" became the site of riots followed by corporal punishment.

Very few states had women's separate facilities until the twentieth century, but Wines' study noted the trend after 1840 to engage more women keepers or matrons. Wines approved the hiring of matrons but with the reasoning that "they would require less pay." One reform-minded matron, Eliza Farnham, initiated

14

classes, provided reading materials and encouraged female prisoners to make handicrafts at Sing Sing. She also arranged a glass case where they could sell them to tourists. From time-to-time, the prison contracted women for such work as button making.

Although not extensive, the progress made after 1840 in the eastern prisons for separate women's facilities did not transfer to Colorado because of the very few women inmates (two to ten at one time before 1900). Colorado women did not have a separate prison until 1936, although the Board of Penitentiary Commissioners hired matrons for their separate quarters in the 1890's. And in the Victorian mode, of course, Colorado followed the routine of domestic service for women.

Incarceration and Labor on the Eve of Colorado's Territorial Prison

Generally, we can delineate several periods of American prison experience. The first, from 1787 to 1820, encompassed a time of trial and error, philanthropic reform, propagandizing, pamphleteering and frustration with good intentions often gone awry. According to Rothman, Americans, by 1820, became disillusioned with the deterrent approach. Fueled by anxiety, the Jacksonians then identified the root cause of crime to be the social environment instead of the misconceived criminal codes; they took a hint from the propounders of human perfectibility and determined to rehabilitate the criminal.[68]

From roughly 1820 to 1840, two separate rival systems of Pennsylvania and New York engaged in long rhetorical battles relative to their merits. During those eras, the former log cabin jails and cave cells evolved into Auburn-like institutions with 500 to 1000 cells housing workshop manufactories that sent varying amounts of profit to state general funds. As newer technology replaced handicraft production, the struggling free workers and artisans mounted objections to the competition from inmate labor. Especially in New York, political intervention mandated some restrictions on inmate labor. Many discipline traditions permeated the whole prison society. For infractions, corporal punishment such as flogging (at that time flogging was upheld in the navy, the school and home), or ducking, the shower bath, the strait jacket and the gag prevailed. Reducing meals to bread and water often changed a hostile attitude. Most inmates wore distinctive garb, lived in small cells without running water or toilets and endured poor ventilation and extremes of temperature. In the few Pennsylvania-type prisons, inmates had water, showers, heat and milder punishment but no human contact. Only when the public paid a fee to "gaze upon the ... human menagerie" did they see what went on behind the walls of ... the forbidding and often monumental prison architecture."[69] The prisons isolated the inmates either psychologically or physically and viewed religion as an agency of reform through Bible reading, chapels and chaplains.[70]

During this second period of prison history, humanitarian zeal for reform flourished not only in many phases of life such as anti-slavery societies and temperance advocacy, but also in asylum reform, a vigorous anti-gallows movement and abolition of imprisonment for debt.[71] But, along with the newer optimism for human progress came the knowledge that the institutions were not fulfilling their promises. Moreover, media disclosures of prison cruelties and visitations by humanitarians like Dorothea Dix placed in motion the third wave of prison concern in the 1840's.

The third period lasted through the Civil War and featured more rhetoric than changes. State prison societies such as the New York Prison Association and various government-appointed investigating committees served to keep some attention focused on the prison systems. The media stirred up interest which led to an attack on some of the old correctional ideas. Still, New York prison historian, W.D. Lewis, argued that no new penal policies could emerge while political circumstances determined leaders and policies. Penologist Z.R. Brockway saw more continuity than change and that pecuniary advantages to the state continually dominated the policies.[72] According to Rothman, confinement and the building of long-lasting prison edifices seemed to be the only option which emerged from the Jacksonian era's design to "house the wicked or luckless." Rothman's summation continues to express the ambivalence and frustration of the incarceration process, "We applaud promoters of change but are horrified at the results of their efforts."[73]

One year before Colorado opened the doors of its territorial penitentiary, Ohio's Governor Rutherford B. Hayes welcomed 130 delegates from twenty-four states, Canada and South America to the first meeting of the American Prison Association. Those post-Civil War reformers articulated their philosophy in their 1870 Declaration of Principles. Though the Declaration centered on the Jacksonian theme that crime was a moral disease requiring moral regeneration, it departed from the Jacksonian regimen of fixed sentences, locked step, silence and isolation to a program for bettering the inmate by cultivating self-esteem and responsibility.[74] In weighing another aspect of prison administration, the Association perceived the problems of contract labor and declared that: "While industrial labor in prisons...is of the highest importance and utility, we regard the contract system of prison labor as prejudicial alike to discipline, finance, and reformation."[75] And when New York's Prison Association director, E.C. Wines, completed his comprehensive post-Civil War study, he concluded that the many lofty goals of the 1870 Prison Congress were incompatible with the reigning system of convict labor.

> Contractors have no interest, *per se*, in the reformation of prisoners. Their interest as contractors and the interest of the prison as a reformatory institution not only do not run in parallel lines, but they are repellant and antagonistic. Let any changes be suggested with a view to giving more time to the mental, moral and industrial improvement of the prisoners; or that the convicts be taught a complete trade instead of such snatches thereof as are now commonly imparted. [and] . . . the contrac-

tors would not consent to such an abridgement of the convict's labor.[76]

Despite the warnings of over seven decades of trial and error experiences, the eastern systems provided the traditional menu from which western prison builders selected their format. Colorado politically located its territorial penitentiary at a quarry site and instituted lockstep, mealtime silence, striped suits, corporal punishment, overcrowding, political patronage and remunerative inmate employment. Just as the eastern prisons experienced their trauma of trial and error, so did Colorado while it struggled with the boom and bust mining economy. Obvious deviations from the eastern traditions included hasty construction with less concern for architectural design, less emphasis on reform and penitence, more mixing of inmates, less rigid discipline and fewer industrial employment opportunities.[77] Although the newly transported westerners patterned the traditional eastern systems, they avoided some incarceration failures — if not by superior leadership, through the adaptations to a new environment.

NOTES - CHAPTER I

[1]*Selected Literary and Political Papers and Addresses of Woodrow Wilson*, 3v. (New York: Grosset and Dunlap, 1921), v. 3, p. 217.

[2]Orlando F. Lewis, *The Development of American Prisons and Prison Customs, 1776-1845* (Albany: J.B.Lyon Co., 1922), p.9. This is the classic reference to which later prison historians referred.

[3]Michael Sherman and Gordon Hawkins, *Imprisonment in America, Choosing the Future*, (Chicago: University of Chicago, 1981), pp. 79-80.

[4]O. Lewis, *Development of American Prisons*, p. 10.

[5]Blake McKelvey, *American Prisons, A History of Good Intentions* (Montclair, New Jersey: Patterson Smith, 1977), p. 1.

[6]David J. Rothman, *The Discovery of the Asylum, Social Order and Disorder in the New Republic* (Boston: Little, Brown and Co., 1971), pp. 57-62. For a discussion of Enlightenment thinking see Marcello Maestro, *Cesare Beccaria and the Origins of Penal Reform*, (Philadelphia: Temple University Press, 1973). The leaders were Beccaria, Bentham, Montesquieu, Voltaire, and John Howard. Locke's social contract argued for the right of punishment by state, Montesquieu urged that punishments be established by law, Voltaire exposed cruel punishments, Beccaria wrote the most famous essay on crime and punishment which affected the western world in its rational and humane reform and John Howard worked for prison improvement throughout Europe.

[7]Ibid.,pp. 58-62. See also, Edwin H. Sutherland and Donald R. Cressey, *Criminology* (Santa Barbara: University of California, 1966), p. 310. In 1875 B.C. Hammurabi's code demanded an "eye for an eye." Torturous punishments prevailed and transgressors were transported. For example, in 1834, England transported 4053 and executed 480 criminals. England's penal colonies were North America and Australia, Portugal's were Brazil and Africa, and Siberia served as Russia's.

[8]McKelvey, *American Prisons*, p. 6.

[9]Joseph M. Hawes, ed., *Law and Order in American History* (New York: MacMillian Co., 1960), pp. 37-8. See Orlando Lewis for an appraisal of Rush.

[10]McKelvey, *American Prisons*, p. 8.

[11]Ibid., pp. 26.

[12]Harry Elmer Barnes, *The Evolution of Penology in Pennsylvania, a Study in Social History* (Montclair, New Jersey: Patterson Smith, 1968), p. 102 for a quotation of the praise written to Philadelphia by the English reformer, John Howard.

[13]Barnes, *Evolution*, p. 139-41.

[14]Edwin H. Sutherland and Donald R. Cressey, *Criminology*, p. 485. This was the ideology behind the medieval church laws also.

[15]Hawes, *Law and Order*, p. 43.

[16]O.Lewis, *Development of Prisons*, p. 125.

[17]Barnes, *Evolution*, pp. 142-3. This was quoted from *A Brief Sketch of the Eastern Penitentiary* by one of its wardens, Robert Vaux.

[18]Ibid., p. 146.

[19]O. Lewis, *Development of Prisons*, pp. 43-46.

[20]Ibid., pp. 48-55. There were fifty-four rooms holding eight each. The dimensions were twelve by eighteen feet.

[21]Ibid.

[22]W. David Lewis, *From Newgate to Dannemora, The Rise of the Penitentiary in New York, 1796-1848* (Ithaca,New York: Cornell University, 1965), pp. 54, 56-57, 67. He based his history of New York prisons on much of Orlando Lewis's careful research which means that the material is often duplicated.

[23]Ibid., pp. 85-95.

[24]Barnes, *Evolution*, p. 173. Tocqueville gathered material for his famous Democracy in America during his prison inspection trip.

[25]Ibid., pp. 174-6. Barnes quoted from G. de Beaumont and A. de Tocqueville, *On the Penitentiary System in the United States and Its Application in France*, tr. by Francis Lieber, Philadelphia, 1833, pp. 19-47. According to Barnes, this work is one of the chief sources for early American penology. See also George Wilson Pierson, *Tocqueville in America* (Gloucester, Mass.: Peter Smith, 1969), pp. 128,

234, 301. Although Tocqueville and Beaumont won a prize for their book, the inspector-general criticized them for not visiting enough prisons.

[26]See in Barnes, *Evolution*, footnote, pp. 177-8 for a listing of sources of articles both supporting and criticizing both systems.

[27]W. D. Lewis, *From Newgate*, pp. 109-10

[28]Barnes, *Evolution*, p. 177. In Europe the separate system was almost universal by 1862.

[29]*Genesis* 4:19.

[30]Harry Elmer and Negley K. Teeters, *New Horizons in Criminology* (Englewood Cliffs, N. J.:Prentice-Hall, 1960), p.524. They quoted a foreign visit to the Philadephia prison in 1796 in footnote which tells that the prisoners made one dollar a day and seemed contented and that the convicts kept accounts of their expenses, clothing, board, and his fine to deduct from his earnings.

[31]Barnes and Teeter, *New Horizons*, pp. 527-32.

[32]James D. Butler, "British Convicts Shipped to American Colonies," *American Historical Review*, II (October, 1896) : 12-23. Butler explained that most women who came had been "public women" and were always "good looking." There were nine female prisoners in Virginia before 1636.

[33]Orlando Lewis, *Development*, p.105.

[34]Ibid., p. 106.

[35]Ibid. This is not to say that New York was first or the only one to use contracts, but Auburn was the widely known model.

[36]Jessica Mitford, *Kind and Unusual Punishment, The Prison Business* (New York: Alfred A. Knopf, 1973), p.195. See also O. Lewis who gives same figures and reasons why contracts failed, p.131.

[37]John R. Commons, et.al., *History of Labour in the United States* I (New York: The Macmillan Co., 1918), pp.344-5. The growth of railroads, roads, and canals aided this movement. The distant markets even included the West Indies which had a market for molasses hogsheads- see O.Lewis, p.183.

[38]Commons, *Labour*, p. 346. Quoted from the Board of Managers of the Prison Discipline Society, Second Annual Report, 1827,p. 121.

[39]W.D. Lewis, *From Dannemora*, p. 181.

[40]Ibid., p. 181.

[41]Barnes and Teeter, *New Horizons*, p. 224-5.

[42]E.C.Wines and Theodore WA. Dwight, *Report on the Prisons and Reformatories of the United States and Canada made to the Legislature of New York, January, 1867* (Albany: Van Benthuysen and Sons' Steam Printing House, 1867),p.261. This is the 570 page report from field notes which came from 70 volumes of material collected by the authors. This work plus Wines continued efforts to bring the prison societies together for prison reform made an impact on world-wide penology as great as John Howard had a century earlier, according to McKelvey, p. 68.

[43]Ibid., p 258. This was for 1860, but in the 1830's, rates were fifteen cents a day according to O. Lewis, p. 131.

[44]See George Cable, *Silent South*, rare books collection,Univ. of Colo. library for a description of the evils of the southern lease system.

[45]Wines, *Report*, p. 262.

[46]Ibid., p. 262.

[47]Ibid., p. 265.

[48]See Commons, *Labour in United States. vol.I*, for a detailed discussion of trade union growth. He wrote that actually the economic conditions caused the workers to look for a scapegoat in the prison labor because prison production was minor. However, most historians recognize that it was special areas where the competition lay.

[49]Ibid., p. 155. This was quoted from *New York National Advocate*, Feb.7, 1823.

[50]W.D.Lewis, *From Newgate*, p. 52, quoted from the New York statutes.

[51]Orlando Lewis, *Development of Prisons*, p. 133. An example was that combs which cost $58. to make in Albany cost only $15.50 to make in prison. The coopers

complained that nearly as many coopers were employed at the Sing Sing prison as in New York City. p. 138.

[52]Ibid., p. 332.

[53]Ibid., p. 137.

[54]Commons, *Labour*, p. 432.

[55]Orlando Lewis, *Development of Prisons*, pp. 138-9. The silk industry never proved popular or feasible. A few mulberry trees were planted, but the contractors refused to give up their lucrative contracts.

[56]Commons, *Labour*, p. 432. An interesting analogy occurred in Cañon City when a local banker could not open a safe and called upon an inmate to ply his trade.

[57]Orlando Lewis, *Development of Prisons*, pp. 137-8.., pp. 143-6.

[58]Ibid., pp. 143-6.

[59]Commons, *Labour*, p. 411. For an interesting description of the Geneva Shoemakers' union case wherein the union was declared illegal, see Commons, pp.410-414.

[60]W.D. Lewis, *From Newgate*, pp. 157-8.

[61]Ibid., p. 159.

[62]Ibid., pp. 171-73. See Glen A. Gildemeister, "Prison Labor and Convict Competition with Free Workers, 1848-1898." Ph.D. dissertation, (Northern Illinois University, 1977), p. 74 for interesting comparisons. For example, of 16,774 convicts sent to Sing Sing between 1849 and 1867, 26% were female. Of 42,621 sent to New York City jails, 35.9% were female. This affirms that women were more likely to commit misdemeanors than felonies.

[63]W. D. Lewis, *From Newgate*, pp. 168-173.

[64]Ibid., p. 175.

[65]Ibid.

[66]Ibid.

[67]Wines, *Report*, p. 71. Again we should note that the evidence that administration is more important than laws because there is a letter confirming the difference in women's and men's jails when the administration was conducted by nuns. The nuns housed the women humanely.

[68]Rothman, *The Discovery of the Asylum*, pp. 107-8.

[69]Orlando Lewis, *Development of Prisons*, p. 329.

[70]Robert L. Norris, "Prisons, Reformers, Penitentials, Publicists in France, England, and the United States" (Ph.D. dissertation, American University, 1985), p. 178.

[71]Merle Curti, *The Growth of American Thought*, Second Edition (New York: Harper and Brothers, 1951), pp. 369-72.
See Norris, p. 72, for an explanation of Beccaria, Montesquieu, Hobbes. Also in Norris's study of sixty reformers, he concluded that reform rhetoric was motivated by humanitarian, religious and scientific impulses -the desire to apply principles of science to a social problem. p. 27. See David Davis, "Movement to Abolish Capital Punishment, 1787-1861," *American Historical Review* LXIII (October 1957):29-46. See Rusche and Kircheimer for the classic Marxist interpretation that forms of punishment correspond to a given stage of economic development., pp. 6-7 and for the relationship of the lower classes to the industrial revolution, p. 73.

[72]Corinne Bacon, compiled, *Prison Reform* (New York: H.W. Wilson and Co., 1917), p. 19.

[73]Rothman, *Asylum*, p. 294.

[74]McKelvey, *Good Intentions*, p. 88-89. This is a good description ot the lofty feelings of the signers of the National Prison Association. Also quoted in Mitford, *Kind and Unusual Punishment*, p. 195.

[75]Wines, *Report*, p. 265.

[76]McKelvey, *American Prisons*, pp. 223-9. There is an overview chapter on western prisons and their early experiences here.

CHAPTER II

THE EMERGENCE OF COLORADO'S TERRITORIAL PENITENTIARY

> *Making governments and building towns are*
> *the natural employments of the migratory*
> *Yankee. He takes to them as instinctively as*
> *a young duck to water. Congregate a*
> *hundred Americans anywhere beyond the*
> *settlements, and they immediately lay out a*
> *city, frame a state constitution and apply for*
> *admission into the Union, while twenty-five*
> *of them become candidates for the United*
> *State Senate.*
> Albert D. Richardson[1]

When coursing Highway 50 westward through Cañon City, Colorado, on the appropriately-named Royal Gorge Boulevard, one passes the walled Territorial Maximum Security Prison. Its historic name distinguishes it from seven other Colorado prisons abutting Highway 50 about three miles east of Cañon City. Today, the prisons in Fremont County compose one-half of the sixteen facilities under the Colorado Corrections System which hosts one of the fastest growing prison populations in the nation (from 1985-1991, federal figures reported Colorado as the fastest growing).[2] The foreboding walls on the west end of the prison city mark the eastern gateway to the spectacular Royal Gorge — the granite-walled canyon through which the Arkansas River drops 2500 feet when it passes from the mountains to the plains. But why and how did Colorado's founders locate its first prison in this attractive valley, the former bed of a prehistoric lake almost ten miles in diameter and bordered on three sides by hills and mountains?

For that answer, we flashback to the days when impromptu governments accommodated Colorado's rapid population influx before it attained statehood in the Centennial year. To be sure, the milieu in which the territorial prison developed differed from that of the eastern prisons which Colorado's transplants took for a pattern. Although many eastern states had built somewhat monumental structures to house their lawbreakers and their industrial workshops, Colorado Territory, in 1871, opened a simple rectangular three-tiered brick cellhouse with no plans for workshops. While the eastern states experienced long periods of colonial and state government before constructing their central prison systems, Colorado dedicated a prison only fourteen years after the first Anglo-Americans found something sufficiently enticing for them to settle in the heart of the "great American desert." Although urgency, expediency and environmental ingredients propelled the formative years of Colorado, tradition and experience from the East guided the western pioneers.

Embryonic Colorado - The People are the Government

When the influx of gold seekers began in 1858, Colorado appeared on the map as part of four different territories (Nebraska, Kansas, Utah, New Mexico). Impatient for a local government, about thirty-five transplants introduced politics into their winter camps around present-day Denver only five months after arrival. On November 6, 1858, they elected Hiram J. Graham to carry their request for a separate territory to Washington. But Congress, in the midst of the territorial slavery debate, tabled the request.[3]

Disappointed but not daunted, the first newcomers pursued another option — statehood. They elected delegates to a convention and adopted a constitution to present to the electorate in September of 1859. To augment interest in a state constitution, the leaders stressed the further threat to law, order and property rights from the oncoming migration of fifty-niners. Those fears were fueled as much by the exaggerated press accounts.[4] In his newly-established newspaper, *Rocky Mountain News*, William Byers expressed a similar conviction:

> Government of some kind we must have, and the
> question narrows itself down to this point: Shall it be
> government of the knife and revolver, or shall we unite
> in forming here in our golden country . . . a new and
> independent state?[5]

While their early efforts for statehood seem presumptuous, some valid reasons existed. The western historian, Earl Pomeroy, in his study of territorial governments recognized the impatience of shifting populations who preferred almost immediate statehood to territorial status. In his words, "Citizens resented the territorial status not only because they were Westerners, but also because recently they had been Easterners."[6] Distanced from the accustomed orderly administrative procedures, they intended to initiate their own. Furthermore, many of them were the same people who had experienced the gold rush to California ten years earlier and had witnessed that area, within two years after the peace treaty with Mexico, become a full-fledged state without going through the territorial stage. Colorado territorial secretary and contemporary historian Frank Hall marveled at the "dashing boldness of these resolute pioneers" and noted that fewer than two thousand were represented; that before they had opened any great mines or any successful agriculture enterprises, those people took measures without authority of law to establish an "independent commonwealth."[7]

Even though events transpired rapidly in this new country where a spirit of self-preservation reigned, providing for orderly elections and constitutions certainly does not convey the stereotypical picture of rash conduct of bearded men in the wild and wooly west. By contrast, many newcomers were experienced officials eager to continue their leadership amd develop the customary institutions.

Despite the campaign for the "State of Jefferson," the general electorate in

September narrowly rejected the plan amidst dubious and varied counts of approximately three thousand ballots cast.[8] Obviously, some voters preferred territorial support from the federal treasury. But while a distracted Congress ignored their petition for separate territorial status, the leaders gambled on a third expedient route — a locally formed "territory." In a speedy three-day session, eighty-seven delegates adopted a constitution for the "Territory of Jefferson" which actually summarized the first document for the "State of Jefferson." A slate of officers appeared on the ballot along with the constitution question on October 24, 1859.[9] In the Proceedings of the Convention, the anxious delegates sent a strong appeal for voter approval. Exaggerating the need for law and order they complained that "Pending the action of Congress in our case, we have no protection for life or property but the code of Lynch Law."[10] With that threat, the voters approved the provisional Jefferson Territory, and for sixteen months the "spontaneous commonwealth," as historian Frederic Paxon called it, endured.

To promote law and order, the provisional government adopted a criminal code of 487 sections and a civil code of 645 sections. But in actual practice, the already functioning autonomous Miners' Districts and "claim clubs" continued to enforce most order-preserving activities. Those groups or clubs exemplified the best tradition of "the people are the government."[11] From necessity and tradition, the people of each mining camp, embryo town and agricultural settlement framed their own simple codes of civil and criminal law and chose officers to administer them. In turn, "Jefferson Territory" and later, Colorado Territory, following the example of California's 1851 legislature, accorded legality to the mining camp governments.

The local law of the miners also won recognition on the national level. Chief Justice Salmon P. Chase described it as "A special kind of law, a sort of common law of the miners, the offspring of a nation's irrepressible march, — lawless in some senses, yet clothed with dignity." The United States Senate received a report stating that, "The rules and regulations of the miners . . . form the basis of the present admirable system arising out of necessity."[12] Of those miners' camps, early Colorado historian Jerome Smiley asserted that law and order prevailed with as much stability as in New England — minus blue law intolerance.[13]

While the central idea of miners' claim law rested on "priority of possession," what was the usual manner of dispensing criminal punishment? One case fittingly reveals a practical method of justice innovated for sparse and new frontier areas. *People vs. William Carl* involved a frontiersman accused of stealing money, tried by a jury of twelve and convicted by a unanimous verdict. The sentencing required no physical facilities for rendering the verdict:

> That the prisoner is Guilty of the Theft . . . and the
> punishment [is] to be Twenty One lashes on the Bare
> Back and Shave the right side of his head and also the
> left side of his Whiskers and Moustache and to leave the
> Mountains in twenty four hours.[14]

At this early stage of settlement, incarceration was impractical so penalties varied according to circumstances. Gregory District's practical stipulation for petty larceny required that the guilty one pay a fine or work on public roads.

Countering the miners' court was the peoples' court which sprang into existence in the agrarian communities to provide for law and order. Usually when a grave offense arose, the people hastily called a "town meeting," organized a "court," elected a sheriff, appointed a prominent citizen as judge, selected a jury and dispensed instant justice. Of course, "justice" sometimes appeared even less formally when an enraged and wronged assemblage spontaneously demanded banishment, whipping, or hanging of the suspect.

While the struggle for territorial recognition continued in Washington, "Governor" Steele and other officers continued to discharge their duties despite some opposition. Although the citizens reelected him on October 22, 1860, obedience to this government had been voluntary. People had refused to pay taxes so Steele proclaimed that "all persons...should bear in mind that there will be no salaries . . . that the General Government will be memorialized to aid us in our adversity."[15] And federal recognition soon came.

Colorado Territory

Serious events in other parts of the nation allowed the deliberation of House Bill Number 366 designating territorial status for Pike's Peak country. After seven southern states seceded, interest in western territorial organization heightened. Soon debaters in the House and Senate settled on the name of Colorado delineating boundaries between the 25th and 32nd meridians and the 37th and 41st parallels. On February 28, 1861, lame duck President James Buchanan signed the Organic Act framing a legal entity for the pursuit of law and order institutions.[16]

Newly-elected President Abraham Lincoln appointed the first roster of officers for Colorado Territory, but only two of them resided in Colorado. Indeed, "carpetbagger" appointees became the pattern for the next fifteen years while Colorado's territorial days coincided with the Civil War and Reconstruction Period. Even though the locals had been in Colorado only a few years before the federal administrators, the "older" residents often expressed discontent with the appointees (carpetbaggers).

In his first official act, Governor William Gilpin from Missouri organized three judicial districts and assigned judges. In only four days, Chief Justice Benjamin Hall, a native of the prison town of Auburn, New York, and a member of Secretary William H. Seward's law practice, admitted twenty-seven attorneys to the Colorado bar.[17] Obviously the Territory suffered no shortage of legal advocates.

Pressure for a Prison

When Governor Gilpin addressed the first territorial legislature in September, 1861, he called attention to the need for a police system and laws for the prevention and punishment of crime. Although the main part of his address concerned the importance of raising a militia, his comments on the 1861 special census (required to determine the number of delegates to the territorial legislature) underscore his rationale for a prison. The United States marshal had reported 18,136 white males over twenty-one years of age, 2,822 under twenty-one, 4,484 females and eighty-nine Negroes totaling 25,331. Gilpin questioned the preponderance of males for having "no recorded precedent in any new society."[18] To him the male population implied increased disorder. In fact, Colorado's settlement began with a sparse and largely transient male population seeking precious metals — unlike the Midwest where pioneers were largely agrarian families.

The concern for order was exacerbated by the complication that one-third of the population openly supported the Confederacy. The possibility of defiant secessionists and more detentions under the new territorial court system with its enlarged staff of attorneys sent out calls for an adequate prison facility. When town and county governments emerged, they provided small jails, but those structures seemed unsafe for long-term convicts. Colorado historian Robert Athearn suggested another dimension to the perceived need for a prison structure when he argued that many saw a prison as "another instrument of control in a growing society that promised to become more complex as time passed."[19] After all, those transplants hailed from areas where imprisonment had functioned as social control.

When Gilpin's successor, John Evans, addressed the legislature, he specifically appealed for a penitentiary. He described the problem of securing prisoners and added, "I trust that an appeal to Congress for aid in the erection of a prison . . . would not be in vain."[20] Two years later, Governor Evans saw a new ray of hope for prison funds. To the Territorial Legislature, he reported that "The course pursued by the General Government towards other territories in making appropriations for the erection of Capitol and penitentiary buildings for them would inspire confidence in making an appeal for these objects for Colorado Territory." Further, he noted that a local prison would save the federal government the expense of taking the Rocky Mountain prisoners to the states.[21] That escape and transportion were expensive is indicated by the Governors' *Record Book* which contains pages of requisitions for the extradition of escaped felons, warrants for arrests amd rewards for their capture.[22]

While the governors sent appeals for help in acquiring physical structures to a Congress harried by a war, Colorado's first United States Marshal, Copeland C. Townsend, also found that his duties necessitated a structure for incarceration. Because of fears of subversion, he received varied orders from the governor to arrest and confiscate the supplies of suspected Confederate sympathizers along the front range.[23] Providing detention facilities became a necessity when the marshal arrested over forty men who were assembling a military unit at Fort Wise. The marshal explained his expedient renovation of a post office building at the corner of Denver's East and Larimer Streets for the first "federal prison" to the Secretary of Interior in October, 1861.

> This Territory, being without any structure in the form
> of a prison, . . . and the secession element here being

rampant and defiant, . . . we have had no alternative but
to fit up a prison or to surrender the government to the
rebels and criminals.

The correspondence between Chief Justice Benjamin F. Hall and Secretary of State
William Seward, revealed that Lincoln ordered the release of most transplanted
loyal Southerners.[24] Despite the temporary nature of Confederate sympathizers, the
marshal incarcerated other lawbreakers in his makeshift prison.

Over and above the turmoil of the Civil War years, other compelling and
perceived needs for a strong central penitentiary emerged. Some Coloradans
complained about the inadequacy of the physical structures; others desired better
protection for a suspect or convicted felon before his sentencing. Law enforcement
officers made long torturous trackdowns only to have "slippery desperadoes"
escape from a local jail, usually some flimsy "crackerbox." A typical example
concerned the escape of a Cañon City mule thief from a log cabin store doubling as
a jail just before he was to be hanged in 1861.[25]

The prevalence of mob action and lynchings also illustrated the urgency for the
safe keeping of a suspected criminal until and after he had his hour of justice.
Denver's first murderer, the "Hungarian," experienced the credo of most courts —
"give-him-a-trial-and-hang-him." A "jury" caught him at Uncle Dick Wooten's
saloon, and within forty-eight hours after his confession the convicted man dangled
from a rope on the banks of Cherry Creek.[26] Local groups of vigilantes, desiring
hasty "justice," occasionally seized a wrongdoer enroute to a jail or broke into a
calaboose to remove a suspect to the nearest tree or bridge for immediate suspension. The documentation of "Boulder's Only Hanging" of an alleged horse thief
details that a mob wrested the accused from the deputy sheriff, but finding no tree
tall enough for the hanging, they expediently strangled him.[27]

Another motivating component in the pressure for an early prison structure
emanated from the cry that lawlessness and violence reigned. Exaggerated
publicity of the type that came from the pen of early traveler and newspaperman
Horace Greeley helped to fuel those fears. Referring to Denver, Greeley reported
"more brawls, more pistol shots in this log city . . . than in any community of equal
numbers on earth."[28]

Undoubtedly the predominant male population exacerbated the problem of
lawlessness. Saloons, brothels, and gambling — all scenes conducive to violence
— attracted young men. Promise of easy money enticed not only the honest, hard-
working prospectors, but also the lawless outcasts, saloon keepers from the East,
smooth-tongued gamblers and gunmen seeking new pastures. In mining camps,
college graduates rubbed elbows with illiterates, and ministers and rogues worked
side by side at the sluice boxes. Mining historian Rodman Paul commented that
"Men with unstable or weak personalities who in quieter countries might have led
innocuous lives, here became wastrels and lawbreakers, and in so doing they found
themselves in congenial company."[29]

One of the most widely publicized incidents of violence involved the Espinosa brothers who randomly murdered about thirty-two Southern Colorado residents and marked some of the bodies with a crude "cross of death." A posse of miners killed one of the brothers near Cripple Creek and purportedly found a note claiming that the Espinosas planned to kill 500 "Americanos" to avenge their losses in the Mexican War. Whether this reign of terror stemmed from that motive is uncertain and irrelevant, but it is interesting to note that Colorado Territory offered a $2,500 reward for the killers, dead or alive. In order to qualify for the reward, Indian scout Tom Tobin took proof (two heads in a gunny sack) of his successful hunt to Ft.Garland, but spent the next thirty years trying to collect his reward from the inadequate treasury coffers of young Colorado.[30]

Obviously environments at certain times augment temptations for crime, and unusual conditions prevailed in the Rocky Mountain mining camps which maximized enticements for criminal behavior. With possessions so scarce, their protection meant life or death to their owners. At one time in 1861, Newsman Byers, who influenced the thinking of many Coloradans whether or not he exaggerated, wrote that horse and cattle thieves had "overrun" Colorado. To counteract that, he urged the organization of secret vigilante committees and tribunals.[31]

Rivalry over unclear mining claims and land suits over preemption furthered violence. "A speedy trial by lamplight" for three strangers who allegedly jumped claims in Hall Valley resulted in a speedy hanging in the 1860s.[32] The content of gold dust, often used in commerce, frequently incited arguments. Byers described a typical method of making bogus gold bricks; the schemer made only one corner of real gold for the assayer and the remaining brick of bogus gold, and a bank fell prey to the scam when it bought 20,000 bogus bricks in June of 1861. Dueling moved west also, but only one fatality is recorded.[33] Perhaps the scarcity of women in Colorado underlay some duels and murders. Desertions and divorce occurred more often on the unstable mining frontier than in the East. Clearly then, some environmental crime and violence persisted.

Inevitably, eastern Congressmen heard about western lawlessness from sources other than from the requests of Rocky Mountain delegates and soon agreed to provide territorial prisons. The Thirty-Ninth Congress on January 22, 1867, legislated "That the net proceeds of the internal revenue of the Territories of Nebraska, Washington, Colorado, Idaho, Montana, Arizona, Dakota" will for the three years, (1866, 1867, 1868) be set aside for the purpose of erecting, under the direction of the Secretary of the Interior, penitentiary buildings . . . in such places . . . as may be designated by the legislature thereof." The law required each of the territories to appropriate $40,000 for its prison except Washington which was allotted only $20,000.[34]

Selection of a Prison Site

Because the federal law authorized the Territorial legislative assembly to select the prison site, vote traders and lobbyists campaigned for the institutional trophy. And when one reads the arguments advanced for the prize — a penitentiary — it becomes obvious that the need to quell lawlessness had not been the main criterion. Players in the contest sought an institution for economic benefits, political rewards, "honor" and even "restitution" for a political slight. Tying the capital location argument to the penitentiary site provided the bedrock for the vote traders.

Acting Governor Frank Hall recommended a "central" location for the prison which triggered a debate in the newspapers and the legislative chambers.[35] Cañon City legislator Thomas Macon, an attorney who only recently arrived in Colorado, spearheaded his city's quest for the prison. Acting Governor Hall himself credited Macon for "some rather skillful trading on the capital and other questions of local importance" to win the prison for Cañon City.[36] Whereas the House and Council *Journals* reveal no details of the vote-trading, Macon himself admitted trading votes. As he explained, he and a small core of southern Colorado legislators supported Denver for the capital over Golden, then hosting the Territorial government. Eventually then, Cañon City earned the votes of a sufficient number of northern legislators to achieve its goal for the prison.

Before Cañon City's victory, however, other towns challenged the small town at the eastern entrance to the Arkansas River Canyon. House Bill #11 to locate the prison in Cañon City passed in the House on December 16, 1867, but awaited action in the Council. In a last minute attempt to influence the legislators, the *Rocky Mountain News* opined that Golden City should be chosen because "this mountain town stands sadly in need of such an institution, and [the legislature] having perpetrated a piece of vandalism in stealing from it the capital will now make restitution by giving the thing in honor."[37] Without a strong and independent base for economic growth, the hope for economic development spurred institutional bidding from many developing towns who quickly tried to amend the location bill in their favor when it reached the legislative floor. Representatives from Boulder City, Mt. Vernon, Black Hawk, Golden, Central City, Burlington, Hamilton, Denver, Idaho, Georgetown, Pueblo, and Colorado City all tried to replace Cañon City in the bill. With its drawing card of mining resources, Summit County's representative even offered to organize a joint-stock company for a mine to be worked by convicts. Nevertheless, all of those efforts failed, and Cañon City seemed to control sufficient votes to prevail in the House, but not without further maneuvering.

Jealousy mounted in Southern Colorado when Pueblo, Cañon City and Colorado City raised the level of invective through letters published in the newspapers. Thomas Macon's letter to the *Rocky Mountain News* explained that on the fourth day of the session, Southern Colorado delegates had met together and chosen Cañon City by a vote of eight to one. In addition, their group had endorsed Denver for the capital prize with the understanding that Cañon City would gain the prison, and, therefore, they regretted Pueblo's objection. To tarnish Pueblo's claim, Macon wrote that Pueblo could not build secure structures because it lacked building stone and lumber, but Cañon City had blue and white limestone, coal, fire clay and iron ore. In a postscript to the letter, Macon promised twenty-five acres at no cost to the

Territory. Adding substance to Macon's letter, five other Southern Colorado legislators signed.[38] Pueblo retorted indignantly that it was Cañon City's buildings that would perish in the wind and also protested its omission from the "secret" meeting where the capital location had been decided, and that, because of Cañon City's inaccessibility, the prison should go to Pueblo or Colorado City.[39] The rivalry had been intense.

In turn, Colorado City boasted of the best resources for building the prison — forests, coal fields, copper, zinc, alum, gypsum, good grazing, good farm land and water power. Generously, its leaders offered one-fourth section of land for the structure and argued that Cañon City had only "adobe soil".[40] In its decision-making, the legislature seemed unconcerned for a location where the availability of resources could provide jobs for prisoners although Colorado City boosters had specifically proffered that possibility. Most assuredly, all proponents of site offers considered the prison an economic asset.

Apparently Byers' compensatory endorsment of Golden for the prison site influenced the Council (the upper house of the General Assembly) when it amended the House bill to read "Golden" rather than Cañon City. However, after a conference committee meeting, the Council relented and accepted the House bill with Cañon City as the site on January 4, 1868.[41]

Complete victory for Cañon City arrived when Colorado's Seventh Session passed the authorizing act three days later. The act stipulated that "the penitentiary for the Territory of Colorado . . . be located . . . at Canyon City in the county of Fremont . . . not more than one-half mile from the business centre." The law also required a donated parcel of land of no fewer than twenty-five acres. Further it provided for the governor to appoint a commission of three who, within sixty days, were to select a site with capacity for irrigation and cultivation.[42] The latter stipulation suggests that the legislators finally became aware during the site selection debate of a need for some resource offering inmate self-support, but the original small parcel substantially limited that prospect.

As power brokers for the local site commission, Acting Governor Frank Hall appointed Samuel N. Hoyt of Lake County, James M. Wilson of Arapahoe County and Anson Rudd of Cañon City. All three later held positions with the prison — Hoyt as construction superintendent, Wilson as a penitentiary commissioner and Commissioner Rudd as warden. At first, Rudd offered twenty-five acres of his own land. Considering Rudd's property too close to town, the commissioners announced the choice of thirty acres donated by a pioneer mercantile store owner, Jonathan Draper.[43]

As time bore out, the site on the west side of Cañon City offered some advantages — proximity to irrigation canals and abundant resources such as limestone, plaster of Paris and sandstone. A mild and pleasant climate prevailed in an altitude of 5,343 feet, and the valley was protected from severe storms by the nearby mountains. The Arkansas River formed the natural boundary on the south, and a ditch providing a temporary water supply ran through the grounds. A series of limestone formations, known as "Hogbacks," provided the natural barrier on the west side of the land and contained valuable limestone deposits. For a time, the building stone found a market in expanding Cañon City, and the lime filled the need for the nearby smelters and ore processing. The natural soda springs adjoining the property became a focal point for Sunday gatherings of tourists and local citizens; for years, while the prison band entertained outside the prison wall, the inmates sold popcorn and their handmade curios.

At first, the chosen site aroused some criticism because the *Rocky Mountain News* retorted in defense that Cañon City was not a "willow-swamp" but an excellent location, close to granite quarries, oil wells, and a natural thoroughfare to South Park and the Western Slope.[44] This is not to say that the land choice had no negative features. One-half mile from a town was too close for a growing community, and, in a few years, business growth reached the prison walls. Colorado's boosters exaggerated growth while seeking statehood and railroads but failed to envision the style of expansion which even a slow-growing community would have. When they perceived the need for a structure in which to confine their lawless, little did they foresee that the prison population soon would exceed the small area they set aside. The small acreage available for gardens proved inadequate. Significantly, Colorado in its formative years drew a pattern for its penitentiary that in later years caused trouble — the selection of a prison site based on insufficient foresight and influenced by political motivation. This proved costly to the government and the inmates during the long struggle to provide housing and work.

The Prison's Milieu - Fremont County and Cañon City

The environs of Colorado's home for miscreants strongly relate to its history. One of the seventeen original counties laid out by the provisional Jefferson Territory, Fremont County lies in the south central part of the state on the eastern boundary of the mineral belt. Today its almost rectangular shape approximately equals the size of Connecticut, but at the time of its selection as the prison locus, it encompassed what is today Custer County and part of Huerfano County. Its altitude varies from 12,000 feet to a low point of 5000 feet where the Arkansas River crosses its eastern boundary.[45]

Knowledge and geography of the region were hazy when Zebulon Pike spent his twenty-eighth birthday in December of 1806 on the northern side of the Arkansas River and built his camp (the first Anglo-American-built structure in Fremont County) near the same hogback where the prison stands today. Later, in 1819, a treaty with Spain clarified the international boundary as the Arkansas River; Major Stephen Long's expedition passed through during the next year. In 1821, the Arkansas River, within the Fremont County area, became the Mexican boundary. Texas, independent in 1836, also claimed jurisdiction of that area of present Colorado, but the United States conquest in 1848 settled that border dispute. On his third expedition in 1845, John C. Fremont, the county's namesake, traversed both sides (Mexican and United

States) of the Arkansas River but never attempted to pass through the forebidding narrow "Grand Canon" (Royal Gorge) of the Arkansas River.

Although the area had been a favorite post for hunters and trappers as well as winter headquarters for Indians, its first Anglo-American settlers included gold-seekers enroute to California but weary enough to stop in Colorado, discouraged prospectors who left the mountain diggings to try farming and mountain miners who wintered in the valley because of its mild climate. Early entrepreneurs envisioned the area which became Cañon City as the gateway to the mining camps of the mountains. In October of 1859, a party of six town builders from Pueblo built a cabin near the soda springs where Pike had rested fifty-three years earlier. They also laid out a road to the Tarryall diggings. But not much developed there until after the spring of 1860 when civil engineers, Buell and Boyd of Denver, surveyed the townsite and delineated an area of about 1280 acres.[46] Soon teamsters with heavily-laden freight wagons stopped to purchase supplies for the mining camps. To supply this market, sawmills, general stores, new buildings, saloons, and a newspaper sprouted. Farmers, hoping to sell their produce at inflated prices in the gold camps, settled and planted their seeds as soon as they could. The first issue of the *Cañon City Times* on September 8, 1860, reported a shingle mill and a steam saw mill, and, by November, the newspaper listed forty businesses.

Booster tactics appeared early in the Cañon City area. Offers of original town shares and evidence of nearby oil, coal, iron, gypsum, marble and limestone enticed settlers. The *Cañon City Times* reported that thirty new residences rose in a two-week period during October of 1860, that stage freights came from Kansas City to the new "El Dorado, the depot for southern mines" and that "thirty to forty wagons and many emigrants arrived on one weekend in June of 1861."[47] Hardly a year old, a voting district encompassing the Cañon City Claim Club area registered 609 males and 123 female settlers on the 1860 census.

Claim jumping incidents motivated thirty-five residents to create the Cañon City Claim Club which existed from March 13, 1860 to January 25, 1862 before county government took charge of all law and order functions.[48] The club issued claims for such purposes as townsite, farming, millsite, lumbering, ditch rights, burial grounds, stone quarry and "oil running." Those claim samples illuminate the diverse topography of the locality. The membership list included 264 men and one woman. A listing of their occupations portrayed a cross section of the kind of people who came to the Arkansas area and probably represented a cross section of other Colorado immigrants — merchants, lawyers, doctors, preachers, farmers, and ranchers, a newspaper editor, a blacksmith, a hotel proprietor, miners, hunters and saloon-keepers. The Claim Club's constitution provided for many facets of local civil government including a building code.[49] Two of those original Claim Club members, Anson Rudd and B.F. Allen, became territorial prison wardens.

But the great expectations for growth disappeared by late 1861 when nearly all men vacated the area to fight in the Civil War, and commerce lessened because miners preferred the trail through Colorado City and Ute Pass to South Park. Called the "father of Cañon City," Anson Rudd later reminisced that the soldiers protecting the southern routes to the mining camps withdrew during the Civil War and protected only the Platte route which helped Denver to grow at the expense of Cañon City.[50] The struggling newspaper, which set its type by hand and required eight days to obtain news from St. Louis, published its last edition on October 7, 1861. This left Cañon City with no newspaper until 1872, one year after the prison had opened. During the Civil War years, the so-called gateway city dozed in a Rip Van Winkle sleep.

One of the few "hangers-on," Anson Rudd, was a distant cousin of Zebulon Pike, who supported his family chiefly with his blacksmith shop. Often playing host to Chiefs Colorow and Ouray, the Rudds generally found the small bands of Utes who drifted in and out of Cañon City more of a nuisance than a threat because they delighted in watching the women cook as well as sampling the food. A train of twenty families from Kansas led by Thomas Macon joined Rudd and his few neighbors in 1864. They became known as the Resurrectionists in two senses. First Rudd saw in them the resurrection of the town when they occupied the vacant stone buildings. Also because they chiefly followed the orthodox Baptist and fundamentalist faith, he referred to them as "resurrectionists."[51] Unlike the miners, those families sought stability in business, farming and cattle raising.

As mining activity increased in the San Juan country and South Park, railroad surveys began. Logs for railroad ties floated down the Arkansas River from California Gulch and Oro City through Cañon City to Fort Dodge. Also the area's high quality coal was in demand for the steam locomotives. Jesse Frazier's introduction of cherry, apple and peach trees titled South Cañon the "garden spot" of the state. Moreover, by the time the prison opened, hot springs, mineral springs, soda springs and oil springs attracted health seekers and hotel entrepreneurs to Cañon. The gateway city became more than a gateway for commerce and service after Macon's leadership in the Territorial legislature won the prison. That prize - the institution - provided a gateway for Colorado's miscreants to pass in and, after a designated residence, out of the "walled city."

After the Civil War, the population grew slowly. The first true census in 1870 showed 1,064 in Fremont County, 817 native-born and 247 foreign-born. Cañon City's share, a large decrease from the 1860 voting claim count, numbered only 213 native-born and sixteen foreign-born.[52] Despite the 1860 claim of over 700 residents in Cañon City, the census shows that it did not again attain 500 until after 1878; this also indicates the transiency of early mining-related populations. The picture, then, is that the site for Colorado's prison was slightly populated and over 100 miles south of the more populated Denver.

Construction of the Prison

Although the Interior Department controlled construction, Territorial officials could recommend a local building superintendent. That sparked another round of lobbying for the political job. Numerous letters recommending various individuals included those commending Anson Rudd, Benjamin Woodbury of Black Hawk or

Columbus Nuckolls of Central City as the "proper and suitable person" to build the penitentiary.[53] However, Secretary of Interior, O.H. Browning, received most endorsements for his final choice, Samuel N. Hoyt, a building contractor. Letters from Company G, Seventh Regiment Infantry of Illinois of which he had been captain and the Loyal Soldiers Club of Colorado endorsed Hoyt. Others praised Hoyt as "an accomplished builder and carpenter," "a highly cultivated mining engineer," "an honest businessman" and "a gentle man of large literary attainments." Former Governor John Evans recommended "Captain Hoyt" on January 28, 1869, as "a gallant soldier in the late war."[54] With all of those endorsements, Hoyt seemed to fulfill the political expectations of many.

Accepting the appointment, Hoyt swore to "support the Constitution and faithfully serve in the position." Sureties to his $40,000 bond included John Hughes who turned in an unsuccessful bid for the prison construction.[55] Hoyt modified and adapted the plans and specifications which the Interior Department standardized for all western territorial prisons. Modeled from the Auburn plan, the government specifications called for a two-wing cellhouse. The allotted $40,000 could provide only one wing. The *Rocky Mountain News* called attention to this discrepancy by reporting that "government architects drew a plan to cost $100,000," but they would have to raise Colorado taxes if they followed those specifications.[56]

The Interior Department approved the modified plans. The federal specifications for Colorado's first institution called for the cellhouse to be 70' 2" x 44' 4" with forty-two cells six by eight feet in size. Each of the three stories contained fourteen cells and one bathroom with an iron bath tub and a slop sink. A lift tank supplied the water from a well. An iron railing led to the two upper stories. Three foot trenches formed the foundation for double-faced walls. The exterior walls consisted of "rubble masonry of the building stone to be found in the neighborhood." "Hard brick" composed the cell walls and brick or flagging stone would be floor material. The window heads were arched and the window sills were formed of split stone. The window frames were boxed with sash two inches thick and their sashes hung with "pullies and weights of cotton sash cord made of thread." One-inch bars on the windows spaced no more than five inches apart provided security. Each iron cell was secured with a "first quality" lock. Specifications described the plumbing dimensions for the drains, lift pumps for the tanks, rain gutters and flues for heating and ventilating. The "best wood in the locality for the floor of galleries" was required. Even the paint was prescribed — three coats of white lead and oil paint for the wood and two coats of red and black paint for the iron.[57]

From his office over the Hense and Company Jewelry Store on Denver's Larimer Street, Hoyt advertised for bids. To the prospective bidders he explained that the designated contractor would receive $10,000 when the building reached the top of the first tier, $6,000 at the second tier, $6,000 at the third and the remainder upon building approval. The bids, due on June 30, 1869, were opened on the following day at ten o'clock in the morning in the presence of Governor McCook and Secretary Frank Hall.[58] Only three contractors bid, and one of those withdrew.

John Hughes from Denver submitted a bid of $37,460, and Thomas Mullen and Benjamin Woodbury of Gilpin County proposed $36,340 — both slightly under the allotment. The Territorial officials recommended the low bid, and Hoyt requested approval from Secretary of Interior Jacob Cox by telegraph because the "building season is fast passing away."[59]

Before accepting the bid, however, Secretary Cox delayed by inquiring about the honesty of the Mullen-Woodbury firm. Governor McCook replied favorably regarding the contractors, but he added that due to some rumor that Hoyt could have had "slippery dealings," he had required Hoyt to take an oath that no impropriety had occurred in the bidding.[60] Among the "citizens of Denver" who underwrote the bond for Mullen-Woodbury was the name of John S. McCook, Colorado's governor.[61] Frontier Coloradans seemed to know and support each other quite readily. Builders Mullen and Woodbury earned trust and respect from their successful penitentiary structure which launched them into a career of building important landmarks. Mullen later built Colorado's capitol at Denver; Woodbury, a former gulch miner near Idaho Springs, built the Wyoming penitentiary.[62]

Almost two months after the bid opening, Hoyt reported from Cañon City that the signed building contract stipulated that the contractors would furnish the materials and complete the work in six months from July 26, 1869.[63] Fortunately for the future of the prison, Jonathan Draper again offered to donate an additional ten acres of adjoining land; Hoyt requested permission to accept it so that it could be used for "workshops and manufacturing."[64] After the cornerstone ceremony on September 12, 1869, the *Rocky Mountain News* praised Superintendent Hoyt as the "right man to push it along." The paper described those attending the ritual as "fortunate" and that the "occasion called out the wit, beauty and brains of the classie town of Cañon City."[65] With few institutions in a new territory, perhaps the newspaper could justly acclaim this event as "an era in our progress long to be remembered." Surely the building of a prison loomed as a phase in the institutional "conquest" of the West or of Colorado.

In good bureaucratic form, Hoyt sent frequent progress reports to the Interior Department. In October, he reported that ironwork came slowly from the East and in November that "lumber is being seasoned at the mills." But in December, he happily reported that Cañon's mild weather had not impeded progress. In fact, with the first tier finished, he requested that the contractors receive the first installment of $10,000.[66] The second tier went up on December 18 and the third story on January 11, but when the six-month deadline rolled around on January 26, 1870, the contractors asked for an extension of ten days because one iron door had not arrived from the East. Finally on February 10, the completed cellhouse awaited inspection. Territorial Governor McCook appointed Territorial Treasurer James B. Thompson to inspect it, and, if satisfactory, to turn over a $16,000 treasury draft to the contractors. Thompson approved the building and collected $112.25 for his services.[67] Throughout the construction period, it appears that the difficulty of collecting remuneration annoyed the contractors. As late as April 6, 1870, the contractors telegraphed the

Secretary of Interior asking for their balance. Even Superintendent Hoyt had to ask for his pay for six months' service.[68] In considering the distance between East and West and the federal government's distraction with the Reconstruction of the South, it seems unusual to find the scrutiny which the Secretary of the Interior gave to the small Territorial prison when he asked Hoyt by what authority he had advertised in more papers than authorized; Hoyt explained that he had advertised in only one more than authorized in order to give the contractors better notification. For whatever motive, Hoyt offered to pay the bill personally if the government refused.[69] Probably he had begun to recognize the extensive bureaucracy.

Without a doubt, Number One cellhouse must have been sturdily built because it lasted sixty-nine years. After visiting the prison, a newspaper editor praised the contractors and superintendent with the opinion that "I consider it one of the most perfect and convenient buildings of the kind ever constructed and one of the attractions of the place."[70] That small stone cellhouse with a mansard roof modeled on the imposing Auburn structure became a symbol of pride to early Coloradans chiefly because so few institutions existed at the time.

Four and one-half years elapsed from the time that Congress passed the Territorial Prison Act until Colorado's penitentiary opened on June 1, 1871. Although the contractors had completed the physical edifice by February 10, 1870, another problem delayed opening. Recall that in order to build the prison for the $40,000 allotment, Superintendent Hoyt had eliminated the administration wing housing the kitchen. Without a kitchen, the convicts could not move in. As a remedy, the Attorney General asked the Secretary of Interior for permission to use the remaining $2,463 (the surplus in the bid process for the cellhouse) to construct "the kitchen and yard accommodations." Charles Helm, a local carpenter built the wooden structure for $549.[71]

Following the many bureaucratic delays caused by the inconvenience of communicating with Washington for decisions, Governor Edward McCook proclaimed the penitentiary ready to receive convicts on June 7, 1871. The name of the first inmate listed in that never-ending prison record book became well-known through repetition. John Shepler, sentenced from Gilpin County for one year for larceny at the age of twenty-four, listed his nationality as German and his occupation as butler. Number 2, thirty-five- year-old William Henderson from Clear Creek County, served only two years of his five-year sentence for manslaughter when Governor McCook pardoned him. The first woman inmate, Mary Solander, Number 60 of Boulder, arrived in the prison's second year of operation and recorded her occupation as abortionist. After only five months behind bars for manslaughter, Governor Elbert pardoned her.[72] During the first six months twenty-three convicts entered the Territorial prison.

Territorial Administration

As with any new institution, even a penal one with only forty-two cells, various problems plagued its administration. Early turmoil in administration arose from the federal-territorial relationship. During its construction, some citizens erroneously assumed that it belonged to the Territory. An editorial comment bemoaning the lack of local autonomy concluded with "At least Uncle Sam opened a dam good stone quarry in Fremont County."[73]

Unsure of how the prison would operate, Colorado's Territorial General Assembly provided a general plan for its administration on February 11, 1870. The prison would receive any convict whose term of incarceration exceeded six months; the governing board would consist of the governor; the auditor and the district attorney of the third judicial district (this included Fremont County); the Territorial treasury would bear the expenses.[74] When requesting approval to build a penitentiary, few had considered the future expense. But the Territorial auditor, N.F. Cheeseman, doubting the financial feasibility of a prison, sent questionnaires to the auditors of Kansas, Nebraska, Nevada and Minnesota. After receiving answers that showed considerable expense in supporting a prison, he suggested to the legislature that Colorado could avoid the expense of officers and guards if "we send our convicts abroad" because an able-bodied convict in a workshop in the East would be self-supporting. He also proposed to "board our lunatics in the East" at half of the cost.[75] His prophetic outlook on the cost of a penitentiary proved true, and finances became an ever-increasing burden.

After the Interior Department had erected the prison, Congress changed the base of authority by placing control with the Attorney-General and Justice Department. In each territory, the United States marshals directly administered the institution with the mandate that prisoners "should be employed."[76] A United States marshal acted as the executive and bursing officer for the Department of Justice. In Colorado's case, Marshal Mark Shaffenburg, one of three Colorado marshals appointed by President Lincoln, designated his chief deputy as warden at the institution so that he could retain his residence in Denver and his office at the Denver Court House.

Transporting convicts to the prison proved time consuming and expensive. In describing his difficulty in conveying convicts to the "gloomy and desolate spot," a sheriff of Arapahoe County provoked a question regarding the suitability of the prison location. First, he had journeyed by train to Colorado City where he hired a wagon team for the forty-three "arduous" miles to Cañon City. The burdensome trip caused "one horse to drop dead in front of the "imposing edifice." Furthermore, the return trip proved even more hazardous when the water tanks froze and they had to push the train over the Continental Divide.[77] While transportation improved, the majority of convicts continued to hail from the more populous northern areas of Colorado - always adding to the expense of incarceration.

Varying critical reports emanating from disgruntled prison employees or the news media destabilized the administration. Charges such as those which had plagued eastern prison administrations appeared — cruelty or leniency to inmates and fraud or inefficiency on the part of the wardens or guards. Invariably, the press, the official involved, the legislature or the governor called for investigations and political maneuvering. During the five years before Colorado became a state, five different wardens faced the glare of criticism. As political appointees with no specific professional training, they confronted enormous challenges from their superiors whose expectations for prison management generally stemmed from an economic base and from the public whose spectrum of concerns varied from rehabilitation to revenge. Examples of the ambivalence regularly appeared in newspapers. The *Denver Daily Times* commented that unfortunately "the only freedom [for the convicts] is an occasional duck shooting along the river on Sunday."[78] On the other hand, a few days later, a newspaper criticized a guard for "savagely beating" a prisoner.[79] Various media charges called forth investigations. Trying to please the public resulted in what might be called the "warden syndrome" resulting in warden roulette.

Escapes provoked much of the criticism directed against the wardens because each escape provoked considerable publicity. Imagine a cellhouse placed in an open space with no wall around it, and "all fourteen inmates" assigned to grading the grounds or to work around the community with only three guards and one acting warden. That situation, as well as the occasional employment of inmates off the grounds, permitted easy escapes; consequently the warden became the target for the darts of blame. When the first escape occurred in December of 1871, Marshal Shaffenburg visited the prison. To ease the situation, he ordered balls and chains for inmates when off the grounds as well as new white woolen suits with stripes "to mark them as jailbirds."[80] The marshal also assigned the inmates to build a makeshift wall of lumber, but almost ten years elapsed before they completed a stone wall. Ironically, not only did the absence of a wall allow prisoners to escape, but the prison itself complained of "intermingling" when it notified Cañon City residents to keep their hogs off prison grounds as "they will not be tolerated here."[81]

Shortly after the prison opened, the *Denver Tribune* began circulating stories of wrongdoings at the prison. The paper charged that Shaffenburg sold supplies intended for use at the prison, that the chief guard, Michael Duber, beat nude prisoners and that the acting warden, Albert Walters, ran the prison with an iron fist. Shaffenburg and the *Rocky Mountain News* called the charges "rumors" and claimed no wrongdoing.[82] Locally, a group of citizens including future warden Anson Rudd visited the prison at the invitation of prison officials to inspect and to interrogate each inmate separately. They reported that thirty-one of the thirty-four said they received satisfactory treatment, and only two thought their treatment bad.[83] Additionally, Governor Elbert appointed a committee consisting of Attorney-General C.H. Allerman, Territorial Auditor J.B. Thompson and H.C. Thatcher of Pueblo to personally investigate the prison. The committee found no basis for the accusations. Regarding a charge of diverting outside inmate labor for private use, the committee specifically concluded that it was positively proved that every cent for such service . . . and every article of building material, wood, or corn received in exchange for convict labor was duly accounted on the deputy warden's books.[84] The latter comment clearly indicates that the inmates, from the beginning, worked for private individuals throughout the community for barter as well as pay while trying to make the prison self-supporting.

Another type of criticism was aimed at the discipline of Acting Warden Walters and his "Prussian or military background."[85] Actually, those "objectionable" rules requiring inmates to take their meals to their cells, to eat in silence and to march in lockstep style derived from Auburn's code of discipline. Undoubtedly, however, many officials who had so recently endured a military experience preferred that system.

For whatever reason, Walters left the prison to go into a business, and J.C. Reed, editor of the Pueblo *Chieftan*, took charge in June of 1873. Within eight months, he too fell victim to the "warden syndrome." While Walters had been too tyrannical, Reed felt the sting of rebuke "for allowing prisoners on the street." Angry exchanges occurred between a guard and Warden Reed regarding the responsibility for one inmate who purchased liquor down town. Reed argued that a guard had given the inmate twenty-five lashes and then sent him for whiskey.[86] Running a newspaper seemed insufficient preparation for administering a prison if, in fact, the various charges of mismanagement contained any accuracy. Reed defended himself against the mismanagement charges hurled by the *Central City Register* by arguing that the false testimony originated from bitter "discharged guards."[87] The *Cañon City Times* supported the prison administration and contrasted the superior conditions at the prison to the "filthy county jails."[88]

Faced with those charges and countercharges, an investigating committee composed of three legislators spent February 4-5, 1874 in Cañon City. They took sworn testimony from various guards, ex-guards and local citizens. The entire testimony attached to their report reveals much of the turmoil which led to the early demise of Warden Reed. Alex Redfield, former guard testified that

> the latest hour at which I have let prisoners in was 2 o'clock in the morning. The convicts let in late had generally been employed at the Warden's house. Have let in the Mexican, Antonio, in a state of intoxication without a guard...Mr. Reed told me when I was tired to put on prisoners and go to sleep.

C. H. Buttolph reported that he had seen "a prisoner out all day Sunday fishing without a guard. Have known prisoners to come in as late as 12 o'clock without guard — life prisoners." Only the brick factory owner who worked the convicts testified in favor of Reed's supervision.[89]

However, the primary duty of the legislative committee had not been to investigate the charges against Warden Reed but to assess whether the legislature should take advantage of a recent law which Congress passed on January 24, 1873. That statute transferred from the United States marshals the "care and custody...and personal property [of the penitentiary]...to said territory." The legal title would remain with the United States, and the Territory would receive one dollar per day for the subsistence of each federal prisoner. The Territory had not acted on the takeover, and the press had prodded the legislature to gain Territorial autonomy of the prison operation.

To assist the legislators, the controversial Warden Reed presented cost information pertinent to their study. He estimated the actual cost of subsistence for each inmate at forty cents per day whereas the Territory had been required to pay one dollar per day for each convict's subsistence to the federal government since its opening in 1871. Thus the figure revealed that the cost of thirty-nine convicts for one year had been $13,486 or $1,004 less than the federal government had required the Territory to pay. In addition the committee learned that profits from convict labor for two years amounted to $4,000 which did not revert to the Territory and that the federal government had no expansion plans for accommodating the growing population. With that knowledge the committee unanimously recommended that the Territory take charge. In addition, the committee foresaw, if the Territory had direct control, more opportunities for "properly utilizing convict labor" and placing the penitentiary upon a self-sustaining basis. Specifically, the inmates could erect new buildings and a wall, plant trees and enlarge the ditch running through the prison grounds. The report concluded by suggesting that discipline could be enforced in accord with the views of the people rather than by federal regulations.[91]

Satisfied with the recommendation, the Territorial Legislature enacted provisions to assume operation. After February of 1874, a board of managers appointed by the governor from each of the three judicial districts would supervise the prison. The board would visit the prison every three months, have justice-of-the-peace powers to inspect the conduct of the "keepers" of the prison and report to the legislature at each session. The warden, appointed by the governor, must reside at the prison; as treasurer of the institution, he would post a bond in the amount of $10,000; in turn his annual salary would be $2,500. When making improvements, the warden must employ inmates, but "he may hire out convicts" and must account carefully for any such labor.[92]

From the time that Congress authorized Territorial control, one year and three months passed before Colorado Territory actually assumed control. The best explanation for the delay rests with the turmoil in the governor's office. President Grant had removed Governor Edward M. McCook, appointed Samuel H. Elbert, removed Elbert and reappointed McCook during that time.[93] Marshal Shaffenburg claimed his readiness for the changeover, but blamed the commissioners and Acting Governor Frank Hall for the delay.[94] Eventually in April of 1874 the Board of Managers appointed by the governor accepted operation of what they hoped would prove to be a less costly Territorial prison.

During the political upheaval, Governor Elbert replaced the controversial Reed with the locally popular Anson Rudd as the third warden (first Territorial warden) in February of 1874. The attitude prevailed that "if anyone could straighten out the prison, Rudd could." Aware of the seeds of unrest under Reed, Rudd fired three guards and appointed some whom he considered trustworthy.[95] Immediately, he put convicts to work building roads, quarrying stone, making brick and terracing the popular Soda Springs adjoining their structure.

As might be expected with the ambivalent attitudes toward inmate labor, some of that work led to an early strain in the "era of good feelings" between the community and the prison. The *Rocky Mountain News* squelched rumors that Rudd had employed convicts to work on his personal irrigation ditch by explaining that the contract allowed prison use of the ditch in exchange for inmate tunnel labor.[96] But when eight dangerous convicts overpowered the inside guard, stole arms from the prison arsenal and escaped to the mining community of Rosita where they terrorized the residents until a vigilante group captured the fugitives,[97] Rudd became the scapegoat. Although the *Cañon City Times* staunchly defended Rudd on the basis that no sturdy wall enclosed the prison, the governor retired him.[98]

In rapid progression, the fourth warden, David Prosser, moved his family into the warden's residence during the prison's third year. One newspaper demeaned Prosser's appointment as an "experimental one" because his qualifications seemed to be only his political attachment to the governor. However, perhaps his skill as a carpenter and Denver builder helped prepare him for his most immediate task - to enclose the penitentiary. With the help of a newly-laid rail track on which to convey the nearby rock, the convicts began a wall twenty feet high and three feet thick "equal to the Great Wall of China" around five acres of the grounds.[99]

Northern Colorado news media praised Prosser for the large amount of work progressing at the prison and for his economy of feeding and clothing an inmate for thirty cents per day. But his work did not please the locals who complained that unguarded inmates worked on the streets and that the warden did not buy supplies locally.[100] Criticism expanded when Cañon City police arrested Prosser for behaving in a "drunken manner" on Main Street. Amidst a glare of publicity, the public figure paid a fine of ten dollars and costs. The press battle seemed to be north vs south when a northern newspaper editor supported Prosser by reporting that the "locals" became jealous because he had purchased supplies in Denver; furthermore, Prosser's drunken appearance had only been a delirium condition from a drug taken for an ailment.[101] Inevitably, Prosser received a letter from Governor John L. Routt asking him to resign because the "commissioners are dissatisfied with your management." Governor Routt accepted Prosser's resignation on December 6, 1875, and turned to Benjamin F. Allen, Cañon City hardware dealer, for the last of the beleagured Territorial wardens.[102]

In addition to the "warden syndrome," only two years elapsed before the ever-increasing problem of overcrowding in the forty-two bed cellhouse began. During Allen's administration, the legislature appropriated money to add a new wing to the forty-two bed cellhouse. The cells in the new west wing were four feet wider and one foot shorter than those in the original east wing.[103] Although Allen's administration produced a new cellhouse and new industries, some rumors of incompetency and fraud in connection with the wall construction circulated. Nevertheless, his administration generally won fair marks for success.[104] With the spotlight on

Colorado's statehood success in the Centennial year, Allen rode out the criticism and served until March, 1877 when prison population reached approximately eighty-one.

With Allen's business sense also came a fair ability to practice good public relations. For example, Allen wrote an open thank you letter to a Cañon City lady for her box of books which had "brought happiness to the convicts" and took advantage of the occasion to describe the "enjoyable" way in which the inmates celebrated the Centennial Fourth of July. To celebrate the historic day, the warden had ordered their chains removed for which the inmates thanked him "with tears" in their eyes. Then they sang patriotic songs for three hours and heard music from the Cañon City brass band and the "Italians."[105] Quite possibly he sent that letter to a northern Colorado newspaper to thank a lady in Cañon City with an eye to promoting his state-wide public relations — something so desperately needed in the warden's role.

For fifteen years, Colorado's territorial government had run concurrently with the difficult Civil War and Reconstruction years. Many would-be settlers had come and many had left in the 1860s, historian Robert Athearn's so-called "decade of disappointment." There had been Indian wars, a mining slump, a national panic in 1873, a locust invasion for two years and a constant struggle to win approval for statehood. Despite the hurdles, the population quintupled in the 1870s and twenty-six counties appeared on the state map in 1876. The thirty-eighth state's heterogeneous population consisting mostly of Anglo-Saxon derivation had increased from 39,864 in 1870 to 194,327 by 1880. When Colorado became a state on August 1, 1876, a total of 195 prisoners had registered at its federally-built prison. Like many other state prison experiences, Colorado's six years of territorial prison management had encountered politics, media exaggeration, greed, scandals among its officers, overcrowded conditions, scant financial support, dishonesty and lack of professional administration.[106] Trying to finance Colorado's incarceration system with the least involvement of tax money led to the difficult problem of finding remunerative inmate labor. As Colorado has always done, it looked to its natural resources to provide inmate employment in the last quarter of the nineteenth century.

44

NOTES - CHAPTER II

[1]Albert D. Richardson, *Beyond the Mississippi* (Hartford, Ct.,: American Publishers, 1869), p. 177.

[2]*Denver Post*, 21 September, 1992, p. 1:4.

[3]*Congressional Record*, 35th Cong., 2nd Sess.,(Washington: John C. Rive, 1859), p. 657. For debate also see p. 1065.

[4]Frederic L. Paxon, "Territory of Colorado," *University of Colorado Studies* IV:2 (1907): 68. See also Robert G. Athearn, *The Coloradans* (Albuquerque: University of New Mexico, 1976), p. 8. See also Rodman Paul, *Mining Frontiers of the Far West,1848-1880* (Albuquerque: University of New Mexico, 1974), pp. 111-113 for an account of towns at the points of departure making a profit with inflated accounts of metal finds.

[5]*Rocky Mountain News*, Denver, Colorado, May 7, 1859, 1:4.

[6]Earl S. Pomeroy, *The Territories and the United States, 1861-1890* (Seattle: University of Washington Press, 1969), p. 106. See also Patricia Limerick, *The Legacy of Conquest, The Unbroken Past of the American West* (New York: W.W. Norton, 1987), p. 80.

[7]Frank Hall, *History of the State of Colorado* 4 vol.(Chicago: Blakely Printing Co., 1889), vol.I, p.185.

[8]Paxon, "Territory", p. 69. An excellent account of the same and the problem of accuracy in voting accounts is Robert L. Stearns, "Colorado: A Study in Frontier Sovereignty", an address given at the Thirtieth Annual Meeting of the American Association of Law Libraries, Denver, Colorado, June 26, 1935, p. 17.

[9]*Rocky Mountain News*, hereafter *RMN*, October 6 and 20, 1859, Stearns, "Frontier", p. 18.

[10]Donald Wayne Hensel, "A History of the Colorado Constitution in the Nineteenth Century" (Ph.D. dissertation, University of Colorado, Boulder, 1957), pp.26-31. He details Byers' influence. The constitution also copied that of Iowa.

[11]James Grafton Rogers, "The Mining District Governments of the West" (An address delivered at the Thirtieth Meeting of the American Association of Law Libraries, Denver, Colorado, June 28, 1935) Pamphlet file, Western History Collection, University of Colorado, p. 5. This article describes the evolution of the

laws. He has included a list with the mining districts and their locations of those whose records are extant. He estimated that there were 150-200.

[12]Charles Howard Shinn, *Mining Camps, A Study in American Frontier Government*, ed. Rodman Paul (New York: Harper & Row, 1965) p. 282 quoted from a Supreme Court decision in December, 1865, and p. 288 and p. 294.

[13]Jerome C. Smiley et al., *Semi-Centennial History of the State of Colorado* (Chicago: Lewis Publishing Co., 1913), p. 659.

[14]Thomas M. Marshall, "Miner's Laws", *American Historical Review* 25 (April, 190): 434-39.

[15]*RMN*, Sept. 19, 1860, Paxon, "Territory," p. 73.

[16]U.S. Statutes at Large XII (1861) pp. 172-177 for the entire act.

[17]Robert G. Athearn, *The Coloradans* (Albuquerque: University of New Mexico, 1976), p. 58. See also Paxon, "Territory," p. 75. It is noteworthy that Gilpin was not a total stranger to the area because he had commanded an army detachment on the Santa Fe trail in the 1840's and had written prophetic books about the future of this area to which he came as governor.

[18]*State Department Papers, Colorado Series*, v.I, #25, Dec.28,1859 -April 22, 1874, microfilm, Federal Archives, Denver branch. Printed message in both English and Spanish.

[19]Athearn, *Coloradans* , p. 66 and p. 59. Furthermore the Republican nominee faced a voting roster that showed three-fifths were Democrats at that time.

[20]*Council Journal*, Colorado, Sess. 2, Evans message to   legislature, July 18, 1862, microfilm, p.18.

[21]Ibid., Sess.4, Feb. 3, 1864, p. 14.

[22]*Governors' Record Book*, v.3, pp. 9-19. #8841-C, Colorado State Archives, Governors Gilpin and Evans.

[23]*State Department Papers, Colorado Series*, v.II, #35, Governor Gilpin's proclamation ordering the specific arrests, Sept. 29, 1861. Warrants for those arrests can be seen at the Rocky Mountain Branch of Federal Archives, Denver, under the category of U.S. District Court, First Judicial Ds., Denver, docket folders for 1861-2. Box #2. Treason cases dated October 13,1861. Ft. Wise, at the mouth

of the Purgatoire River, was named for a governor of Virginia by a cavalry officer in 1860. It was later renamed Ft. Lyon in honor of General Lyon killed in a Missouri battle. After a flood, it was moved twenty miles down the river.

[24]*State Department Territorial Papers*, vol. VI, #54, letter from Hall to Sec. of State Seward, April 25, 1862.

[25]*The Cañon City Times*, Colorado Terr., July 11, 1861 and July 22, 1861.

[26]*Denver Post*, May 7, 1978, Empire Section, Olga Curtis, p. 71.

[27]*RMN* reprint of June 29, 1867, clipping in pamphlet file, Western History Collection, University of Colorado, Boulder. Reference was to the amount of shock Boulder residents felt. The building of prisons did not end lynchings. All of the recorded five lynchings in Cañon occurred after the prison was built.

[28]*The Denver Post*, May 7, 1978, Empire section, p. 71.

[29]Paul, *Mining Frontiers*, p. 166.

[30]Donna Taylor, "Memories from the Foot of the Royal Gorge," (Cañon City High School Printing Class: 1969),pp. 24-8. Pamphlet file, Western History Collection, University of Colorado. Also see Henry Priest, interview of March 19, 1863, "Deadman's Gulch", *Colorado Magazine 8*, Jan. 1931, p.34. Espinosa Peak near Cripple Creek so-named for where the first brother was killed; there are two Colt revolvers at the Colorado Historical Museum supposedly belonging to them; another story is that the head of one was kept in alcohol at Ft. Garland until 1899. This is described in Rosemae Wells Campbell, *From Trappers to Tourists, 1830-1950* (Palmer Lake, Colo.: The Filter Press), p. 37.

[31]Byers, *History of Colorado*, MS., p. 11. Often his viewpoints resulted in violence aimed at him.

[32]*Denver Post*, Sept. 1928, Magazine sc. clipping, Western History Collection at University of Colorado.

[33]Byers, *Centennial State*, Manuscript, Bancroft Collection, Western History Collection, University of Colorado, 1884, p. 6 and 59.

[34]*U.S.Statutes at Large 14*, George P. Sanger, ed. Dec., 1865-March, 1867, Jan. 22, 1867, (Boston: Little, Brown, 1868), p. 377.

[35]*Council Journal of the Legislative Assembly of the Territory of Colorado*, 7th Sess. (Denver: Collier, 1868), Hall's message announcing the law on Dec. 3, 1867. p. 22.

[36]Hall, *Colorado* I, p. 450.

[37]*RMN*, Dec. 18, 1867, 4:4.

[38]*RMN* Dec. 17, 1867, 1:3. Also in Dec. 20, 1867, 2:1.

[39]Ibid., Dec. 30, 2:1.

[40]Ibid., Jan. 2, 1868, 2:2.

[41]*Council Journal*, Sess.7, Dec. 24, 1867, pp. 85-7, 120.

[42]*Revised Statutes of Colo.*, Seventh Sess. of the Legislative Assembly, Dec. 2, 1867-8 (Central City: Collier, 1868), pp. 475-6.

[43]*Deed Record Book B*, Jan. 28, 1868, Fremont County Clerk's office, p. 60. Also see the deed in *Terr.Papers*, Colo. Series, August 18, 1869. The *RMN* on Feb. 8, 1869, published the territorial audit indicating that $888.88 had been spent in locating the capitol and the prison with $166.67 "undrawn."

[44]*RMN*, June 26, 1868, 4:3.

[45]Fremont County lies in the south-central part of Colorado on the eastern boundary of the mineralized belt. A collection of *Colorado Maps*, 1861-1913, at the Colorado Historical Society library shows that Fremont was reduced in 1868 by the Seventh Territorial Assembly and in 1877 by the First General Assembly.

[46]"The Story of the Arkansas Valley," (Denver:1919)   Western History Collection, Denver Public Library, p. 15.

[47]*Cañon City Times*, October 15, 1860, p. 3, Jan. 12, and June 16, 1861.

[48]The Claim Club record is part of the official archives of Fremont County. It is listed as Entry 81 and is described on pages 44-45 of the *Inventory of the County Archives of Colorado, No. 22, Fremont County*, prepared by the Historical Records Survey. Also in Rosemae Wells Campbell, *Fremont County, Colorado, 1830-1950* (Palmer Lake, Colorado: The Filter Press, 1972), p. 33.

48

[49]George L. Anderson, "The Cañon City or Arkansas Valley Claim Club, 1860-1862," *The Colorado Magazine* XVI, (Denver:State Historical Society), Nov., 1939, p. 209. There is a copy of the constitution on p. 203.

[50]Anson Rudd, "Reminisces of Early Cañon City," Colorado Magazine 6-7, 1929-30, p. 111·

[51]Campbell, *From Trappers,* p. 43.

[52]*Statutes of the Population of the United States, Ninth Census* (Washington: GPO, June 1, 1970), p. 16 and p. 95. At that time Colorado recorded a population of 39,864.

[53]*Interior Department Territorial Papers, Colorado, 1861-88,* "The Penitentiary at Cañon City," microfilm #M431. Rocky Mountain Branch, National Archives, Denver. The letters are unnumbered.

[54]Ibid., Letter from Evans to Secretary of Interior.

[55]Ibid., letter from Hoyt to Sec. of Interior, Mar. 7, 1869.

[56]*RMN*, Feb. 3, 1869, 1:2. When New Mexico built its larger prison in 1884, the cost was $138,726. In 1805, Massachusetts spent six years building its prison and $170,000 and employed a foremost architect.

[57]*Interior Department Terr. Papers*, handwritten list with no date. Printed also in the *RMN* June 1, 1869, 1:4.

[58]Ibid., printed copy of the advertised bid which also appeared in *RMN*, June 1, 1869,1:4.

[59]Ibid., letter from Hoyt to Sec. Cox, July 1, 1869.

[60]Ibid., letter from McCook to Cox, July 23, 1869.

[61]Ibid., memo showing Mullen-Woodbury bond, no date.

[62]Pamphlet, no author or date but with this notation, Fremont County History Room, Cañon City Public Library.

[63]*Interior Department Papers*, letter from Hoyt to Cox, copy of the contract, Aug. 1, 1869.

[64]Ibid., letter from Hoyt to Cox, Sept. 15, 1869. Abstract of land is there.

[65]*RMN*, Sept. 13, 1869, 1:4 and 1:2.

[66]*Interior Department Terr. Papers*, letters from Hoyt to Cox, Oct. 1, Nov. 2, Dec.1, 1869.

[67]Ibid., memo Feb. 15, 1870.

[68]Ibid., telegram from Mullen to Cox, April 6, 1870.
and letter from Hoyt to Cox, Feb. 10, 1870.

[69]Ibid.,letter from Hoyt to Cox, May 10, 1870.

[70]*RMN*, May 16, 1870, 2:2.

[71]*Interior Department, Terr. Papers*, letters from Att. Gen. A. T. Sherman to Columbus Delano, Sec. of Interior, April 15, 1871 and July 8, 1871.

[72]*Prisoner Record Book, CSP*, State Archives, Denver, pp. 1 and 3.

[73]*RMN*, Feb.26, 1870, 4:2.

[74]*General Laws of Colorado Territory Passed at the Eighth Session*, (Central City: Collier, 1870),p.33.

[75]*Council Journal of the Legislative Assembly of the Territory of Colorado*, 8th Sess., (Denver: Byers, 1870) Jan. 4, 1870, pp.62-6. Kansas described its prison as having been built on the Auburn plan and not by the federal government.

[76]*Congressional Globe*, 41st Cong, Third Sess., Part III, Appendix, Ch. XV, p. 330.

[77]*RMN*, Nov. 10, 1871, 1:4.

[78]*Denver Daily Times*, Feb. 15, 1873, 4:2.

[79]*Canon City Times*, March 20, 1873, p. 1.

[80]*RMN*, Dec. 24, 1871, 1:3.

[81]*Cañon City Times*, April 18, 1872, 3:4.

50

[82]*RMN*, June 21, 1873, 4:4.The charges aslo appear in June 5, 1873, June 21, 1873, 4:4.

[83]*Cañon City Times*, March 20, 1873, 4:4.

[84]*Cañon City Times*, June 26, 1873, p. 1. Also see *RMN*, June 21, 1873, 4:4.

[85]*RMN*, June 5, 1873, 1:4.

[86]*RMN*, Feb. 10, 1874, 4:5, Feb. 11, 1874, 2:1.

[87]Ibid, Feb. 1, 1874, 2:3, Feb. 10, 1874, 4:3.

[88]*Cañon City Times*, Feb. 26, 1874.

[89]*General Laws*, Tenth Session, 1874, "Report of Joint Committee of Council and House of Representatives of Colorado Territory," Feb. 9, 1874, Appendix, pp. 282-7.

[90]*Congressional Globe*, 42nd Cong., 3rd sess., pt. III, 1872-3, Appendix, p. 234. Also appears in *RMN*, Jan.23, 1874, 4:3, and Jan. 24, 4:3.

[91]*General Laws*, Tenth Session, 1874, "Report", Appendix, p. 284 and pp. 289-90.

[92]*General Laws*, Tenth Session, Feb. 13, 1874, p. 206.

[93]Smiley, *Colorado I*, pp.375-7. Read for interesting details of political maneuvering and complaints of Colorado citizens regarding the appointed governors.

[94]*RMN*, March 5, 1874, 2:3.

[95]The original certificate of appointment is on display at the Rudd House in Cañon City, dated Feb. 16, 1874. Michael Welch, "Yesterday," prison clipping file, Fremont History Room, Cañon City Public Library.

[96]*RMN*, April 30, 1874, 2:2.

[97]*The Daily Tribune*, Denver, May 28, 1874. Also *Cañon City Times*, June 11, 1874, 3:2 and June 18, 1874, 2:3.

[98]*Cañon City Times*, June 25, 1874. Also see *Executive Records, Colorado*, vol. II, letter from Acting Governor John Jenkins to Rudd, June 18, 1874, State Archives, Denver, p. 327.

[99]*RMN*, May 2, 1875, 4:2 and June 13, 1875, 4:2.

[100]Ibid., June 16, 1875, 4:2. Also see Ruth Stinemeyer, collector, pamphlet file, Fremont History room, clipping from the *Cañon City Times*, but undated.

[101]*RMN*, Oct. 1, 1875, 4:1.

[102]*Governors Correspondence, 1875-89*, vol. I, Box 8919, Colorado Archives, Denver, October 19, 1875, p. 116.
In this box also is the letter of acceptance of Prosser's resignation by Governor Routt, p. 165 and the letter of appointment for Allen, Dec. 6, 1875, p. 166.

[103]*Minutes of the Board of Commissioners*, 1874-1930, Box 19382 A, Colorado Archives, Denver, Feb. 16, 1876, p. 4.

[104]*RMN*, Feb. 25, 1877, 4:4. Also see Stinemeyer, Prison File, Fremont History Room for the assessment.

[105]*RMN*, July 9, 1876, 4:3.

[106]A footnote to the scandals regarding the prison also involved the U.S. marshals. Three of the five territorial marshals faced accusations of wrongdoing. Socially prominent Mark Shaffenburg earned two years of hard labor at the federal prison in Leavenworth for signing false affidavits and vouchers while serving as marshal. For the stories see Charles Calvert, "U.S. Marshals, Colorado, 1861-1958,", typed MS., Western History Library, Denver, June 30, 1958, pp. 2-8 and the *RMN*, Feb. 25, 1877, 4:2.

CHAPTER III

AT HARD LABOR - NINETEENTH CENTURY

No prison can be considered complete which
does not afford the means of hard labor.
Elizabeth Fry[1]

Historically, incarceration and inmate labor became bedfellows for a variety of reasons. Whether inmate labor served for punishment, for reform or rehabilitation, for profit to the state or to pay the cost of incarceration, for discipline or to control certain segments of society, it persisted as the *sine qua non* of imprisonment. Nineteenth century prison reformers had reached an almost universal conviction that hard work and discipline reformed criminal behavior. Consensually, taxpayers resented the burden of supporting miscreants. Of necessity, the search for some form of lucrative employment became the constant but elusive and even slippery theme of nineteenth century prison management.

Long before Colorado had a prison, the search for inmate employment to ease the responsibility of earlier eastern taxpayers had resulted in serious objections from free labor, unions and manufacturers with whom cheap convict labor competed. Determined to avoid some of the earlier pitfalls, the Centennial state prison managers molded some of the more successful inmate labor practices to their local resources. Nevertheless, Colorado's prison employment yielded a troubled history. Even though Colorado's selection of the penitentiary site had been politically motivated rather than labor oriented, the choice near a quarry site resembled New York which had also designated a profitable quarry site at Sing Sing for its prison. Consequently, traditional hard work and a rock pile symbolized early Colorado prison labor. And Colorado imitated other tried-in-the-East patterns of convict employment such as Auburn's silent congregate workdays and its system of contract labor within workshops - all enforced with strict discipline, lockstep and striped prison garb. To this pattern, Colorado's managers added expediency and pragmatism in seeking remunerative work for their comparatively few inmates.

Colorado Updates its Legal Framework
Quite naturally, the first years of prison operation under different jurisdictions — the federal government, Colorado Territory and finally the state — proved to be fraught with confusion. Even before Colorado built a prison, Colorado Territorial lawmakers had given the sheriffs and county commissioners authority to work inmates.[2] Congress also instructed the United States marshal and the Territorial governor to secure employment for the inmates.[3] With this policy already formulated, it is no surprise that Territorial Governor Samuel Elbert, in his farewell legislative message asked that the "labor of the convict should be made to defray the expenses of his prosecution, custody and keeping."[4]

Anticipation for profitable convict labor also appeared in the reasoning for transferring the prison from the United States marshals to the Territory in 1874 because "The Territory receives nothing for the labor of the convicts, . . . and it would be the wisest and cheapest plan for the Territory to take charge of the institution."[5] When Colorado became the thirty-eighth state in 1876, the General Assembly updated laws for what would become Colorado State Penitentiary. The Board of Managers became the Board of Penitentiary Commissioners appointed by the governor for two year terms. The policy-making Board operated within legislative guidelines not only for administration but also for inmate labor. Board members received a yearly stipend of $400 for quarterly meetings and reported all proceedings to the governor and biennially to the legislature. The warden, also appointed by the governor for two years with the consent of the senate, received a salary of $2,000 and reported to the commissioners regularly and to the legislature biennially. Specifically, the warden would keep a "business-like record of all transactions" concerning "the profitable employment of the convicts" and "an account of all articles manufactured in the workshops" and then deposit the earnings with the state treasurer for credit in the penitentiary fund. Aware of graft possibilities, the legislators wisely forbade all officials and employees to receive any prison supplies, money from convicts or from their labor.[6]

Although the legislature provided that all "male convicts" confined in the penitentiary must perform labor as prescribed by the board of commissioners, they also allowed "good time," i.e., they could earn a deduction of sentenced time for cooperative service. By specifying "male convicts," did that imply that females did not work? In reality, the few incarcerated women had no remunerative work, but performed the housekeeping duties of the prison and the warden's residence.

Further legislation instructed the warden to "hire out the labor of the convicts to the best advantage, but in no case shall a convict be allowed to go out to labor without being under the custody of a guard or overseer of the penitentiary."[7] By this clause, Colorado clearly recognized the state's responsibility for those it had incarcerated — a policy contrary to that which granted sole custody of convicts to a lessee who might exploit the labor. Another clause required that the warden record each convict's name, earnings, place of work and length of time. In sum, those regulations provided the Board of Penitentiary Commissioners and wardens with the first blueprint for inmate labor. Legal adjustments evolved only when labor experiences and public attitudes demanded change.

A final clause relating to inmate labor authorized the possible relocation of the penitentiary "to a place where the labor of the convicts can be made more remunerative to the state" if the general assembly should so order.[8] Having won the institution, Cañon City retained a firm control on the entire prison system with options for local expansion until only recently when several other towns have won economic and political campaigns for new prisons.

Setting the Stage during the First Decade of Inmate Labor

During the first decade - the 1870s - 226 convicts signed the prison record book. With only one cellhouse, necessary construction and ground work occupied the inmates for some time. By 1874, they had built an office for the guards, a warden's brick house, a carpenter shop, a blacksmith shop and two outhouses. But the quest for remunerative labor became paramount for the prison officials. Obviously early wardens seemed to lack incentives for agriculture production because the lists of vouchers for purchased supplies included most of their food. This lack of self-support quickly concerned a vigilant investigating committee which reported to the legislature in 1874 that there are forty acres of ground connected with the Penitentiary, a good deal of which is tillable. All the vegetables required for the prison could be raised by convict labor.[9]

With so much confusion in the Territorial days, agriculture developed slowly. Thinking more in terms of workshops, Warden J.C. Reed recommended productive labor along the pattern set by the Auburn prison when he reported that

> The labor of the convicts has been utilized to some extent in making brick, getting out rock, and getting wood. If there were workshops in connection with the institution, the convict labor would be remunerative; as it is now, there is little or nothing for the prisoners to do in the winter.[10]

But workshops, too, would await the next decade and never attain the profit shown in the eastern prisons.

For the first two years, the receipts only totalled $4,000, all accrued from convicts "working off the grounds" or in private contract labor. The inventory accompanying the changeover from federal to territorial operation revealed that convicts built houses for local residents, hauled and quarried stone at $4.50 a load, and that the warden contracted them to Fremont County at $1.50 per day.[11] Consider that the expenditures on the labor account amounted to $3,585 to supply "a guard for every gang of fifteen," and the result was only a profit of about $500.[12]

While prisoners might be legally "hired out," leased or contracted, Colorado practiced those options quite modestly when compared with other state inmate labor operations. Aware of the notorious examples of leasing the entire body of convicts to the total disposal of private contractors, Coloradans disdained the system which led to abuse of the arrest system to gain black labor, cruelty leading to frequent overwork and deaths of convicts, graft for lessees or fraud in the state governments. Expressing the general consensus of disapproval, Governor Benjamin H. Eaton told the Legislature in 1887:

> Any proposition to farm out the labor of the convicts can not be entertained. ... The civilization of the State

would revolt against it. The people of the State are not
ready to embrace a public shame to escape taxation. The
disgraceful disclosures of barbarous brutality where the
system has been tried in the Southern States are known
to our people and would leave us without even the poor
excuse of ignorance in attempting such a shameful
experiment in our proud and enlightened commonwealth.[13]

Both realistically and environmentally, the widespread use of the contract system
in Colorado proved impractical because few industrial workshops prevailed in the
nineteenth-century West. However, Colorado became the only Rocky Mountain
state in which, for a time, a contract labor policy allowed a manufacturing firm to
work the inmates within the walls.[14] Common in the East, this policy aimed at
fulfilling the philosophy of making the prison pay for itself.

Indeed, as soon as the federal government relinquished control to the Territorial
government, some minor random contracting occurred when the first Territorial
warden, Anson Rudd, negotiated a trade with local ditch companies. Ditch
construction and repairs by inmate labor were bartered for prison usage of the
ditches and irrigation water from the Arkansas River. When Fremont county
commissioners contracted for inmate labor on roads, the local newspaper approved
and reported that "they are as well-guarded as the stingy appropriation will allow."
Less permissible was Warden Prosser's attempt to contract for a slaughter house on
the Arkansas River bank; this ended quickly when local officials invoked a law
forbidding that type of discharge into running water.[15]

With few opportunities for contracting labor, Warden Prosser turned to the
resources at hand by concentrating on the market for building stone. Even though
shackled with balls and chains, the inmates learned to dynamite the sandstone from
the hogback, shape the blocks with hammers and chisels and smooth them with a
carborundum type stone. Years of sandstone removal left scars on the reduced
hillsides but supplied building material for prison additions and other area structures
as well as cash earnings.

Pressing for prison workshops, the *Rocky Mountain News* criticized the prison
for the "low value" of its lime and stone labor, and opined that, until workshops are
built, "the prison must be an expense rather than a revenue."[16] Expressing a similar
viewpoint, the Board urged the warden to work "all able-bodied convicts" regularly.[17] Dutifully, in 1877 the warden sought more far-reaching contracts by
advertising bids for the labor of seventy-five convicts. The winning bidder, A.
Cohen, who had hired 600 convicts at Joliet, Illinois, paid Colorado fifty cents for
each inmate's nine and one-half hour day. Additionally, he furnished the salaries for
the extra guards at his downtown shoe factory until the Board ordered the inmates
to build a three-storied shoe shop on prison grounds.[18] Contractor Cohen enjoyed a
new shop furnished by the prison — one of the benefits for a prison contractor.

Organized as the Colorado Shoe and Boot Company, Cohen's company employed inmates from January, 1878 to January of 1881 when they ended the contract ten months before its expiration by mutual agreement.[19] Colorado officials had learned what the eastern prisons had often experienced. When outside contractors and their foremen intermingled with inmates, they introduced favoritism and rivalry, gave bribes and caused general dissension. As tensions rose in March of 1880, the Board of Commissioners prohibited the warden from allowing any extra pay or private agreements with convicts for overwork.[20] Obviously, affairs did not improve and, in January of 1881, the Board prohibited all company employees from entering the prison grounds because some of the employees passed contraband to inmates and the company chose their foremen from the ex-convicts who had learned the trade while in prison.[21] As a consequence, the Board issued strict new rules governing the relationship between outsiders and inmates.[22]

The profit of the shoe contract is difficult to determine because of incomplete and vague records, but some generalizations can be proposed. While in the downtown shop, the company could only accommodate forty convicts, but when the inmate-built shop opened on the grounds in November of 1879, up to seventy worked. One newspaper account stated that seventy-seven inmates produced a weekly quota of eighty dozen pair of heavy work shoes.[23] Warden M.N. Megrue's report for 1879-80 listed only the total earnings from inmate labor of all kinds as $22,023, but he recorded the exact days of labor in the shoe shop. Count those days and the total is 28,476 inmate work days, multiply by fifty cents which the contractor paid for each day, and the likely cash earning to the prison was $14,230 from the shoe contract for that biennium.[24] Of all earnings for that two-year period ending in 1880, the shoe contract contributed 64.6 percent. But with the early demise of the contract, shoe shop earnings for the next biennium dropped to $515.[25] Nineteenth-century bookeeping seldom calculated the amount expended on shop upkeep so the "earnings" figures reflected only the exact amount turned over to the state treasurer as "earnings."

Despite the problems with the Cohen Company, the profits of the shoe contract encouraged them to try again, so the Board attempted another contract with an outside shoe shop manufacturer, Herriman and Hirsch Company. An incentive to hire more inmates appeared in this company's contract. For the first forty inmates, the contractor paid fifty cents per day, but for the next forty only forty cents. The contract included a clear stipulation for expulsion if the contractor violated any prison rules that upset the discipline.[26]

The local paper touted the shoe workshop as a "boon" to Cañon City because twenty local citizens also found employment with the prison shoe factory. Because manufacturing was uncommon in Fremont County, the news article detailed the process for its interested readers. First, five convicts soaked the leather in vats in the basement, then sixty-five inmates with twelve foremen did the cutting on the main floor, and finally twenty convicts on the second floor finished the boots and shoes for marketing throughout the western states.[27]

But once more a shoe contract ended prematurely when that company completed only one year of its five-year contract. Its departure must have left some disappointment over the loss of local jobs. Although contract shoe manufacturing failed in Colorado, some states found it highly profitable. For example, statistics for 1880 reflect that Colorado's inmates made only about 3 percent of the small amount of shoes manufactured in Colorado, while in Rhode Island and South Carolina, inmates crafted the same amount as free labor did; in Nevada, inmates fabricated two and one-half times more than free labor produced.[28]

With earnings low and appropriations from the legislature insufficient for the growing inmate population, the search for self-support stretched in many directions. Emulating eastern prisons, Colorado's Board introduced in 1877 the 25 cent fee for viewing life inside the bars.[29] The Board earmarked the fees for religious services, books and organ rental because the legislature appropriated nothing in this category. Earnings in the "visitors fund" for the biennium ending in 1882 were $640.[30] Visitor fees increased each biennium as curious travelers passing on the highway in front of the prison conveniently stopped for the tour. After the legislature placed the first chaplain on the state payroll in 1884, the visitor fees became "library" fees.[31]

As succeeding wardens tried to report profit, they also sought cost-reduction in management by substituting inmate labor for hired labor, discharging personnel and employing convict labor in the office. Warden M.N. Megrue cancelled the contract with the Denver and Rio Grande depot for hauling and furnished his own team for the inmates to haul water and other supplies; the state, however, purchased a harness and wagon for the team. Even the few employees felt the inadequate funding when the prison exhausted its appropriations, and during the year of 1878 resorted to payroll certificates of indebtedness; this imbalance actually added fifteen percent to the maintenence cost. The Board of Penitentiary Commissioners blamed the Legislature for its failure to appropriate the requested $30,000 (usually the legislature adjusted the requested budget downward).[32]

While officials were finding it impossible to keep all of the inmates employed, the institution was buying convict-made goods from other states. For instance, the iron doors for the second cellhouse came from the Illinois prison at a cost of $3,000. And the warden had not captured the building stone market when the builders of the Horace Tabor Center in Denver bought convict quarried "machine dressed limestone" from Illinois and "buff-colored sandstone" from Amherst, Ohio.[33] Colorado prison stone cutters, however, became more competitive later.

Despite the scarcity of jobs for inmates, a variety of jobs awaited local entrepreneurs which boosted the economy of Cañon City. Locals supplied the ever-increasing roster of guards and foremen and furnished food and other supplies to the prison. At his discharge from the prison, a convict received a suit of clothes which a local company provided for seven dollars.[34] Frequently, the warden hired wagons and horses to pursue escaped convicts and granted rewards for their capture.[35] An interesting contract appeared in the Board *Minutes* indicating the purchase of a wagon and exhaust boiler for Harry Parker who had the "rights" to haul the excrement from the prison vaults for five years.[36]

Not only did the prison provide opportunities for the local free labor, but the supply of convict labor often benefited the community. When emergencies occurred, sometimes inmates assisted. One such example stirred the local news reporter to applaud the help at the W. C. Catlin fire by writing that "too much cannot be said in praise of the boys in stripes who worked with a will and to great effect."[37] When the warden "hired out" inmates, it was the local residents and city and county governments which could utilize them easily. The local newspaper reported that convict labor keeps "the alleys just as clean as our streets and our ditches."[37]

Of course, the enlargement of facilities at the prison site added to the inventory value, but construction contributed no cash earnings. The precise amount of cash earnings for the first decade is indiscernable, but the total barely reached $35,000. The actual figure for the last biennium of the 1870s amounted to the greatest portion of the total — $22,023.[38] Of course, the successful period of the shoe contract had contributed most of that. As measured by some eastern prison standards, Colorado's first prison decade ended with little success in finding profitable employment for the 544 men and four women who passed through the facility.

Although the Board authorized the deputy warden to study workshops at prisons in Ohio, Illinois and Kansas, circumstances pointed toward natural resource utilization as a better direction for Colorado State Penitentiary. Hence, the scenario for the next two decades shifted to brick, lime and quarry products which found a market in the building and mining segments.

Brickmaking

The "author of the first brickyard" in Cañon City had found brickmaking much more lucrative than his mining in California Gulch. Settling on one of the city's first four homesteads in 1864, William C. Catlin and his wife, both immigrants from Lincolnshire, England, obtained clay from the Temple Canyon Road for the profitable brick factory. From the first, Catlin learned the value of contracting with the prison to supply various services. He sold beef or bricks and later leased his land for prison gardens. In 1879, Catlin formally contracted for inmate labor. The terms stipulated that each party furnish one-half of the pay for the guards and share the bricks equally with the sale price set at seven dollars per thousand.[39]

Because the brickyard was located across from the penitentiary on the south side of the Arkansas River, the inmates had to cross a bridge and walk almost one mile to the workplace. This snake-like line of lock-stepped prisoners clad in their striped suits and accompanied by three or four guards became a daily sight to local residents. On one occasion, either their appearance or some unusual antics frightened a team with a wagon injuring "an English passenger" in the incident.[40]

Particularly in Cañon City, that daily visibility of convicts walking to work augmented ambivalent attitudes regarding inmate labor. Just as Easterners had complained, assorted groups and individuals questioned favoritism in contracting inmate labor as well as the frequent hiring of inmates around the community. One reporter revealed that "Laboring men are so scarce who are willing to work that Mr. Sell was compelled to hire a gang of convicts to help do his threshing this week."[41]

Pushing for a change in the law, influential Cañon City legislator B. A. Rockafellow presented an "eight-foot petition" to prohibit the convicts from working off the grounds while advising the Assembly to give up some of the profit that "these striped-suited convicts earn disbursed around the area."[42] Heeding his request as well as others eager to end outside labor, the lawmakers in 1883 forbade convict employment off the grounds "except as incident to the business and management of the penitentiary."[43]

But this law threatened to end the lucrative brick-making contract if the convicts could not leave the grounds, so the warden searched for some circumvention of the law. When contract renewal time appeared, the warden devised a plan to act as agent for the penitentiary and, in turn, to form a partnership with Catlin for a three-year lease of the brickyard. Catlin as the "first party" furnished the premises, machines, tools, molds, expertise and the labor for the night burning of the bricks while the inmates slept behind the walls. In compliance with the letter of the law, the property lease became "incident to the business of the penitentiary." Warden C.P. Hoyt as the "party of the second part" furnished the labor and the wood for kiln burning. Additionally, the prison paid rent for the "leased" brickyard to Catlin at the rate of $5.00 per 1,000 bricks manufactured or 200 of every 1,000 bricks.[44]

In addition to providing building material for prison construction, convicts manufactured an average three to four million bricks per year and sold them throughout the area for five to eight dollars a thousand. Attempting to tune into market demands, the Board urged the warden to check into the "market size of bricks to suit the Leadville market."[45] According to Warden Joseph A. Lamping's 1890 biennium report, they had sold 1,812,539 bricks, had used 551,350 to build a new cell house and 41,425 for general improvements as well as to pay their lease rent in bricks to Catlin. In addition they had an inventory of over 100,000 bricks. The cash earnings amounted to $12,465 from an average price of $7.20 per thousand, and those used on the grounds were valued at $4,149. The brickyard totaled $5,922 in production expense. Generally, the reports only listed cash earnings, but this report does indicate that, after expenses, brickmaking was profitable. For the decade of the 1880s, $38,168 went to the state treasury from brickmaking, and this represented 12 percent of the total cash earnings. Yet fewer than fifty convicts made bricks, and during months of inclement weather, the yard closed.[46]

During the last decade of the nineteenth century, the cash earnings from brickmaking dropped to $12,648 or 7.54 percent of the total cash earnings. Opposition by labor unions who refused to work with convict-made bricks had limited the market. In 1900, Warden Hoyt, in his third term, gloomily reported:

> We started out in the spring of 1899 with prospects for
> a good trade in brick, having an order for 4,000,000 to
> start with. After making 350,000 so many objections

were raised against this line of work that we were forced
to discontinue it. If I could have gone on with this work
there would have been no deficiency for this biennial
period.[47]

Thereafter, the prisoners confined brickmaking to the grounds chiefly for state use.
In a climate of states that experienced less union and political activity, such as New
Mexico, brickmaking remained profitable because of the low cost of production.

Lime and Quarry Work

Fortunately, the site of the prison near rock outcroppings provided the most
gainful inmate labor. The following table is prepared from the cash earnings listed
in the succeeding warden reports and illustrates the approximate value of those
resources:

Percent of Total Cash Earnings

	Lime	Stone Quarries
1882-1890	65.2%	7.1%
1892-1900	50.%	8.9%
1902-1910	56.%	9.4%
1912-1920	5.3%	11.48%
1922-1930	unclear	9.3%
1932-1940	unclear	475 working

From this it is evident that, for over three decades, the sale of burned lime
provided more than half of the earnings, and the sale of building stone elevated the
earnings to almost two-thirds. Large numbers of inmates could work during all
seasons, and the minerals provided much of the prison building material. The
burned gray lime provided flux for the smelting process and builders bought white
lime. Of course, the sales fluctuated with the rise and decline of the mining and
building industries.

Only three years after Colorado became a state, the Board proposed to expand
employment by acquiring the adjoining quarry grounds belonging to the Colorado
Coal and Iron Company. They entered into an agreement with the owners
requesting an appropriation of $2,500 to pay for twelve acres adjoining the
penitentiary which "includes the whole lime quarry and a portion of the stone
quarry." The prison, at the same time, traded seven acres of its unusable land to the
Colorado Coal and Iron Company. In substantiating the need for the land, the
commissioners argued that "Colorado does not afford opportunities for contracting
its convict labor to manufacturers as most of the other States of the Union."[48] That
purchase would allow them to supply the growing market for lime and building
stone. Although the Third Session of the General Assembly in 1881 authorized the
purchase, the legislators did not appropriate the money until February of 1883;

nevertheless, during the interim the prison worked the quarries and paid rent to the Colorado Coal and Iron Company.[49]

Before June 1, 1881, the prison had lime sales of only $602, but in the next eighteen months lime sales rose to $27,862. To support production, the warden added fifteen horses, more wagons, carts and other tools as well as a new three-storied brick horse stable with sleeping quarters for the guards.[50] On the lime ridge, they built twelve lime kilns with a capacity of 1,250 bushels of lime per day. As a humane gesture to the stone-cutters who had no protection from the sun or the storms, the inmates constructed a roofed shed. Increased demand from the smelters led to the purchase in 1885 of another lime ridge for $5,000 and the building of a half-mile tramway from the east lime quarry to the kilns for $3,500.[51]

In the true capitalist and industrial manner, the prison officials sought marketing contracts to enhance lime sales. In 1881, "Smith and Stiff" appeared before the Board to seek the exclusive right to sell prison-burned lime in Leadville, Silver Cliff and Pueblo for two years at seventeen cents a bushel. Agreeing to their request, the Board further stipulated that the company must "put in a railroad switch to the kilns, pay one half the expense of grading the track for the switch at the rate of one dollar per day per man for convict labor used in the construction of said switch." After completion of the switch, the price was sixteen cents per bushel, but the company had to promise not to sell any lime other than prison-burned lime and not to ship any unburned limestone to those named places. In addition, the Board closed a contract with former Warden M.N. Megrue to sell lime in Denver.[52] In another contract, the firm of A.W. Duggan and Company won the sole and exclusive right to sell prison lime at "Salida and all points on the line of the Denver and Rio Grande Railway running northerly from Salida for three years." Their price in 1882 was fourteen cents per bushel "loaded on the cars at Cañon City."[53]

Periodically one of the "middlemen" failed to fulfill his contract, causing troublesome negotiations for the Board. The agreements, requests and uncollectable debts to the prison of one lime salesman, John Flintham, occupied copious notes in the *Minutes* of the Board's meetings for over twenty-six years. In some areas, the Board had to order the warden to take over the sales of lime.[54]

When private companies protested the low prison lime price, Warden Robert A. Cameron argued that the state-owned lime quarries provided the only low price which the smelters could afford, and that if the price increased, the smelters would resort to the use of unburned lime.[55] Here Cameron, a former general who fought with General Grant, defended his position versus the problems of his environment — to keep the prisoners busy with profitable work versus private enterprise's need to compete versus an industry dnmanding cheap raw materials to stay in business.

In the interest of augmenting economy and inmate labor, both the Board and the warden in 1888 dared to tread on the domain of private enterprise by recommending that the state purchase coal lands for forty or fifty dollars an acre. With the lime burning operation and heating needs requiring over twenty tons of coal a week, the administration saw the practicality of owning coal lands.[56] Even earlier, Warden

Hoyt had made a similar suggestion after visiting the coal mine operation in Kansas.[57] But this idea was an exercise in futility while mining remained Colorado's leading industry so no politically sensitive legislature could allow that type of inmate labor.

Actually, the General Assembly had restricted convict labor further in April of 1887 with a law which forbade persons, corporations, county or city governments from hiring convicts or from bringing in convict labor from other states and prohibited the importation of convict-prepared material for the "erection of or repairing of any public building."[58] Consequently, in Warden Hoyt's second term, he discreetly refrained from delivering lime or brick near the prison to avoid competition "with the laboring masses." Even so, Hoyt recorded the highest cash earnings of the nineteenth century in the 1887-1888 biennium when he marketed 277,312 bushels of gray lime for twenty cents a bushel and 13,323 bushels of white lime for 23 cents.[59]

During the next biennium, the fifteen lime kilns required repairs according to Warden Joseph A. Lamping who complained that they were "old style because the rock and coal screenings or slack with which we burn lime were being fed in from the top." Lamping's report also contained one of the few break-downs between cost and earnings — the lime expense had amounted to $16,510 to produce cash earnings of $32,196.[60] A ballpark deduction as to the general lime profits could be that the cost of production usually equalled one-half of the profits.

The cut stone trade for building foundations had been producing around $5,000 biennially besides providing material for a new cell house, the stone terrace and the new execution chamber (the state had ordered that executions be held in private at the penitentiary instead of being carried out in the county of their crime as they had been until 1891). But when private-cut stone sold for less than prison-cut, the Board advised the warden to lower the price to the free level.[61] Obviously, the moneyless society "inside the wall" endured the same price fluctuations of the volatile mining industry as did the outside community.

Only 132 inmates among an average number of 635 toiled in the stone and lime routine in 1896; this motivated both Governor Albert McIntire and Warden John Cleghorn to suggest that they again look into a shoe and boot industry. Governor McIntire claimed that the state bought convict-made shoes elsewhere while Colorado supported its inmates in idleness and allowed their families to live in abject poverty.[62] But the law of 1887 had forbidden all contract labor. Faced with this technicality, the General Assembly amended the older law to allow convicts to work with "the least conflict to free labor." The state then appropriated $10,000 for productive employment,[63] and the Board sent Warden John Cleghorn to inspect the *modus operandi* of eastern prison workshops. This inspection trip both opened and closed the warden's eyes to the contract system. Cleghorn's deduction was:

> Every convict in these penal institutions who is em-
> ployed . . . under the system of contracts now in vogue
> comes in direct conflict with the common weal by

actually superseding and taking the place of some poor
but honest laboring man; and I predict that as soon as
free labor is thoroughly aroused to this injustice the
contract system will be forever discontinued.[64]

In a rare instance of returning tax money, Cleghorn returned the $10,000
factory appropriation to the state. After this experience, the warden unsuccessfully
asked that Colorado acquire some mineral land with low grade ores for the location
of a branch penitentiary.

Two years later when lime sales were still producing one half of the cash
earnings, Warden Hoyt, in his third term, relined twelve lime kilns with 100 loads
of boulders, 2,800 fire brick and 50,000 common brick and built 2,000 feet of
roadway to reach a new stone quarry. He also added a supply of shovels, picks, and
wheelbarrows.[65] Enlarging that industry seemed justifiable when considering that,
in 1900, smelting and ore refining composed 43.4 percent of the state's entire
manufacturing industry.[66] When the supply of lime rock reached exhaustion by
1903, the enterprising Board paid the City $700 for its rights to another new
limestone ridge just north of the former quarry.[67]

As the nineteenth century closed, the familiar problem of underemployment
mounted. Fewer than one-third of the 600 prisoners worked on the rock quarries.
The sale of lime decreased when strikes in the mineral industry closed mines and
smelters.[68]   By the second decade of the twentieth century, the lime earnings
dropped to only five percent of the total. This phenomenon characterized private
enterprise also. Although the 1919 *Colorado Yearbook* listed fourteen limestone
enterprises employing 228 workers, that accounted for only one percent of the entire
mining activity.[69] Clearly the quest for other pursuits had to increase.

Other Nineteenth-Century Projects
Since brick, stone and lime accounted for more than two thirds of all cash
earnings, other sources brought minimal returns.   In 1892, Warden Lamping
expressed the concern that "A prisoner, after having engaged in digging in a stone
quarry or helped about a brick-yard or lime kiln, is little advanced in the trades to
make a living for himself when released."[70] Linking recidivism to the lack of
employment skills, penologists stressed that inmates needed to learn trades so that
they could cope on the "outside."

While trying to find more trade-skill jobs, the pressing consideration was to
alleviate the taxpayers' burden. Unhappily for the wardens, many Coloradans
continued to compare the amount of self-support in some of the less scrupulous
states with Colorado's small prison. Enviously, the Denver *Times* reported that in
Alabama "where they work the convicts in cotton fields and coal mines, they turned
over $75,000 surplus." After Warden Hoyt's unsuccessful plea for a shop to
manufacture hollow ware, he retorted that a half dozen states presented no drain on
the taxpayers, and that Minnesota returned $6,000 while Coloradans bought

imported convict-made goods because "politicians are afraid of organized labor."[80]

Faced with the dilemna that the convicts must work but present no competition to free enterprise, prison leaders experimented with some options which, though not remunerative, helped to set the stage for the successful road building era of the early twentieth century. Several ideas regarding land reclamation and development motivated the Board of Commissioners to direct prisoners into reclamation work, a trend supported by many groups.[72] In 1888, their suggestion was:

> There are large tracts of land on each side of the Arkansas river, now worthless, that would become valuable for agricultural purposes, if sufficient water could be furnished for irrigating. We, therefore, recommend the construction, with prison labor, of two large irrigating ditches, . . . one on each side of the river, starting at the mouth of the Grand Cañon, [called the Royal Gorge today] running in an easterly direction as practicable to work with prisoners.[73]

They proposed to pay for it by selling water rights, thus helping the prison to become "self-sustaining." Only an appropriation of $10,000 for teams and equipment would be needed, they believed. Agreeably, the Seventh Session of the General Assembly granted the request. The state highway engineer would select the feasible routes and the penitentiary commissioners could lease the water rights to the public.[74]

The survey located the headgate about four miles west of Cañon City on the north side of the river. From that location, the ditch would proceed easterly to a point about nineteen miles north of Pueblo where it would cross Fountain Creek. The first work occurred on a tunnel where the ditch had to pass through the hogback near Cañon City. After the prison had drawn only $1,482 of the appropriation, the auditor discovered that "no more could be used" because appropriations stemmed from certain funds such as land sales and often were insufficient to uphold the legislative appropriation. To continue the work, the Board issued certificates for $9,207 bearing seven percent interest, payable in water to nearby land-owners.[75]

Further appropriations of $50,000 in 1891 and $40,000 in 1893 allowed more construction, but obtaining funds from the legislature became a frustating yearly situation. Lack of funds caused frequent suspension of work on the ditch. By statute in 1893, the supervision of the project passed from the Board of Penitentiary Commissioners to a State Board of Control with the authority to administer the certificates of indebtedness at five percent interest.[76] But with the depressed times after the Panic of 1893, money was not forthcoming. Four years later, two lawmakers, Maxey Tabor and Cañon Citian B.F. Rockafellow, appeared before the Board with assurances that they would exert all efforts to obtain funds to carry on the work.[77]

Following the course of the project reveals the successes and frustrations of State Canal Number 1. The state engineer in charge reported that by the end of 1892, the convicts had completed one and nine-tenths miles of ditch and 270 feet of tunnel excavation at an expenditure of $54,558. At a fair contract price, the value of the earthwork would have been $104,668.[78] At the end of each quarter, the Board *Minutes* noted a payroll for free labor on the canal which ranged from one to six thousand dollars during the years. Obviously, the project moved along as a happy compromise between free and convict labor for a time. Although work had temporarily stopped from January to April of 1894, Warden Frank McLister reported that 122 prisoners resumed work each day in April, 135 in May and June and 131 in July.[79]

Another glitch in the plan surfaced when a survey of the canal revealed that private companies held all of the water supply and a new source would entail costly reservoirs. During 1893-94, the work had cost $44,813, but a private contract would have amounted to $109,980.[80] When Governor James H. Peabody of Cañon City gave his inaugural address to the Fourteenth General Assembly in 1903, he explained that lack of available water because of prior appropriations had stopped work on the canal after $200,000 had been spent. He urged that it be completed to its intake and turned into a feeder for a chain of reservoirs from the Royal Gorge to the Fountain River; hopefully, he projected, flood seasons would fill the reservoirs providing plentiful water to sell. Again that proposal did not materialize, and the General Assembly finally appropriated $35,000 in 1907 merely to clear the indebtedness of State Canal Number 1.[81] For many decades, Cañon City received water via a pipeline laid through the convict-built tunnel and along the right-of-way.[82] Today, only history recalls that project with the name of the street, Canal Street, running where the canal had been planned.

An interesting side light to the tunnel blasting connected prison labor history with the Benedictine nuns at nearby St. Scholastica Academy and filled pages of the Board's *Minutes* as well as occupying some debate on Capitol Hill. Much of the tunnel work required blasting through hard rock. Consequently, the boring of 1,160 feet of rock in two tunnels for almost three years reverberated throughout the community. When this steady blasting appeared to cause cracks in the old military college housing the Catholic school, the Board hired Architect John J. Huddart for fifteen dollars to examine the building. His lengthy report concluded that, besides faulty construction, the "damage was caused by the blasting done in the adjoining hills, at a distance of about 1600 feet and might have been assisted by the blasting in the quarry, a distance of 900 feet."[83]

For the next three years, the Benedictine Sisters, forced to vacate the building, lived in a small shed on the property while they beseeched the Board and the legislature for compensatory reconstruction. For some reason, the Board did not heed Hoddart's recommendation to repair the building, but hired Architect D. A. Bradburg to draw plans to rebuild the structure at a cost of $5,000.[84] After much debate as to whether the state could extend any funds for a "Catholic order of nuns," the General Assembly finally appropriated $8,000 to "erect such a building equal to the one" which sustained damage by the construction of the Hogback tunnel and State Canal Number 1.[85] Although the architect received his payment for the plans in 1895, the Sisters were still camping in the shed a year later. Finally, after Sister Rose's fifth visit to the Board, the warden purchased the necessary material to complete the building in March of 1896.[86] Warden Cleghorn reported the cost of the rebuilt convent as follows:

Amount of appropriation for lumber $8,000
Furnished from penitentiary:
8,412 feet rubble rock 672
1,876 feet pitched face ashler 375
449 feet cut stone sills 157
399,228 brick 1,966
306 loads of sand 306
1,320 loads of lime 265
633 feet flagging 373
Total $12,116

Guards for the convicts working off the grounds to replace the structure cost an extra $1,230.[87] Certainly that incident illustrates the many facets of prison-community relationship, i.e., bureaucracy, prejudice and controversial culpability.

When work on Canal Number 1 had seemed to be progressing satisfactorily, Mesa County leaders, eager to irrigate dry land, conceived their plan for a canal constructed with convict labor. To implement the idea in 1891, the legislature passed "An act to construct, maintain and operate a state ditch in Mesa County." It stipulated that the people of that western slope valley raise $50,000 for the purpose and pay the expenses of the convicts engaged in the work. To supervise the work, a member of the Board of Penitentiary Commissioners, Captain D.J. Nichols, would receive a salary of $2,500 per annum. After a prominent Grand Junction businessman, T. C. Clayton, raised the subscription money, an argument erupted involving the superintendency. The local interests preferred their own superintendent, but the law clearly provided that the Board's official take charge. Locked in disagreement, they scuttled the entire project.[88]

Women Inmates

To complete the picture of nineteenth-century inmate labor, consider the women inmates. The wardens' reports contained no details until 1898 when one matron added a short report, but then no more information appeared until 1906. Commenting on the few incarcerated women (two or three a biennium in the 1880s), Governor Pitkin asked, "Are men so gallant or women too good in the West?"[89] Throughout the reports, one finds only an occasional small expenditure or an occupational listing of "housework" or "nurse" which possibly indicated a woman inmate. Undoubtedly women performed only domestic chores in the nineteenth century.

Female quarters consisting of six cells, a small kitchen and bath were located "over the laundry and bath houses adjoining the old wall." A gate and stairway from the prison yard gave access. The warden unsuccessfully requested $10,000 to provide a workroom in 1890.[90] But the new Board of Charities and Corrections appointed in 1891 recommended a matron and a new cellhouse to "enable the female prisoners to receive the same care and attention that is bestowed on the males."[91] Two years later, the male inmates built a new two-storied cellhouse containing forty cells for twelve inmates. A wall fourteen feet high within the main wall enclosed the female inmates. Warden Cleghorn predicted:

> Work in the sewing room, the laundry, the kitchen . . .
> will give them ample opportunity for inculcating habits
> of neatness and industry which will be useful aids
> toward their reformation.[92]

The different treatment for women included the purchase of "corsets," the banning of tobacco in the female department and the prohibition of "paddling" female inmates.[93] When the matron requested facilities to establish a cooking school, she reported that the twelve women inmates in 1898 had no employment.[94]

Generalizations

Some significant generalizations portray nineteenth century inmate labor. As in all prisons, the majority of those incarcerated were the young, poor, unskilled and transient. Unlike the older prisons, Colorado could not find much profit in the contract industrial system and actually restrained it through legislation (See chapter IV for an explanation of the obstacles). Unlike many other states, Colorado never legally allowed its inmates to be worked without regular prison guards in charge. Therefore, death rates were lower than in other prisons (undoubtedly climate accounts for much of that), and abuse incidents were rare. Since most of the inmate labor involved unskilled work, it is obvious that inmates learned few skills applicable on their release.

With no wall around the penitentiary for some time and the problem of taking the convicts four to twelve miles to work on leased gardens and roads, escapes were numerous — 133 fled in the first 29 years and over 50 were not recaptured.[95] To accommodate growing numbers of inmates, building expansion continued. The media and special interest groups influenced prison policies as well as the direction of inmate labor. The resources provided some remunerative work but much less self-support or profit than some eastern industrial prisons had managed. As the twentieth century arrived, officials continued to search for sufficient funds and inmate jobs for the growing institution.

NOTES - CHAPTER III

[1]Helen Varick Boswell, "Women and Labor," Annals of the American Academy of Political and Social Science 46 (March, 1913): p. 17.

[2]*Laws Passed at Sixth Session of the Legislative Assembly of the Territory of Colorado at Golden, 1866-67* (Central City: Collier, 1868), pp. 61-2.

[3]*Congressional Globe*, 41st Cong., Third Sess., Part III, Appendix, Ch. XV, p. 330.

[4]See Elbert's Message., *Cañon City Times*, Jan. 15, 1874.

[5]*General Laws, Tenth Session, 1874*, "Report of Joint Commission of Council and House of Representatives of Colorado Territory," Feb. 9, 1870, Appendix, p. 282.

[6]*General Laws, Colorado, Acts for years -1870-76 and Laws Enacted at First General Assembly of Colorado*, Nov. 1, 1876 (Denver: Tribune Stean Ptg. House, 1877), ch. 57, pp. 685-9, p. 693, pp. 695-6.

[7]Ibid., p. 696.

[8]Ibid., p. 698.

[9]*General Laws*, "Report of Joint Committee",Feb. 9, 1874, p. 283.

[10]Ibid., p. 282.

[11]*General Journal*, Colorado State Archives, Box # 19382, April 14, 1874, p. 11. Ads for selling stone also in *Cañon City Times*, Feb. 18, 1875, 2:5. Ibid., July 16, 1874, 5:4, has the note of the county commissioners contracting labor for six miles to the Butler ranch.

[12]*General Laws*, "Report of Joint Committee", pp. 282 and 284.

[13]*First Biennial Report of Bureau of Labor Statistics of the State of Colorado, 1887-88* (Denver: Collier and Cleaveland, 1888), pp. 397-8. Also see George Cable, *The Silent South* (New York: Scribners, 1885) for the complete story.

[14]Georg Thomson, "The History of Penal Institutions in the Rocky Mountain West, 1846-1900." (Ph.D. dissertation, University of Colorado, Boulder, 1965, p. 127.

[15]*Cañon City Times*, Aug. 13, 1874, 5;;4, 2:4.

[16]*RMN*, Feb. 15, 1877, 4:3, Aug.1, 2:2.

[17]*Minutes*, July 10, 1876, p. 11.

[18]*RMN*, Sept. 21, 1877, 4:2. October 14, 1877, 4:2.

[19]*Biennial Report of the Commissioners, Warden, and Physician, 1881-82*, (Denver: Tribune, 1879), p. 11. Hereafter called *BR*. Also see *Minutes*, Sept. 3, 1878, p. 41.

[20]*Minutes*, March 9, 1880, p. 65.

[21]*Minutes*, Jan. 27, 1881, pp. 106-7.

[22]*BR*, 1881-2, pp.76-7. List of shop rules.

[23]*RMN*, April 18, 1880, 5:1.

[24]*BR*, 1879-80, p. 39.

[25]*BR*, 1881-82, p. 22.

[26]*Minutes*, Sept. 12, 1882, pp. 116-7.

[27]*Fremont County Record*, Nov. 4, 1882, 1:2.

[28]*Second Annual Report of the Commissioner of Labor, 1886*, "Convict Labor," (Washington:GPO, 1887), p. 192.

[29]*Minutes*, March 12, 1877, p. 20.

[30]*BR*, 1881-82, p. 22.

[31]*BR*, 1885-86, p. 22.

[32]*Minutes*, July 12, 1877, pp. 24-5, Jan. 8, 1878, p. 31 and July 9, 1878, p. 39.

[33]*RMN*, Aug. 1, 1877, 2:2.

[34]*Minutes*, June 3, 1879, p. 53.

[35]*General Journal*, Prosser, State Archives, Box 19382, April 14, 1874 - March, 1881, p. 11.

[36]*Minutes*, March 9, 1880, p. 68.

[37]*Canon City Times*, March 27, 1873, 3:2.

[38]*BR*, 1879-80, pp. 12-13.

[39]*Minutes*, June 7, 1880,p. 73 and March 6, 1879, pp. 43 and 68.

[40]Printed interview with Mrs. Claude Rogers, May 1, 1942, Prison file, Fremont History Room, Cañon City Library. Also this is mentioned in *Fremont County Record*, July 16, 1881, 4:2.

[41]*Fremont County Record*, August 13, 1881, 4:2. There are also items in Oct. 28, 1882, 2:2.

[42]Ibid., March 10, 1883. 2:2.

[43]*Laws Passed at Fourth Session of General Assembly*, Feb. 11, 1883, p. 246.

[44]*Minutes*, May 10, 1884, pp. 171-2.

[45]Ibid., June, 1885, p. 204.

[46]*BR*, 1889-90, p. 14.

[47]Ibid, 1889-90, pp. 6 and 15.

[48]Ibid, 1879-80, p. 7.

[49]*Laws Passed at the Fourth Session of the General Assembly of Colorado*, (Denver: Times, 1883), pp. 25-26. Approved Feb. 13, 1883.

[50]*BR*, 1881-82, p. 8.

[57]Ibid, 1885-6, p.4. This was purchased from Captain B.F, Rockafellow who served with the Michigan cavalry and whose father came to Colorado in 1866.

[52]*Minutes*, Sept. 2, 1881, pp. 98-99.

[53]*Minutes*, Dec. 9, 1881, pp. 103-04.

72

[54]Ibid., Dec. 6, 1889, p. 346.

[55]*BR*, 1885-6, p. 10.

[56]Ibid., p.6.

[57]*RMN*, Nov. 20, 1883, 6:2.

[58]*Laws Passed at the Sixth Session of the General Assembly of Colorado.* April 2, 1887, p. 232. There was controversy over the use of convict-made materials in the new capitol building at the time.

[59]*BR*, 1887-88, pp. 14-15.

[60]Ibid, 1889-90, pp. 15-6.

[61]*Minutes*, Dec. 1, 1893, p. 540.

[62]*BR*, 1895-96, pp. 11 and 22. also see *Biennial Message of Governor Albert W. McIntire, 1895*, pamphlet, (Denver:Smith-Brooks, 1897), pp. 39-42.

[63]*Session Laws*, April 28, 1897, p. 32.

[64]*BR*, 1897-98, pp. 8-10.

[65]Ibid, 1899-1900, pp. 14-5.

[66]*Biennial Report Bureau of Labor Statistics, Colorado, 1901-2*, (Denver:Smith-Brooks, 1902), p. 414.

[67]*BR*, 1903-4, p. 4.

[68]See Harold V. Knight, *Working in Colorado*, (Boulder: University of Colorado, 1971) for a history of the strikes in mining areas in 1903.

[69]State Board of Immigration, *Yearbook of the State of Colorado, 1920*, (Denver: Welch-Haffner Ptg., 1920), p. 185.

[70]*BR*, 1891-2, p. 28.

[71]*Denver Times*, August 2, 1898, 8:3 and June 28, 1899, 4:1.

[72]See table on cost comparisons in appendix from *First Biennial Report of Labor Statistics, 1886*, p. 405.

[73]*BR*, 1897-98, p. 18.

[74]*Session Laws*, April 19, 1889, p. 285.

[75]*BR*, 1889-90, pp. 9-10.

[76]Supreme Court letter in response to Governor Davis Waite's inquiry, Waite's box 26693, State Archives, and *Session Laws*, 8th sess., April 8, 1891, p. 335.

[77]*Minutes*, May 23, 1897, p. 163.

[78]*BR*, 1891-92, p. 25. This was directly opposite the mouth of Grape Creek.

[79]Letter from Warden McLister to Governor Waite, April, 1894. State Archives, Waite's box #26692.

[80]*Fremont County Record*, Dec. 1, 15, 22, 1894.

[81]*Session Laws*, 16th session, 1907, pp. 166-7. See also *Biennial Message of Gov. James B. Orman and Inaugural Address of Gov. James Peabody, 14th Sess*, (Denver: Smith-Brooks,1903), pp. 96-7.

[82]Interview with former city administrator, John R. McGinn, Nov. 20, 1989.

[83]*Minutes*, May 15, 1893, pp. 468-70.

[84]Ibid.,July 13, 1893, p. 485.

[85]*Session Laws of Colorado, Tenth Session*, (Denver: Smith-Brooks, 1895), April 8, 1895, ch. 7, p. 36.

[86]*Minutes, II*, June 7, 1895, p. 15 and March 31, 1896, p. 90.

[87]*BR*, 1895-6, p. 18.

[88]*Minutes*, Jan. 30, 1892. Clippings from an unidentified paper, probably Grand Junction, in Dave Nichols file box #1380 at Western History collection in University of Colorado, Boulder.

[89]*RMN*, Jan. 5, 1883, 2:2.

[90]*BR*, 1889-90, p. 7.

[91]*Second Biennial Report of the Board of Charities and Corrections of Colorado*, (no listed publisher) Nov. 30, 1894, p. 55.

[92]*BR*, 1895-96, pp. 19-20.

[93]*Minutes*, Dec.7, 1893, pp. 509 and 528. vol.I1, Nov. 28, 1899, p. 273.

[94]*BR*, 1897-98, p. 60.

[95]*BR*, 1899-1900, p. 19 and table on p. 36.

Colorado's Territorial Cellhouse, built one-half mile from the small town of Canon City.
Courtesy of Colorado Historical Society.

Convicts excavating for the Canon City water works.
Courtesty of Denver Public Library.

Top: *Marching single file to brickyards across the Arkansas River.*
Bottom: *The mineral water spring facing Highway 50.*
Courtesy of Colorado Historical Society

Top: *Six-mule team and road plow worked by convicts on roads.*
Bottom: *A reporter tours the road camp.*
Courtesy of Colorado Historical Society.

Two views of Colorado State Penitentiary about 1884 with lime-
stone hogback looming behind.
Courtesy of Colorado Historical Society.

CHAPTER IV

PARADOX OF INMATE LABOR

*It is true that a nail cannot be driven by a
convict or by any man, in any place or under
any circumstances, without competing with
another man who desires to drive the same
nail.[1]*

Colorado's rocky historical road toward employing convicts during the nineteenth century and the interacting parodoxical elements which changed the entire perspective of inmate labor by 1936 require closer consideration. How and where to implement a convict's sentence demanding "hard labor" continued as one of the most debatable and ambivalent of all incarceration policies. Fearful of competition from inmate labor, free labor and private enterprise together pressured for state and national legislative restrictions which forged the final roadblocks to the era of competitive prison labor.

Competition with Free Labor and Manufacturers

Somewhat like the foundation of Cañon City as a supply station for miners entering the mountains, the early prison as an institution became a channel of labor for private industry, farming and public works. Cheap convict labor helped to maintain Cañon City's streets, alleys and ditches as well as to provide building stone, lime, and brick at lower prices. At the same time, the prison provided a market for struggling merchants and farmers while it offered opportunities for various local jobs, especially as guards. When the shoe company contracted inmates, it also hired at least twenty locals to assist in the process.[2] Just as the prison factory had become an economic entity in the eastern prisons, Colorado State Penitentiary proved, as its founders expected, to be an economic asset - albeit somewhat different. But this interchange of labor did not long remain a perfect marriage, and the flaws appearing in the relationship required constant mending.

Inmate labor presented competition to free labor and private manufacturing in Colorado, but for several reasons Colorado's legislature resolved it with somewhat less acrimony and tension than the eastern states did. Of course the fewer numbers of inmates and lesser quantities of production involved played a key role in easing Colorado's approach to inmate labor, but heritage also proved a great asset. Having learned of the fraud and convict abuse when institutions relinquished total custody of prisoners to private lessees or entrepreneurs, Colorado only permitted outside inmate labor when under prison guard. To Colorado's credit, it was one of the few western states that never resorted to the lease system (private companies managing prisoners for their work and a fee) as did Nebraska, Oklahoma, Kansas, Washington, Oregon, California, Montana and Wyoming.[3] The wardens were the first to become skeptical of the presence of manufacturing foremen and instructors and the problems which their interchange with inmates often caused. As noted in the early growth years, the prison targeted the open market for the available natural resources of stone and lime. Also, the slow but never-ending institutional expansion and development of water and sewer facilities busied the inmates and reduced the demoralizing aspects of idleness.

But even with the limited industrialization in the Colorado State Penitentiary, the rapidly growing labor unions, tutored by more sophisticated eastern unions, helped to channel the course of inmate labor. If it seems curious that early labor unions in sparsely settled Colorado could wield considerable power, consider the fact that one of the two oldest functioning organizations in Colorado is a union whose history began in 1860, only two years after the first gold seekers arrived; then five printers brought their charter across the plains on a freight team and organized the Denver Typographical Union No 47. Interestingly by 1888, Colorado had more labor organizations in proportion to its population than any other state.[4] And during the 1880s, the decade when Colorado experienced its greatest percentage of population increase, unions, especially railroad unions, multiplied.[5] Colorado's first labor census revealed union membership at 8,894 members in 1888, but it almost doubled to 15,789 four years later. Indeed, with 28,089 members in 1900 and another sizable spurt two years later when the rosters totaled 46,946, unions sustained some clout in Colorado.[6]

While many unions actually saw no competition from inmate labor, they gained an awareness of potential problems from eastern union organizers. Most unions were affiliated with the Knights of Labor which adopted eight recommendations pertaining to "evil" or unfair competition of convict labor as early as 1886 in Richmond, Virginia. In essence, unions stressed the importance of locals working with their state legislatures to restrict inmate labor and to demand that inmates earn money for their families. Other union goals were to prevent convicts from working for the federal government and to disseminate information against convict labor.[7] With this orientation, Colorado unions actively pursued a political role.

Alerted to the need for protecting their newly-won five-dollar wage for an eight-hour day, the Brick-Layers' International Union of America struck at the prison brick-making contract and the "circumvented" leasing arrangement between the warden and brickyard owner W.C. Catlin.[8] By refusing to use convict-made bricks, the unions and some private Cañon City brick manufacturers gradually reduced the prison brick sales until, by the late 1890s, the convicts only produced bricks for state use.[9] Not only brick but also the sale of prison-cut rock generated complaints locally and statewide.

Cheap labor threatened other Colorado trades which began unionizing in 1878 and continued in the 1880s. Soon the carpenters, miners, cigarmakers, horse-shoers, stone masons and stone cutters managed to raise their pay scales to four and five dollars a day. To consolidate their strength, fourteen unions joined together in 1882 to form the Trades Assembly which sought, among other labor objectives, "reforms in prison labor so as to prevent the product of the convict coming into competition with honest industry."[10] They began to think about non-competitive forms of employment for the inmates, but did not offer any viable solutions at that time.

During a legislative battle over convict labor in 1885, Colorado labor unions played their first key political role. Having won a successful strike against the Union Pacific Railroad in 1884, the enlarged Knights of Labor elected "several members to the House of Representatives" and adopted a plank outlawing convict labor.[11] Joining with the Trades-Union Assembly, they successfully fought an ill-conceived legislative plan to reduce the cost of prison maintenance. The proposed bill would have leased convict labor to a private company and paid that lessee fifty-two cents a day for twenty years.[12] To the chagrin of the senators who introduced the lease plan, a concerted outcry erupted. The unions, claiming to represent "15,000 working men," mobilized their strength, sent resolutions and lobbied against Senate Bill No. 117. One resolution stated that the bill would be "injurious to labor and capital and detrimental to the reform . . . of the convicts" because the company had interest in profits and none in the convicts.[13]

As the unions mapped strategy to protest on the Senate floor, they also stated that Governor Evans "and hundreds of others were at this moment fighting our battle, talking to senators at their houses." They cited the dangerous situation in Nebraska where convicts did all of the state printing and fabricated almost all of the harnesses. Other objectors raised the question as to why the legislature would offer to pay more for the maintenance of the convicts than the state was currently spending (the average cost was forty-seven and one half cents per day). Combining self-interest with humanitarian concern, the unions also argued that Colorado's prison death rate was less than one percent, while in Texas, where they "farm them out," it was 14.7 percent.[14]

When the Senate bill reached the House floor, it met with "merciless opposition and was dead on arrival."[15] Defeating the bill saved the state from adopting the lease system, which, as shown by experience elsewhere, invited bribes and fraud among officials and mistreatment of convicts such as beatings, death, starvation, overwork, loss of humanity and racism. Seemingly the *Rocky Mountain News* spoke for many when it reported that the killing of the penitentiary "farm bill meets approval of the press of the state."[16]

Anti-convict labor forces won another legislative victory in 1887 when they lobbied the Colorado Legislature whose membership included eight labor union members.[17] Their efforts terminated the private contracting of inmate labor and banned any "giving of free labor." Specifically, the 1887 law forbade the "hiring out" of convicts to individuals, corporations, counties or cities, forbade the state from bringing in any outside convict labor or from importing any convict-prepared material for the "erection of or repairing of any public building."[18] Arguments which promoted this law ensued from a wide variety of interested parties — each demanding that its ox not be gored. Contractors who did not hire inmates were jealous of those who did; some groups complained about the importing of or the buying of cheap convict-made products from other state prisons; the building trades unions feared the importation of convicts as strikebreakers.[19]

While free workers, tradesmen and small manufacturers had won legislative restrictions on the flow of convict goods and abolished the contract system in some states, still those states could not legally enforce the limitations on products imported from other state prisons. Jobbers could flood the states with cheap unmarked convict products even though they restrained their own prison competition. Consequently, state laws could not protect convict competition adequately. The solution seemed to lie in obtaining a federal law which would allow the states to police convict-made products coming from other states.

Conditions Necessitating Federal Regulation

In 1886, a group of manufacturers organized for that very purpose of obtaining federal protection against convict labor. The vice-president of the Mitchell and Lewis Wagon Company of Racine, Wisconsin, invited manufacturers to meet at Chicago's Grand Pacific Hotel. There, they organized the National Anti-Convict Contract Association with the second article of their constitution defining its object as

> the thorough investigation of the subject of convict labor, for the purpose of discovering and securing the adoption of that method of employing the prison population in the various states which shall be the least burdensome to all labor and least oppressive to manufacturing interests.[20]

They specifically resolved to assist in the passage of a federal law to prohibit the sale of convict-made goods outside of the state where manufactured and to inform Congress and the legislatures of the various methods which might be suitable to replace the lease and contract methods. A Coloradan, W.J. Kinsey, president of the Kinsey Implement Company of Denver, numbered among the twenty-seven officials of lumber, furniture, farm implement, stove, shoe and wagon companies. The products of those companies comprised some of the major money producers in prisons, but note that Colorado's Mr. Kinsey would not have found any farm implements under manufacture behind the walls in Cañon City. Obviously, Kinsey's interests stemmed from a broader base or perhaps a future concern.

In the midst of the struggle between capital and labor, the unions explored another avenue. To validate their charges of unfair competition, the proponents of legal restrictions needed actual data regarding the amount and effects of prison-made products. They lobbied for state and federal Bureaus of Labor which could prepare data helpful to labor's causes. By 1887, eighteen states, including Colorado, and the federal government established such bureaus with resources to pursue the kind of convict employment information desired.

Faced with requests for regulation, Congress approved a joint resolution asking the United States Commissioner of Labor to conduct

> a ... full investigation as to the kind and amount of work
> performed in the penal institutions, ... as to the methods
> under which convicts are or may be employed ... and
> the influence of the same upon the industries of the
> country ....[21]

The outcome was a five hundred page study of convict labor based on extensive testimony included in the *Second Annual Report* in 1888. According to the evidence, the product of inmate labor constituted only .54 of one percent of all production, but that fact did not invalidate the claim that "locally and in certain industries the competition may be serious and require legislative attention."[22] The Bureau of Labor authorized a second convict labor investigation in 1905 which revealed that prison labor in specific industries had practically driven free labor products from the market; specific industries included stoves, hollow ware, saddletrees, whips and cooperage (especially in Chicago). Other products causing severe loss to free labor involved shoes in eleven states, furniture (a single company controlled seven prisons) and workshirts.[23] With the controversy still flourishing, the United States Commissioner of Labor ordered extensive convict labor reports again in 1923 and 1940.

At no time did the opponents of convict labor advocate idleness for the inmates; they presented two options for productive work — public works and state-use. Always they were in accord with the idea that if honest men had to work for a living, the dishonest should. They opposed competition, not prison labor. Their proposition presented at the American Federation of Labor convention in 1897 stated: "The labor ... shall be used for the manufacture of such articles as are required for use in the various state ... institutions," and, when possible, to raise suitable farm products. Further, the plan suggested only an eight-hour day and that all manufactures be carried on by hand labor.[24] These specifics were the same as those adopted by the Industrial Commission on Prison Labor which Congress established in 1898. Continuing to deny charges that unions opposed prison work, Samuel Gompers again stressed their viewpoint in 1911:

> Prisoners should be required to work not for the private
> profit of contractors, nor even for the financial profit of
> the state, but for their reformation and for the benefit of
> their dependents.[25]

Clearly, the goals for the opponents of convict competition lay in promoting an end to contract labor and the adoption of the state-use plan. Through the unceasing efforts of the National Anti-Contract Association, organized workers, free manufacturers and social workers, the federal government prohibited any contracting of federal prisoners to private corporations or individuals in 1887, the same year in which Colorado had done so.[26] After struggling for three-quarters of a century, New York became the first state to adopt the state-use system in 1897.[27] Private profit was out, and New York inmates toiled in some twenty diversified industries such as manufacturing desks for schools, shirts for firemen, brooms for street-cleaners, and shoes for policemen. The unions heaped praise on New York's state-use plan and noted that the reform features led to a decrease in the number of prisoners even though the population was increasing.[28] Some states followed New York, but on the eve of World War I, twenty-four states were still contracting inmate labor to private companies. Only in a few states had the proponents of confining inmate labor to state-use achieved a satisfactory level of non-competition. Most states, however, utilized several systems of inmate labor.[29] For example, Colorado forbade contract labor with private parties but sold prison goods on the open market and employed inmates on public works and roads, the systems being public account and public works.

Following the contemporary trend, Colorado created a Board of Charities and Corrections in 1891 to investigate and advise on policies regarding its institutions. This advisory board recommended that prison employment should be shop and educational work and allow some compensation that could be used toward the inmates's maintenance and his family's support. That plan would promote productive work for prisoners and also protect free labor by selling closer to market prices.[30] Those recommendations, along with the effort to reduce Colorado's inmate maintenance cost (the highest of fifteen prisons tabulated — in Connecticut, Illinois, Indiana, two in Iowa, Kansas, Massachusetts, Missouri, two in New York, Ohio, two in Pennsylvania and Wisconsin), spurred Colorado's lawmakers into relenting somewhat on their 1887 ban on outside labor.[31] By adding a clause to the prison labor statutes, the General Assembly allowed a convict to work where there was "the least conflict" to the free market; from his earnings should be deducted the cost of maintenance with the remainder going to his family or saved for his discharge.[32]

But this plan proved unworkable when the "not so gay nineties" decade in Colorado became one of economic recession due to the decline in silver prices. Colorado's unemployment rose to twenty-one percent in 1900; this meant 47,000 were out of work or 2,000 more than had lost their jobs during the "Panic of 1893." Understandably then, free labor vigilantly guarded against efforts by prison officials to create work for their ever-increasing numbers. Even though Colorado legalized unions in 1889, this had not signified that the General Assembly was pro-labor, and mining unions continued to face severe hurdles from the governors and militia.[33] The lobbying by private enterprise strengthened the unions on the issue of prison labor.

The active miners'organizations, joined by the farmers, loudly objected when Warden Cleghorn requested the legislature to acquire some mineral land for a branch penitentiary or to set aside state land for commercial agriculture. The warden reasoned that those pursuits would comply with inmates employed in occupations of "the least conflict," a clause of the law of 1897.[34] Trying to alert the public *via* a news interview at Denver's Windsor Hotel in 1898, Cleghorn blamed the lack of appropriations for inmate idleness and the inability to set up shops for production of clothing and shoes for all institutions.[35]

Idleness was still an issue when Cleghorn's successor, C.P. Hoyt, accepting a third non-consecutive term in 1898, proposed to employ inmates by setting up shops for the manufacture of bottles, window glass and hollow ware. Since there was no hollow ware manufacturer west of the Mississippi River, those products would be of "least conflict" in Colorado.[36] Despite its merits, the hollow ware plan met the familiar roadblock for new prison ideas — the legislators' unwillingness or inability to appropriate funds.

And yet another obstruction to prison sales arose when some members of the Denver Trades and Labor Assembly visited the prison and reported "discoveries" that Hoyt was making and selling cigars, brick, lime and dressed stone.[37] The warden denied selling cigars or laying brick, but admitted that they were selling brick, stone and lime because he was obeying the law "to keep convicts at work."[38] Credible rumors, nevertheless, still persist in Cañon City where various homeowners assert that convicts built their brick or stone homes. This illustrates the paradox — one man's profit by cheap labor or product is another's loss of a job or sale. Only a few jobs performed outside the prison escaped criticism. No "job" complaints arose when a Cañon City banker, unable to open his safe, called a non-union safe cracker from behind the stone walls to perform his "expert" service.[39]

On the eve of the convention of the Colorado State Federation of Labor in 1899, a news article indicated strong reaction to proposals by the Penitentiary Board and Warden Hoyt to develop some "least conflict" industries within the prison such as hollow ware, bottles and window glass. "The question will probably form the foremost topic of discussion at the convention, it having a vital bearing on the future of the working man," the spokesman predicted.[40] During Hoyt's last year in office, "the most animated meeting ever held within walls" transpired. The Board of Penitentiary Commissioners and Governor Charles Thomas heard the grievances of the Colorado Federation of Labor delegates. The Board explained that if the Legislature appropriated more money, they could stop the competitive sales. In turn, the governor pledged to work with the unions to change the law and to ask for more canal work for the convicts.[41] Hoping to avoid any competition, the emphasis shifted to the hoped-for inmate work on public ways and roads by the end of the century.

In sympathy with nationally organized anti-convict labor groups who were urging restrictive state laws, Colorado further impeded prison sales. In 1903, the legislature set some specific rules for out-of-state vendors of convict-made products. The dealer had to obtain a yearly $500 license, post a $5,000 bond, record all transactions with the secretary of state and label products as being "convict-made" with the date and place of manufacture.[42] Branding products informed the public what they were buying, but even when a state adopted such a law, problems remained. For example, whereas Colorado's law limited prison labor to products that created "least conflict" with free labor, other states could still legally send in their prison products, conform to the labeling and sell to those who chose lower prices. Many agents from other states practiced uncurbed deception by sending unmarked prison-made goods for sale. Only a federal law could restrict this interstate practice because various state laws prohibiting unlabeled packaged goods had been declared unconstitutional. Several bills had passed in the House of Representatives, but the Senate opposed interstate restriction until 1928.[43]

When Congress appointed an Industrial Commission on Prison Labor in 1898 to gather information on the employment of inmates, the facts pointed to progress in reducing competition. While the value of convict-produced goods sold on the open market in 1885 had amounted to $24,271,078, it had dropped to just over $19,000,000 ten years later although the total number of inmates had increased by 13,000.[44] Along with the other Rocky Mountain States, Colorado, with its paucity of manufacturing and its imposition of restrictions, ranked the lowest in value of prison-produced products.[45]

Even so, efforts to align Colorado with the national movement to reduce prison sales continued. To inform Colorado readers of the harm of penitentiary-made goods, the *Colorado Manufacturer and Consumer* reprinted an eastern magazine article in 1925. The Colorado editor prefaced the article with "the facts presented . . . should be of interest to every manufacturer and merchant" because "nearly fifty industries [are] losing sales to this $100,000,000 competitor." The author compiled the facts from the 1923 investigation made by the United States Department of Labor and revealed that the severity of competition to certain industries had prompted Commerce Secretary Herbert Hoover to appoint an investigating committee.[46] In that same year, the Colorado Federation of Labor urged Coloradans to support the national movement against prison contractors whom the union described as "viscious leeches, corrupt politicians and a secret Prison Factory Trust which can be killed by publicity." Because the published list of prison contractors contained none from Colorado, the Federation was obviously aiming at the shipment into the state of prison-made products such as textiles, harness, shoes and furniture. Like a modern day Ralph Nader, the Federation urged the public to check with each store for the brands of those contractors, and if there, then boycott the store.[47]

On the other side of the coin, a portion of the citizenry argued against the efforts to limit convict labor with a variety of comments:

> Idleness drives them crazy. We should not allow idle-
> ness at state expense when they are sentenced to hard
> labor. Work is reformation. They should be self-
> supporting. Other prisons pay their own way. Teach
> them discipline and a trade. Unions don't pay all the
> taxes. Why not buy "made in Colorado" rather than
> from other states?[48]

Those arguments clearly illustrate the ambivalent attitudes which the officials and the lawmakers had to sort out.

Deceptions Relating to Inmate Labor

Trying to please the public and stay in office, the governors, legislators and wardens engaged in devious political exercises. For the most part, a wardenship and the Board of Penitentiary Commissioners were political rewards and even after civil service began, the margin for politics remained. Under pressure to run workshops and diversified work programs efficiently while attempting to balance their budgets and administer the prison plant, the wardens had to deal with the ever-inquiring media. Undoubtedly, confusion within their often-times unprofessional accounting procedures provoked much questioning. Also it was a given that favoritism and competition did occur among prospective vendors, suppliers and contractors.

Investigation after investigation in Colorado resulted from hasty and some-times unfounded news media charges that hampered the work programs. Such comments appeared as "There seems to be something very rotten in the lime business," or "One person refused to serve because he felt like holding his nose after a visit."[49] A description of one investigation illustrates the hindrances posed by jealousy and political favoritism to the continuity of the labor program. In 1894, one of the penitentiary commissioners, F.A. Raynolds of Cañon City, bore the brunt of a series of charges. Contrary to state law, the warden had regularly deposited a large amount of the cash earnings from inmate labor in Raynolds' Cañon City bank which paid the state no interest. The warden had purchased flour, sometimes without a bid, from a mill partially owned by Raynolds and leased Raynold's land for prison gardens upon which the inmates made physical improvements. J.W. McCandless, well-known pioneer of Florence, made the charges to the *Rocky Mountain News* and set off another investigation. When most of the charges were confirmed, the political tumult resulted in personnel changes in both the warden's office and the Board.[50]

For the most part, the public lacked awareness of the magnitude of inmate idleness, and the warden's job depended upon his public relations. Accordingly, his reports to his superiors usually contained glossy accounts of economic improvements and only targeted deficiencies which the warden hoped the legislature would remedy. Wardens had consistently camouflaged much idleness by assigning more men than needed for each job. With that kind of information — and that appeared mainly in the warden's reports which were not widely read by any other than officialdom - how could the public attain an accurate picture of inmate labor? In reality, much of the public did not care to know; generally the attitude was "out of sight, out of mind." Only when a crisis such as a riot, a deficit, a scandal or cries of unfair competition reached the press did reaction crystallize into some expedient policy.

Nor was the public aware of the violations of the labor laws unless the abuses surfaced. One vivid experience represents the ways in which prison officials scuttled and violated the protective laws. Imprisoned for her socialist and pacifist views in 1917, Kate Richards O'Hare became one of the foremost journalists to publicize the evils of contract labor. Incarcerated in the state prison of Missouri because no federal prison existed for women, she not only experienced but wrote about the common violations. Although federal law forbade working federal prisoners, she was sold to Missouri's state prison for eighteen dollars a month, and, in turn, was illegally contracted to the Oberman Manufacturing Company for fifty cents for a nine-hour day. In a further deception, her work there was to sew company names on prison-made garments as "exploitation for the profit of the political party in power and the prison contractors." For fifty cents a day, O'Hare returned work normally paid at $4.50 to $5.20 and regretted that "the pittance paid me did not go into the treasury of the nation I was presumed to have injured, nor into the treasury of the state of Missouri, but into the pockets of the prison contractor."[51]

When released by President Wilson in 1920, Kate O'Hare publicly articulated prison labor reform and eventually became assistant director of California prisons. Soon her revelations of wrongdoing in the labor systems helped to create a concerned atmosphere for restrictions on prison labor. She publicized many cases like that of a man imprisoned for selling a bale of mortgaged hay; while his labor was worth $6.00 a day, the state received fifty cents — a flagrant example of "sending people to prison for fraud and compounding fraud."[52] Consequently with a heightened recognition of inmate labor problems, more interest turned to legislative remedies.

United Advocacy Produces a Federal Law and the State-Use System

After more than a century of struggle to restrict competitive prison labor through state laws, President Herbert Hoover signed the Hawes-Cooper Bill on 19 January 1929 and divested prison-made goods of interstate character by subjecting them to state laws.[53] In tracing that legislative battle, it is clear that pressure groups actuated the changes chiefly through economic motivation. And a unique alliance of chiefly three groups - organized labor, industry and the General Federation of Women's Clubs - forged the significant milestone. That unified effort of normally competitive groups may seem unique, but, as in the case of protective tariffs, they lobbied from common objectives for the necessary federal legislation that would relieve them from what they regarded as "unfair" competition.

Obviously the American Federation of Labor feared the lowering of wage scales and the loss of jobs while the Manufacturers' Conference on Prison Labor did not like to compete with lower prices of products made by convict labor, but can it be said that the National Federation of Women's Clubs was also economically motivated? After examining the testimony at Senate Hearings, the answer is *yes*. In 1909, a group of women shirt makers in Baltimore complained of the large quantities of shirts manufactured in Maryland prisons and sold at low prices in New York which disallowed its own convicts from selling on the open market.[54] Interested in women's wages, the clubs investigated and resolved that:

The products of convict labor should be consumed by
the State, and that the profits therefrom above the just
cost of his keep should be used to support such dependent family as he may have.[55]

Furthermore, in 1909, the Federation helped to launch the National Committee on
Prisons and Prison Labor, an activist body which consistently appeared before the
governors' conferences to encourage an end to contract labor. So from their initial
interest in the betterment of women's economic plights, the Federated Women
added some compelling humanitarian arguments to the ongoing wage and price
struggle over convict labor.

The arguments presented in the lengthy Congressional hearings regarding the
passage of the Hawes-Cooper bill generally included economic, humanitarian,
reform, constitutional and inmate employment issues. While the economic reasons
for restricting prison competition have been set forth, the others require further
exposition. The following testimony for legal changes sent by the Federated
Women to Senator Harry Hawes appeared at hearings of the Senate Committee on
Interstate Commerce in February of 1928 and illustrated many issues:

Prisoners... must work, not only for their own good and
to support their families, but also for the good of the
State and society. ... Women workers suffer bitterly
from the unfair competition which results from the
prison contract system. Approximately 40 percent of all
work shirts now sold on the markets of this country are
prison-made; 35 percent of the work pants and 10
percent of the overalls are prison-made. Such garments
are manufactured exclusively by women outside the
prison ... both their opportunity for steady work and
their wages are seriously affected. ... The blind also
suffer from the commercial exploitation of the prisoners
by private business interests. Broom-making is the best
industry for the blind.... The prisoner is another victim
... he does not receive a trade he can use when released.
... The prisoner who sews a false label in a prison-made
garment ... knows that he is forced to become a liar and
a cheat.[56]

Many contemporary humanitarian thinkers concurred with the Federated Women's
points of view.

One of the compelling deterrents to the passage of a law similar to the Hawes-
Cooper bill had centered on the constitutionality of restricting interstate commerce.
Although the House of Representatives had passed three similar bills, the Senate

continued to reject the idea of subjecting interstate convict-made goods to the rules of the destination state.[57] On the final day of the debate in the Senate Committee of the Whole on HR 7729, some senators persisted in the argument that it was unconstitutional for the federal government to use its "police powers" on articles that were not "evil," that prison goods were not injurious to the morals of the states, that there was distinction between "commerce" over which Congress did have authority and "manufacture" over which it did not, that Congress should not interfere with the state's right to make its own laws and that citizens have the right of freedom of trade into and through other states. In support of regulation, Senator Hawes argued that the states still would make their own laws, but that this federal law would allow them to protect themselves against harmful prison goods from elsewhere.[58]

Among those opposing the Hawes bill were government officials eager to cut costs, wardens with their needs for labor and discipline, some of the tax conscious public, some of the lawmakers who feared the destruction of their prison markets and of course prison contractors. As the debates continued in December of 1928, seventeen states saw this bill as a disaster since they sold the bulk of their prison products out-of-state. A group of western wardens including Colorado's F. E. Crawford sent a petition which represented this opposition. They opposed Hawes-Cooper because it would destroy their markets and the opportunity for some institutions to be self-supporting. Furthermore, they explained that even when most states operated on the state-use and public works plan, they had a surplus labor which could produce some sale items. Finally, the objectors demanded the right to correct their own prison labor abuses and handle their own domestic problems.[59]

With a most specific reason for objecting to the bill, Warden Crawford referred to his biennial report of 1928 that indicated the greatest farm profit in history accrued largely from out-of-state sales.[60] Although some senators had attempted to exempt farm products from the law, they failed, and the Senate passed the bill with a vote of sixty-five to eleven and nineteen abstentions. As to how the Colorado senators voted, the only clue comes from a Senator George who said that because he was paired with Colorado's Senator Lawrence Phipps who would have voted "no" had he been present, he, George, could not vote although his own vote would have been "yes."[61] The junior Colorado Senator Charles Waterman did not vote either. Seemingly one-fifth of the senators preferred not to take a stand by abstaining.

Although the Hawes-Cooper bill passed in 1929, it did not go into effect for five years to allow the prisons to make necessary adjustments for sales. This also meant that the law's constitutionality could not be tested until 1934 after the law became effective. Meanwhile some states continued to contend that the law would illegally deprive penal institutions of an outlet for their products — equivalent to taking property without due process.[62] Still protesting, the Wardens' Association in 1929 asked for the repeal of the law.[63]

The opportunity to test the law arrived when Asa Whitfield sold shirts made in an Alabama prison in Cleveland, Ohio and received a fifty dollar fine. In 1936, the Supreme Court ruled that no violation of the interstate commerce clause occurred because transportation had come to an end when the goods arrived in Ohio; thus, the state could rule on "evil" products, the Court had upheld the Hawes-Cooper act.[64]

Even after the passage of the federal law, the work of the pressure groups did not end because the statute was simply an enabling act permitting states to make their own laws regarding the sale of prison labor products in their own states. Led by the American Federation of Labor, the propaganda campaign to promote restrictive laws continued within the states. By 1933, Colorado and nineteen other states had passed limitations against open market sales. Colorado's state-use plan, similar to many others, prohibited convict-made goods from being "stored, used, sold, or consumed" by any one other than the state institutions, and all such goods entering the state were subject to the same rules as the Colorado convict materials.[65] A month later, the Colorado General Assembly specified that prison labor could only be used on highways or roads or for institutions and agencies, and that the Board could purchase real estate on which to erect the necessary buildings for new prison industries. In line with the idea of running industries as business, the law also required a business management accounting of labor and materials. One final provision clarified the objectives of inmate labor as both vocational training and production of goods.[66]

Still this type of restriction did not solve all the problems. Enforcement of those state laws was difficult, if not impossible, because the interdicted goods mingled freely in commerce making them unrecognizable until Congress passed an enforcement bill. In contrast to the lengthy debate on Hawes-Cooper, the Ashurst-Summers bill passed easily in May of 1935 with an endorsement from Secretary of Labor Frances Perkins. This enforcement law prohibited the transportation of convict-made goods into any area where such goods were illegal. A second clause required total marking of contents, place of origin and address of consignee with a fine and forfeiture of goods for violations prosecuted in federal courts.[67] It too passed the Supreme Court test of constitutionality. But on October 14, 1940, the third and most restrictive of the prison labor acts banned the interstate transportation of all convict-made goods with the exception of agricultural commodities, repair parts for farm machinery, federal prison-made goods going to other federal institutions and prison-produced commodities purchased by any other state institution.[68]

Effects of the Restrictions

Exactly what effect the restrictive laws had on prison labor is difficult to measure because of other major contributing factors in the 1930s - the depression, the increase in prison population and the failure of the prisons to adjust their programs to the changing industrial scene. But as noted, the immediate reaction to the Hawes-Cooper Act was that the states passed restrictive legislation which caused prison products to virtually disappear from the market. Colorado's Warden Roy Best complained in his 1934 and 1936 reports that the canning factory profits were down because of the Hawes-Cooper Act.[69] During the biennium of 1931-2, the canning factory had received $66,000 from canned goods which it produced and shipped out of state, but afterwards most states cut off Colorado's market.

The findings of the 1940 United States Bureau of Labor Statistics showed that the contract and piece-price systems had practically disappeared; that open-market sales involving interstate transportation were relatively unimportant, only about $1,500,000; that thirty-six states produced no goods that went into markets outside the state of manufacture.[70] Explaining the collapse of the contract system to the American Prison Association, James V. Bennett revealed:

> All the big distributors have refused to handle prison products, most of the prison contractors have walked out, and only in a few of the states is any real attempt made to market prison products to anyone except farmers who purchase the binder-twine made in mid-western prisons.[71]

Of course, this meant an increase in convict idleness with 61 percent of those productively employed in 1923 dropping to 44 percent by 1940.[72]

However, legal restrictions did not cause all of the inmate idleness because lack of planning on the part of the state also exacerbated idleness. As early as 1931, the United States National Commission on Law Observation and Enforcement blamed the prison administrators for not developing adequate state-use industries, adding that "their lack of business acumen, daring, and ingenuity suffer in comparison with the entrepreneurs of the free business world."[73] In turn, prison administrators indicated that lack of state finances to start prison industries fueled idleness as well as restraining them from furnishing all of the goods needed in state institutions; in reality, inmates only produced one-tenth of institutional needs.[74] This was no new complaint for Warden Cleghorn had noted this phenomenon back in 1898 when he complained that the prison could make all the clothing and shoes for institutions if the legislature would make an appropriation to set up shops. He also said that only one-sixth of his prison population had work "all the time."[75] Not until 1927 did Colorado legislate that all institutions must buy clothing items manufactured by the Colorado State Penitentiary.[76]

After many states had implemented the state-use plan, the problem then was to force other institutions to utilize convict-made goods. By 1937, Colorado was one of twenty-two states that had attempted to create a market for state-use industries by requiring tax-supported agencies to purchase prison products.[77] At first glance, this would seem to be a satisfactory solution. Such was not the case. Many states only required state institutions to purchase prison-made goods and omitted the market for such jurisdictional agencies as cities and schools. Purchasing agents changed specifications so that prison products did not comply, and then they could evade the law by buying elsewhere. One of the American Prison Association directors observed the warehouse full of furniture at the Illinois prison and gave a practical and commonplace reason as to why governmental agents did not buy prison goods: "The seller for the private company can give them a big dinner and slip them fifty dollars and the man that represents the State can't do it," he said.[78] Competition to supply institutions continued with private jobbers often underbidding prison goods. Colorado tackled this obstacle by legislating that the various institutional Boards could only purchase outside products if they were ten percent less than the state products and of equal quality. In that same law of 1937, Colorado created a purchasing agent to handle convict goods.[79] But with the ten percent regulation, governmental agencies still had a quandary — paying up to ten percent more for Colorado prison goods could be too costly for their budgets. A further obstacle to inmate employment evolved when some states prohibited certain goods from being manufactured by prisons even for state-use.

Lastly, how did the Hawes-Cooper Act affect the federal government? After the various groups turned to the federal government for relief from competition with prison product, it is only natural to suspect that an increasing federal role in state prisons would follow, especially when compounded with the crisis of the Great Depression. In line with increased federal intervention during the decade of the thirties, various governmental commissions relating to prison labor appeared. First was the Wickersham Law Commission which reported to President Herbert Hoover that there were serious problems in all of the prisons.[80] Then the short-lived National Recovery Act aimed to create a market for prison products by raising prices of convict-made goods to market level. Finally, President Franklin Roosevelt appointed the Prison Industries Reorganization Administration under Chairman Joseph N. Ulman which investigated state prisons only at their request. The Administration then could suggest possible prison industries. In its 1940 investigation of Colorado, the Prison Industries Reorganization Administration reported that Colorado ". . . has a good start toward industrialized employment for State-use production," but there should be more cooperation among agencies and strict compliance with the laws.[81]

In predicting the future for the paradoxical labor problem, the Chairman of the Prison Labor Committee, Howard Gill, stressed the need for business management methods, for trained industrial engineers to relieve the wardens and for sound accounting procedures.[82] Recognizing the seriousness of increased inmate idleness, Chairman of the Prison Industries Reorganization Committee Louis N. Robinson denied that free labor and manufacturing interests had been the chief cause. On the contrary, the obstacles to good prison labor lay in poor management, town locations instead of country locations for prisons and the absence of any settled public opinion. In his belief, jobs should be fitted to the man, not the man to the job.[83] This would require serious classification and profiling of inmate qualifications. The earlier American tradition of a prison supported by the labor of inmates had gradually given way to a new standard — convicts working to learn trades for their reformation and release while avoiding public markets. Beyond all of the outside hurdles, many barriers to employment resided in the prison population itself, and these bear scrutiny.

Profile of the Available Labor

What obstacles did the characteristics of the inmates present to those who planned work programs? Who were the inmates? Surely, they were not generally willing workers unless motivated with a privilege, and they often committed sabotage. Since the average two-year period of confinement was only two years, there was a 100 percent labor turnover within that period. Consider the consequences if private industry faced that turnover. To gain more insight into who the inmates were, I developed a generalized profile by dividing them into two time periods — those who inhabited the prison before 1900 and those between 1900 and 1940. The compilation is derived from the wardens' reports and averaged at five-year intervals (See complete tables in appendix).

First period- 1871-1900

Not until 1882 was a native-born Coloradan incarcerated. By 30 November 1900, names of 5,042 convicts appeared in the "Prison Record Book," and 26.3 percent of them were listed as foreign-born. During that period, the average number of foreign-born residents in Colorado comprised 19 percent of the total population.[84] Thus, a higher percentage of foreign-born were behind walls than resided in Colorado, but this too followed the typical national paradigm. In Colorado, most of the foreign-born inmates came from North Europe, predominately English and Irish. In 1900, only 6.9 percent of the foreign-born listed Mexico as their birthplace. Because the officials varied in their manner of listing nationalities, race and literacy, it is difficult to be totally accurate.

Exactly what definition pertained to an "illiterate" convict is not always clear, but some broad generalizations do appear. The average number of illiterates seems to be about 15 percent, and it is clear that the largest proportion of illiterates was "Mexican." Much racial prejudice existed at the time as indicated by the terminology in listing Hispanic native-borns as "Mexicans." More than half of the inmates were single, and the average age was 26 including many teen-agers. Early details on religion were unavailable, but by 1900, 64 percent were Protestant, 32 percent were Catholic, one-half of one percent were non-Christians and 3.3 percent listed no religion. Eighteen percent of those received were known recidivists.[85] Not surprisingly in a recently settled area, birthplaces indicate that few originated in Colorado; only fifteen of the 390 inmates admitted in the 1899-1900 biennium were born in Colorado, and the majority emigrated from more populous eastern states.

In focusing on inmate labor, it is relevant to examine the occupational background of those convicted of crimes ranging from murder, assault, larceny (most often listed), rape and abortion to horse thieving. For purposes of categorizing what the convicts recorded as their occupations, the category of "trades" includes barber, machinist, painter, cook, tinner, weaver, waiter, carpenter, railroader, mason and stone cutter. Although miners appeared as a separate category in the record book, probably most tradesmen and laborers worked for the mining industry or hoped to at one time. Another detraction from accurate statistics is that there was no way to determine how many were unemployed when convicted. For those connected with agriculture, there are two categories -"farmer" and another "farm B" which includes herder, cowboy, rancher, stockman. The data does not allow delineation as to who might have owned farms. The "professional" designation includes lawyers, teachers, doctors, nurses, engineers and druggists while "white collar" categorizes clerks, salesmen, peddlers and bookkeepers (the largest number). Laborers listed themselves as such. Where or if they worked is unknown, but more than half committed their crimes in Arapahoe County (the Denver area).

From the incomplete data then, only a general profile of the talents of the inmates emerges. The cumulative percentages of each category for the nineteenth century was as follows:

Trades	49.3 percent
Farmer	6.5 percent
Farm B	6 percent
White Collar	5.7 percent
Professional	2 percent
Laborers	22 percent
Miners	8.3 percent

There is no evidence to indicate which prisoners found jobs suitable to their talents, but certainly a few did. For a time, one "printer" worked at the local newspaper office. Another designed the prison hospital, some had clerical jobs, the few women performed the housekeeping jobs which the Victorian era seemed to dictate. The prison obtained a band and a choir toward the turn of the century which obviously matched skills acquired before incarceration. Much construction work and plant maintenance required some of their skills. During the nineteenth century, the greatest number worked in the quarries and lime kilns which might have corresponned to the skills of laborers and miners. By and large, the major consideration of this period was to keep inmates busy and adapt them to remunerative jobs. For a time, some were hired out about the county. Some inmates must have been talented because they produced and sold a variety of trinkets on their own.[86]

Because most were young with many years of life remaining after release, reformers urged the teaching of skills enabling inmates to obtain work when released, but the Colorado State Penitentiary (CSP) had few industries during the nineteenth century and little education other than in the chaplain's religious education program.[87] Despite this, however, many inmates must have left prison with newly acquired skills, work habits and discipline. Some might have obtained work as brickmakers, stone cutters, cooks, plant engineers, or in shoe shops or in many areas of construction. Whether these skills prevented them from further crime is unknown and beyond the scope of this study, but prison time did not have to be wasted during the first thirty years.

Second Period - 1900-1940

During these forty years, the number of convicts registered at CSP rose from the 5042 to 16,846, meaning that 21,888 had entered in the period of this study — the first seventy years. One of the questions to explore here by using the same methods is how the inmates differed from those of the nineteenth century. The most obvious change occurred in the number of foreign-born. Up to 1940, an average of 15.85 percent of the inmates were foreign born, but most of them had come in the first twenty years because the rates decreased from 22.7 percent in 1916 to 2.65 percent in 1940. But, foreign born in Colorado's total population had also dropped from 19 to 7 percent in this time span. An unusual statistic here is that the foreign-born inmate population in 1940 was lower by 4.5 percent than the state's total foreign-born population (see table in appendix). Another change was that the portion of the foreign-born inmate population labeled "Mexican" increased from 4.9 percent to 31.6 percent. In 1900, only 4 percent of the inmates were native Coloradans, but forty years later, 23 percent were. As inaccurate as the measurement of illiteracy is, the data indicates a drop of about five percent from 1900.

Using the same occupational categories, the major changes occurred in the numbers of farmers and miners. The number of incarcerated miners dropped by about one-third in the twentieth century. That is easy to explain because it resembles the overall population ratio. In Colorado's population in 1900, miners comprised 13 percent of the total occupations but in 1940 only 4 percent.[88] To explain the ratio of incarcerated farmers to the free is questionable because free men in agriculture totaled 21 percent in 1900, but in 1940 only 17 percent.[95] Yet the number of incarcerated farmers almost doubled (see table in appendix). Possibly the Prohibition Law caused the rise in those listed as "farmers" on the prison register. About one-fifth of the inmates were incarcerated for violations of that law, many for possessing a still. Another explanation could be that, with the depression and the dust bowl in Colorado, unemployment grew faster than the national average in the 1930s so that more transients listed themselves as "farmers".

For the remainder of the occupational categories, little change occurred in the second period. The average occupational composite was:

Professional	1.8 percent
White Collar	7.4 percent
Laborers	16.45 percent
Farmers	14.86 percent
Farmers B	4.44 percent
Trades	48.9 percent
Miners	5.85 percent

Prison jobs of this period offered more diversity when small industries began in the 1930s. The expansion of leased farms with extensive specialization in livestock, conservation methods and fruit growing offered more opportunities to improve those skills. Road work with hard labor and more emphasis on training in honesty provided new latitude. Otherwise, similar prison jobs of maintenance, construction and quarry work continued in the twentieth century. Throughout the period, shops included metal work, tailoring, shoe repair, clothing manufacture, food canning, and then the license or tag plant.

With no data to determine how well those occupations served the inmate upon his release, it is again only plausible to conclude that some might have learned useful skills. Through incentives for decreased sentences such as "good time" which Colorado provided in the twentieth century, efficiency and better work habits developed, but the obstacles to good production continued. The prison had not yet become a vocational school, and the wardens were still trying to find remunerative inmate jobs within the guidelines of state-use.

BIRTH AND LITERACY RATINGS

Year	Foreign-Born			Illiterate		Total
1875-76	28	30.4%		15	16.3%	92
1879-80	62	27.4%		39	17.2%	226
1885-06	69	23.1%		46	15.4%	298
1889-90	125	32%	*3.8%	?		390
1895-06	129	24%		71	13.3%	535
1899-1900	82	21%	*6.9%	19	4.9%	390
1905-06	81	16.3%	*4.9%	46	9.2%	497
1909-10	143	22.2%	*22.4%	?		643
1915-16	167	22.7%	*22.7%	123	16.7%	735
1919-20	119	22%	*51.2%	83	15.4%	540
1925-26	208	20.5%	*45.7%	81	9.9%	1014
				**19	8%	
1929-30	160	15%	*25.6%	65	6%	1065
				**62	5.7%	
1935-36	61	5.5%	*44.2%	55	4.9%	1113
1939-40	30	2.65%	*33.3%	22	2%	1131

*Proportion of foreign-born from Mexico.
**Inmates could read and write foreign language only.
Compiled by author from Wardens' reports.

INMATE BIRTHPLACES

Biennium	Born in Colo.	Foreign Born	Total
1899-1900	15 (4%)	82 (21%)	390
1939-1940	267 (23%)	30 (2.6%)	1131

Compiled from the Wardens' Reports by author.

AVERAGE PERCENTAGE OF OCCUPTIONS
AS LISTED BY INMATES

	Prof.	White Collar	Laborer	Farmers	B	Trades	Miner
1875-1900	2%	5.7%	22%	6.5%	6%	49.3%	8.3%
1905-1940	1.8%	7.4%	16.45%	14.9%	4%	48.9%	5.85%

Farmer B indicates sheepherders, cowboys, stockmen.
Compiled by author from Wardens' Reports.

NOTES - CHAPTER IV

[1]"Convict Labor," *Second Annual Report of the Commissioner of Labor, 1886* (Washington: GPO, 1887), p. 390.

[2]*Fremont County Record*, Cañon City, Nov. 4, 1882, 1:2.

[3]Blake McKelvey, *American Prisons, A History of Good Intentions* (Montclair, N. J.: Patterson Smith, 1977), pp. 218-234.

[4]*First Biennial Report of the Bureau of Labor Statistics of the State of Colorado, 1887-88* (Denver: Collier, 1888), p. 70·

[5]Harry Seligson and George Bardwell, *Labor-Management Relations in Colorado* (Denver: Sage, 1961), p. 40.

[6]*Eighth Biennial Report of Bureau of Labor of Statistics of Colorado, 1901-2*, (Denver: Smith-Brooks, 1902), p. 84. See pp. 64-82 for a complete listing of unions.

[7]"Convict Labor," *Second Annual Report*, 1886, p. 365.

[8]*Eighth Biennial Report of Bureau of Labor·1902*, p. 72. There were locals in Florence, Cripple Creek and Cañon City.

[9]*Biennial Report of Colorado State Penitentiary, 1900* (hereafter CSP), (Denver:Smith-Brooks, 1900), pp. 6-15.

[10]*First Biennial Report, Colorado Bureau of Labor Statistics, 1888*, pp. 70-91, p. 451 and p. 416.

[11]Seligson, *Labor-Management*, pp. 80-1.

[12]*First Biennial Report, Colorado Bureau of Labor, 1888*, p. 402.

[13]*Rocky Mountain News* (RMN), March 16, 1885, 1:2+.

[14]Ibid.

[15]Ibid., April 2, 1885, 2:1.

[16]Ibid., April 8, 1885, 6:1.

[17]Seligson, *Labor-Management*, p. 81.

[18]*Laws Passed at Sixth Session of General Assembly*, April 2, 1887 (Denver: Tribune, 1887), p. 232.

[19]*RMN*, March 7, 1880, 5:2. This also describes the use of stone for the Tabor building.

[20]"Convict Labor," *Twentieth Annual Report of the Commissioner of Labor, 1905* (Washington:GPO, 1906), p. 366.

[21]*Second Annual Report of the Commissioner of Labor, 1886*, p. 3.

[22]Ibid., 371.

[23]*Twentieth Annual Report of Commissioner of Labor, 1905*, p. 49.

[24]Corinne Bacon, compiled, *Prison Reform* (New York: H.H. Wilson, 1917), p. 202.

[25]John P. Frey, "Trade Union Attitude Toward Labor," *Annals of the American Academy of Political and Social Science* 46, March, 1913. These words came from a speech at the AF of L convention.

[26]The law is quoted in the *Second Annual Report of the Commissioner of Labor, 1886*, p. 604.

[27]Corinne Bacon, *Prison Reform*, p. 222.

[28]_____ "Solving the Convict Problem," *American Federationist*, January, 1899, p. 220.

[29]*Twentieth Annual Report of Commissioner of Labor, 1905*, pp. 302-312.

[30]*Third Biennial Report of State Board of Charities and Corrections, 1896* (Denver: Smith-Brooks, 1896), pp. 10-11.

[31]*First Biennial Report, Colorado Bureau of Labor Statistics, 1888*, p. 409. Colorado cost was $347.34 per year; next highest was $222.78.

[32]*Laws Passed at Eleventh Session of the General Assembly* (Denver: Eames Brothers, 1897), p. 32. Law approved on April 28, 1897.

[33]Harold V. Knight, *Working in Colorado* (Boulder: Center for Labor Education, 1971), p. 33.

103

[34]*Biennial Report of the CSP, 1897-8*, pp. 8-9.

[35]*Denver Daily Times*, July 31, 1898, 2:1

[36]Ibid., June 28, 1899, 4:1.

[37]*Denver Daily Times*, Sept. 18, 1899, 8:6.

[38]Ibid., Dec. 17, 1899, 8:1.

[39]*Fremont County Record*, Dec. 8, 1894, 1:2.

[40]*RMN*, June 5, 1899, 1:2.

[41]*Denver Daily Times*, Dec. 19, 1899, 6:2 and Dec. 17, 1899, 8:1.

[42]*Session Laws*, 1903, pp. 374-7.

[43]Frank T. Flynn, "The Federal Government and the Prison Labor Problem" (Ph. D. dissertation, University of Chicago, 1949), p. 102.

[44]*Report of the Industrial Commission on Prison Labor,* v.3 (Washington: GPO, 1900), p. 41. The number of inmates went from 41,877 to 54, 244.

[45]*Twentieth Annual Report of the Commissioner of Labor, 1905*, p. 49.

[46]Allen Murphy, "Penitentiary-Made Goods," *Colorado Manufacturer and Consumer*, Feb. 1927, p. 10. The industries were shoe and boot, textiles, garments, furniture and cordage.

[47]*Colorado State Federation Yearbook*, 1925, pp. 39-40.

[48]*Denver Daily Times*, June 11, 1899, 4:1. Also see *Third Biennial Report of Board of Charities and Corrections*, 1896, p. 10.

[49]*RMN*, June 24, 1883, 4:1.

[50]Letter from committee investigating Board member F.A.Raynolds to Governor Davis Waite, Nov. 29, 1894, in Governor Waites' box #26693, Colorado State Archive.

[51]Philip S. Foner, ed. *Kate Richards O'Hare* (Baton Rouge: Louisiana State University Press, 1982), p. 29, p. 314, p. 321.

[52]Kate R. O'Hare, "The World Tomorrow," *Nation* 8, May, 1925, pp. 137-8.

[53]*Congressional Record*, 70th Cong., 2nd Sess., April 3, 1928- Jan. 4, 1929, pp. 872-3.

[54]*U.S. Senate*, 70th Cong., 1st Sess., "Hearings of Interstate Commerce Committee," Feb. 7, 8, 9, 17, 1928, p. 70.

[55]Ibid.

[56]Ibid., p. 71.

[57]Frank Flynn, "The Federal Government," pp. 34-52. He details the discussions of the forerunners of the Hawes-Cooper.

[58]*Congressional Record*, 70th Cong., 2nd Sess., "Hearings," Dec. 18, 1928, pp. 874-6.

[59]Ibid., pp. 872-4 and pp. 864-73.

[60]*Biennial Report, CSP*, 1928, p. 10

[61]*Congressional Record*, 70th Cong., 2nd Sess., p. 876.

[62]*United States Bureau of Labor Statistics*, "Laws Relating to Prison Labor in the U.S. as of July 1, 1933," Bulletin No. 596 (Washington: GPO, 1933), p. 5.

[63]*Proceedings of the American Prison Association*, 1929 (New York: The Assoc.,1930), pp. 288-9.

[64]____ *Monthly Labor Review* 42 (Washington: GPO, 1936), p. 907.

[65]*Laws Passed at the Twenty-Ninth Session of the General Assembly*, 1933, p. 392. It was approved April 20, 1933.

[66]Ibid., May 19, 1933, pp. 783-6.

[67]*Congressional Record*, 79th Cong., 1st Sess., July 15, 1935, p. 11824.

[68]Frank Flynn, "The Federal Government," p. 107 and p. 113. Minnesota and Wisconsin tried in vain to exempt binder twine and farm machinery by reporting that Minn. had turned over $20,000,000 in 26 years to the treasury in profits. Wisconsin turned $1,250,000 in 25 years to its treasury.

[69]*Biennial Report*, CSP, 1934, p. 8.

[70]*United States Bureau of Labor Statistics*, 1940, p. 11.

[71]James V. Bennett, "Prison Labor at the Crosswords," *Proceedings of the American Prison Association*, 1934, p. 245.

[72]*United States Bureau of Labor Statistics*, 1940, p. 8.

[73]Frank Flynn, "The Federal Government," pp. 131-8.

[74]Ibid., p. 139.

[75]*Denver Daily Times*, July 31, 1898, 2:1.

[76]*Laws Passed at the Twenty-Sixth Session of the General Assembly*, 1927, pp. 540-1.

[77]Ibid., 31st sess., 1937, p. 922.

[78]*Proceedings of the American Prison Association*, 1930, pp. 147-8.

[79]*Laws Passed at the Thirty-first Session of the General Assembly*, 1937, p. 922.

[80]Judith R. Johnson, "For Any Good At All, A Comparative Study of State Penitentiaries in Arizona, Nevada, New Mexico, Utah, 1900-1980'" (Ph.D. dissertation, Albuquerque: University of New Mexico, 1987), p. 148.

[81]"The Prison Problem in Colorado," *The Prison Industries Reorganization Administration*, (Washington: GPO, 1940), p. 44.

[82]Howard Gill, "The Prison Labor Problem," *Annals of the American Academy*, 1933, p. 98.

[83]Louis N. Robinson, *Should Prisoners Work?* (Chicago: Winston Penn Co., 1931), pp. 248 and 301-2.

[84]Seligson, *Labor-Management*, p. 310. This table was compiled from 11th, 12th, 13th, U.S. census figures and lists 20 % for 1880, 20% for 1890 and 17% for 1900 so I averaged that into 19% for the period. See copy of this table in appendix.

[85]*Biennial Report CSP*, 1899-1900, p. 12.

106

[86]*Sixth Biennial Report of the State Board of Charities and Corrections*, 1902, pp. 84-5. The sales of over $25,000 had resulted from trinkets, - canes, inlaid boxes, etc. The prisoners had sold these through the mail in "begging letters."

[87]*Biennial Report CSP*, 1890, p. 10.

[88]Seligson, *Labor-Management*, p. 312 and pp. 316-7. The population of Colorado was 539,700 in 1900; in 1940 it was 1,123,296. Tables are reproduced from census.

CHAPTER V
HONOR ROAD CAMPS

*The state has a property right
in the labor of the prisoners.*
Stagg Whitin[1]

The above quotation rests legally on the language of the Thirteenth Amendment to the United States Constitution which prohibited involuntary servitude except as a punishment for crime. At the same time, it reinforces the widely-held philosophy that convicts must perform hard labor as part of their incarceration sentence. Thus, in the early twentieth century, after several states began using convict labor to build roads, Stagg Whitin, chairman of the National Committee on Prison Labor, became a leading proponent for aligning the necessity of convict employment with the public need for better roads. He reasoned that "Convicts and roads both being state property, the maximum of efficiency is possible through their joint operation."[2] In this sense, then, the quotations are relevant to Colorado's convict road-building era. Add to the belief in the state's right to the inmate's labor the problem of finding work which offered the least competition to free labor, and Colorado had completed the equation. It was Colorado's solution to this equation which achieved national acclaim for its honor system of inmate road building during the first quarter of the twentieth century.

Background of Road Work

Whereas the penitentiary had been chiefly a product of the nineteenth century, convict labor on roads was certainly not a new concept; in fact, it had been a traditional role for *servi poenas* (slaves of punishment or convicts) during the Roman times, if not before.[3] Early examples of road work in America included a 1658 statute of the Virginia Colonial Assembly compelling the convicts to perform road work. Similarly, Governor Bienville ordered the convicts to clear the swamps in 1718 for the foundation of New Orleans. But in 1786, when the convict street work amidst Philadelphia's dense population led to embarrassing interchanges between convicts and the public, officials decided to build a penitentiary so that prisoners could work behind walls and out of view.

On the other hand, in the South where the plantation system existed along with a sparse population and a mild climate, the lease of convicts for outdoor work — such as in the mines, in the lumber and turpentine industry, in laying railroad track or on farms — proved practical if not always humane and aroused little criticism. But the historic moment for convict road work surfaced with the advent of the bicycle in the 1890s, the need for better communications through good roads and a final stimulus from automobile technology. Near the end of the nineteenth century, Delaware worked convicts on a first phase of road construction by preparing stone for the process and soon California did likewise.[4]

To discuss road building and convict labor in tandem reveals further reasons why they came into focus at the turn of the century nationally as well as in Colorado. First, while the federal government had fostered its industries with a protective tariff, developed its railroads through land grants and had expended millions on harbors, canals, and inland waterways, it had left highways — the basic communication between the farm and city — to local development. Not surprizingly, local governments had found no satisfactory solution for the expense of building sorely-needed roads to reduce the cost of transporting food products to market as well as to distribute industrial products in rural areas.

Another concern was the isolation resulting from scarcity of roads in both the West and the South which retarded not only economic development but also cultural advancement. Addressing this problem as far back in time as the 1880s, Radical Republican Senator Charles Sumner declared that "the two greatest forces for the advancement of civilization are the schoolmaster and good roads."[5] Reaffirming that argument in the first decade of the twentieth century, the president of the National Highway Association presented statistics to prove that poor roads prevented accessibility to educational facilities. Illiteracy rates were 600 percent higher for rural areas than urban areas.[6]

As noted in Chapter IV, mounting pressure from manufacturers and labor unions caused many states to legislate against the contract-labor system and the sale of prison-made goods and then to seek less competitive inmate employment. Since commercial, educational, transportation and industrial interests all clamored for better roads, the need for convict employment conveniently seemed to fit the economics of road building. Indeed, contemporary thought categorized inmate road building as non-competitive with outside labor and beneficial not only to the inmate himself but also to the state.

As the demand for improved roads increased, Colorado, like much of the West, was seeking a solution to its surplus inmate labor that would alleviate its over-crowded facilities and would be of least conflict to free labor. At the turn of the century, Governor James B. Orman expressed his concern that "the most vexatious question" is employment, and because older states have not solved the problem, Colorado has no guide.[7] Hence, Colorado's leaders, aware of older prison experiences marred by the complaints of competition from manufacturers and free labor and lack of humanitarian concern for the inmate, cautiously approached the philosophy of productive work for the public. Leading the way for implementation of this philosophy at its 1885 convention, the Colorado Democratic Party adopted a resolution for convicts to receive "permanent employment in the construction and improvement of public roads."[8]

Other promoters of developing good roads with inmate employment included the newspapers and citizen groups. Among the advocates was the *Cañon City Clipper* which urged that the local "sand" roads should be covered with crushed rock so that "our roads are as good as in the East," and that the convicts should do the rock crushing.[9] While commenting on the successful work on State Canal No.1, the editor of the *Rocky Mountain News* promoted public road work as a successful operation for the inmates.[10] According to the *Denver Daily Times*, the convicts could improve their physical conditions through outdoor work and "make the penitentiary and its inmates worth something to the state instead of a burden on it."[11]

In his 1899 Inaugural Address, Democratic Governor Charles S. Thomas also recommended road work for the convicts.[12] A labor paper, the *Pueblo Courier*, maintained that the unions did not oppose convict work if controlled by the state.[13] A prison city paper requested that convicts leave the prison for employment on the roads.[14] Even more ambitious, the *Rocky Mountain News* endorsed proposals to build irrigation reservoirs and to allow convicts to dig a railroad tunnel under the Continental Divide. This latter proposal, however, incurred the opposition of Governor Albert W. McIntire concerned over the cost of maintaining a second prison at the work site and the "inefficiency of convicts as miners."[15]

Responding to the various suggestions, the General Assembly in 1899 provided for an experimental program of public road building by appropriating $18,460 for a wagon road from Pueblo to Leadville. The breakdown of expenses for a two-year-period was:

$2,400 .... salary of the superintendent
$6,400 .... eight guards
$3,200 .... four overseers
$1,500 .... equipment
$1,200 .... teams and wagons
$1,500 .... bridge
$2,260 .... headquarters for the convicts[16]

Road superintendent John Chetelat reported to Governor Charles S. Thomas in 1899 that the working period extended from May 12 to December 18 with twenty prisoners and eighteen reformatory inmates on duty, and only three trusties attempting escapes. The Fremont County surveyor followed practical route along the Arkansas River from Pueblo to Nathrop (six miles below Buena Vista). They situated the bridge at Bray's Crossing and trailed the old Cañon City-Leadville stage road to Buena Vista, Riverside, Granite and Leadville with a reduction of grade from 20 percent to 7 percent.[17]

Chetelat's second report revealed that crews of twenty-four prisoners and eighteen reformatory inmates worked from March 5 to October 20, 1900. To avoid the inefficient method of transporting the convicts to and from the work site, they built one stockade — the forerunner of the road camp — three miles south of Cotopaxi and another nearer to the reformatory at Buena Vista.[18] After two seasons and two additional months of work, Chetelat had spent most of the allotted $18,460 and released the equipment and remaining funds of $1,041 to the warden. A rough estimate would be that the convicts "improved" about 45 miles of roadways while hewing much of the difficult route from the granite cliffs of the Arkansas River. During the process, the *Cañon City Times* praised the small road gang for advancing 100 feet per day through difficult terrain.[19]

On the other side of the coin, the Board of Charities and Corrections (the gubernatorial advisory board of six persons established in 1891 to overlook all state social institutions) called the road experiment "unsatisfactory" and recalled that the "project to employ prison labor on the Gunnison tunnel, authorized by law two years ago, was found impracticable."[20] Probably their disillusionment stemmed from the fact that only a small number of inmates were actually involved while the prison housed a population of 621 in 1902. Above all else, this group's perspective concerned the welfare of the inmates, and they, like the Philadelphians of old, had criticized off-site work because "the present method of working the prisoners in gangs away from the prison gives them an opportunity for degrading, boastful prison talk, and should be discouraged." As a substitute, the Board recommended a more extensive pursuit of the individual trinket sales wherein inmates manufactured and sold items through the mails and local shops.[21] Despite some criticism, this road experiment helped to chart future more extensive roadbuilding.

After Warden John Cleghorn's recall to service in 1902 (he had served two terms from 1894-98), he directed more interest toward public work. By introducing a report from the Office of Public Road Inquiries to the Board of Charities and Corrections, he helped to dispel one of the negative responses to public work. The Board had feared the practices in some southern state where ". . . the negro convict is a slave . . . more deplorable than in ante-bellum days." By contrast, the report praised New Mexico's successful convict labor on mountain roads in exchange for "good time" rewards broadened their tolerance.[22] Soon this group of social institution advisors also lent their support to a plan similar to that of New Mexico Territory.

The Lewis Road Bill and the Origin of the Honor Camp

Road work received the go-ahead from the fifteenth session of the General Assembly when it passed the Lewis Road bill (introduced by the senator from Fremont County) in April, 1905. County or city commissioners could send written requests to employ convict labor for road or street work, but those governmental bodies must pay additional guard expenses and furnish all necessary materials. As a quasi-compromise between the demands to protect skilled labor and the need to employ convicts, the law prohibited inmates from performing any skilled labor or from building bridges. The Board of Penitentiary Commissioners could grant additional "good time" for such convict service.[23] The incentive of a reduced sentence in return for work was pivotal to this law's practicality because it improved the convict's behavior and alleviated the overcrowded prison housing.

As with many non-specific laws, the Board of Penitentiary Commissioners requested a legal clarification as to who would pay the extra subsistence for convicts away from prison. The Attorney General opined that the state must be responsible.[24]

With that knowledge, Warden John Cleghorn, an ex-sheriff and San Juan county clerk, began to implement this law and establish camps. At the same time, the local newspaper boasted that "Fremont County will derive the greatest benefits . . . by reason of its close proximity. . . . it was not intended the convicts should be taken very far away from the penitentiary for the purpose of doing this sort of work."[25] Despite the reporter's lack of foresight, other counties did remove the convicts a greater distance, but unquestionably, as had been intended when campaigning for the prison locus, Fremont County did profit the most from convict labor.

Almost immediately, Cañon City civic leaders negotiated with the warden for inmate labor to build a scenic road along the summit of the 800 foot limestone ridge (hogback) on the northwestern boundary of the prison. Through the efforts of the local leaders, they raised sufficient funds (about $1,200) for the blasting powder, picks, shovels and private teams needed to build the one and one-half miles of scenic highway.[26] Today Skyline Drive snakes along the narrow ridge offering an unobstructed view for miles in all directions. Just as the newspaper predicted, the "driveway . . . would be the first step in the utilization of Cañon City's natural advantages as a resort." In the early days, only horses and hikers traveled the roadway, but after 1910, a few cars puffed their way up and over the road, often scaring the horses. In deference to the horses, the city council limited the horseless carriages to two days a week until horse-drawn carriages became a remnant of the past.[27] In 1906, the governor and many inmates attended the dedication of a stone tablet designed and made by convicts honoring Warden Cleghorn. Importantly, Cleghorn had initiated the "honor" system at Skyline, a distance of one to three miles from the institution.

Cleghorn continued to implement the honor system at greater distances "without gun guards or other protection aside from the overseers in charge of the work." A "gang" of twenty-five inmates lived in tents in 1906 and worked on Fremont County roads about ten miles distant from the institution. During 1905-06, 183 inmates logged 25,533 days' labor and gained ten days of "good time" for every thirty days of work. With no attempted escapes, Cleghorn reported that "the prisoners have all been anxious to secure a place with these gangs."[28]

Clearly, the advantages for road work from Cleghorn's perspective outweighed the extra expense of providing quarters for inmates away from "home." At that point, Cleghorn suggested to the governor and the legislature that, with small appropriations, road work could expand and garner many advantages such as: less state expense than establishing a manufacturing plant, public benefit of better roads and relief of the crowded condition at the penitentiary with less competition to free labor.

Finally two years after Cleghorn's appeal, the General Assembly, in 1908, appropriated $10,000 for a state road from the New Mexico stateline south of Trinidad to Ft. Collins.[29] In May, Cleghorn dispatched ten inmates in the charge of one officer to establish a camp near Starkville near the New Mexico northeastern border. They transported $4,666 worth of equipment — horses, mules, wagons, scrapers, tools and tents. When the camp was prepared, eighty men went by rail to begin work on May 13, 1908. After some initial disharmony, good discipline reigned without the services of an armed guard at night. The only civilians employed at the camp were the superintendent and overseers of the work. Again Colorado's prison implemented its concept of an honor system — this time about 150 miles from the institution. This is not to say that all of the so-called trusties proved "honorable" because the warden reported twenty escapes for the biennium, all from the work outside the prison on roads and farms where "it was impossible to use gun guards."[30] The system, nevertheless, improved as the method of trusty selection evolved and the incentives for honesty increased.

Although this type of road work added nothing to the prison cash earnings, there was another method of computing its value — that of cost comparisons between free labor and convict labor. In presenting the following comparisons, Cleghorn used twenty and one-half cents a day as the cost of maintaining each prisoner in the camp. For the work done from May 13 to September 1, 1908, the contract price would have been $14,823 and the actual cost was $7,009.[31] From the above figures, it is obvious that, with convict labor, the State actually saved fifty-two percent of the value of the work even at the beginning of operations when more delay and confusion existed.

Giving his appraisal, the state engineer, Mr. Jaycox, wrote:

> Aside from the moral and physical influence upon the convicts of an out of door life and a camp managed entirely on the honor system and the advertising which this State is receiving...it would appear from the above that the experiment has been a very successful one.[32]

Also pleased with the results, Cleghorn exhorted the legislature to make liberal appropriations to continue the work. In return for some appropriations, the taxpayers received the lasting benefit of new and better roads.

In February of 1909, the Board dispatched Warden Cleghorn to Denver for a week of lobbying for appropriations. The Board treasurer, George Stracy, said, ". . . it is hoped that the incoming legislature will make provision to continue the construction of good roads."[33] When a $5,000 appropriation materialized, the auditor "held it up" because they "had not determined to what class of appropriation it belonged."[34] Complicating the appropriation procedure was the process of distributing the highway funds, of selecting from which source each amount should come and of collecting from the counties two times the dollars spent by the State.[35]

Also in 1909, the General Assembly established the Colorado State Highway Commission to preside over the state road program. During that year, further legislation provided $9,120 for convict labor on the Colorado Springs to Cañon City road and specified that the Board of Penitentiary Commissioners adopt a special rule of good time "applicable solely to convict employment on public work." A further provision granted all trusty prisoners good time for outside work with a maximum of ten days per calendar month. Regular inside duties were not eligible for good time rewards.[36] This allowed the expanding number of inmates employed on farms to gain a work incentive and also limited the Board of Penitentiary Commissioners from giving more than ten days as work incentives.

Warden Tynan Extends the Honor Camp

Without detracting from the accomplishments and initiatives of Cleghorn, the warden best known for convict road building was Thomas J. Tynan, a traveling salesman. To please his Pueblo constituents who had elected him, Democratic Governor John F. Shafroth appointed the active Pueblo Democrat. Because Tynan liked "to dabble in politics," he was more than willing to take a salary cut for the warden's $208 monthly pay.[37] Following Republican Cleghorn's non-consecutive terms totaling eleven years, this stocky Irishman held the office for eighteen years (longer than any other until Roy Best's twenty-year tenure from 1932-1952). Commenting on Tynan's inexperience in criminology, western historian Robert Athearn said that the West historically valued practical ideas.[38]

True to that assessment, Tynan, without joining the professional warden's association, launched a widescale program of farm work and publicized his road work so well that he and the work synonymously reached the national spotlight. Moreover, his sales background enabled him to embellish his nine biennial reports as no other Colorado warden had, although they all had tried. Indeed, he achieved good public relations with his boards, governors and legislators. Characteristically, Tynan portrayed the routine economic facts regarding the prison improvements and outside work in glowing terms to enforce his initial pledge:

> It has been my ambition to make the institution as nearly
> self-supporting as possible. I have endeavored to return
> to the State, in the product of convict labor, an equiva-
> lent for every dollar spent by the State upon the peniten-
> tiary. And this has been done without leasing out the
> men, or incurring an increase in the loss by escapes, and
> also without entering the men into competition with the
> free labor of the state.[39]

To substantiate this pledge for his first biennium in 1909-1910, Tynan calcu-lated as follows: cash earnings of $38,185 plus $106,746 (saved when convict labor rather than free labor handled the permanent site improvements) plus $155,460 (saved by convict road work) plus $16,890 (farm products consumed by inmates) to equal $317,221. Then subtracting the state's appropriation of $250,000, he claimed a victory for "returning dollar for dollar" and even an excess of $67,221.[40] Certainly, the essence of his reports was that, if the taxpayers of the counties paid the inmates for road building and the state paid them for institutional building, the state taxpayers would have a profitable prison. Ironically, Tynan's logic bears out the "rob Peter to pay Paul" adage. Without criminals, the need for institutions is non-existent.

Of course, this is only one perspective of prison finance, but Tynans's reports routinely compare the accomplishments of convict labor with what the work would have cost on the open market. Consequently, Tynan's reports presented a picture of a self-supporting and contributing institution despite occasional deficits in his budget. The discrepancy, of course, resulted from the fact that there was no actual pay for most convict labor. Importantly, readers must understand that misinterpretations from the above figures often appear in articles about the profitability of Colorado's road-building. In the *Journal of Criminal Law and Criminology*, for example, the author distorts the potential figure of profits as actual and claims huge prison profits; this truly misleads and confuses readers and taxpayers.[41]

During Tynan'a first biennium, the convicts built almost fifty miles of road with an average of 104 men working 610 days. The work in the four Southern Colorado counties of Las Animas, El Paso, Pueblo and Fremont actually cost $56,700, but would have cost $212,160 at contractors' prices. He described the most spectacular work as blasting the Royal Gorge highway out of solid rock. This scenic winding road opened tourist traffic to the top of the eight-square-mile Royal Gorge Park. While Fremont County paid $6,400 for the project, it would have been unaffordable with free labor at a cost of $40,000.[42] At the International Good Roads Congress in Chicago, Governor John F. Shafroth boasted:

> In the Grand Canyon of the Arkansas River there is a very narrow gorge with mountains rising almost perpendicularly on each side to a height of 2,500 feet. It could easily have been bridged, but it has been felt that the scenery should never be desecrated by bridging. There is a flat place on the top of the gorge, probably six or eight acres, and the warden of the penitentiary felt that if a road could be constructed up there so that people could look down into that great chasm, the scenic beauty of the gorge would be shown to advantage, and it would be a great place for tourists to go[43] (The famous high suspension bridge has since been added for the delight of tourists)

To illustrate the early significance of this Royal Gorge road, consider the dedication ceremony in May of 1911. In addition to Governor Shafroth, three former governors (Adams, Thomas and Peabody) and 2,000 visitors attended. Governor Shafroth told the crowd that the road would make "Colorado the playground of the nation." Warden Tynan praised the hard work of the inmates even though some construed it as "buying their freedom," and further noted how it had alleviated the prison labor problems.[44]

After Tynan's second term, he reported that "Our largest single item of labor . . . was of course, road work." For 610 days, 132 prisoners labored on 157 miles of roads in Mesa, Fremont, Larimer, Weld, Boulder, Jefferson, El Paso and Pueblo counties. Because so much of the work in Mesa County consisted of blasting and required skilled workmen, Tynan used higher pay rates than the two-dollar-a-day standard for computing the value of road work. He assessed four and five dollar daily pay rates for skilled blacksmiths, masons and driller - skills actually being performed by some inmates. While probably accurate, the resulting estimation equalled almost six times what the counties actually paid for the roads.[45] In this context, inmate work did not compete with free labor because the counties could not afford private contractual construction.

When Tynan sent his 1913-14 report to Governor Elias M. Ammons, he claimed that "had this institution been paid, on a basis of free labor, for its production in labor on roads, ranches, and improvements, it would not only pay back to the taxpayers its full cost of maintenance, but it would show a profit of $202,980." Six large camps with 226 men and 26 teams worked 508 days to complete 149 miles of roadway.[46] By law, the inmates worked only eight-hour days whereas free labor had not yet won that limitation in Colorado. Listed in the State Highway Report were the specific camp sites:

> Larimer County - Fall River Road above Estes Park and the Poudre Canyon Highway.
> Weld County - Platte River road from Morgan County to Greeley.
> Boulder County - Boulder Canyon between Boulder and Nederland.
> Fremont County - along the Arkansas between Parkdale and Texas Creek.
> Pueblo County - on the Pueblo-Fowler road, Pueblo-Beulah road and the Colorado Springs road.
> Garfield County - on the Glenwood Springs-Rifle road and the Glenwood-Newcastle road.
> Mesa County - completed a portion of road up Plateau Creek.[47]

In his road inspection report, the State Road Supervisor particularly praised the convicts at Parkdale for the excellent drainage work.

Not only did roadwork inflate the prison estimations of profit, but the same method of calculating improvements revealed profits for the prison. One example will suffice. By the end of 1916, "skilled" inmates had installed toilets and running water in all of the cells both at the penitentiary and the reformatory, and a daily average of 207 convicts had constructed 145 miles of roadway. Consider the 1915-1916 biennium of Tynan's accounting:

Inmates gave to the state:

roadwork valued at $465,000,
products consumed 41,000
improvements 20,000
cash earnings 39,373
total 565,373
tax appropriation 203,000
PROFIT .... $362,373[48]

When the wartime prison population decreased, the number working on the roads dropped by one-third to 119 trusties. Nevertheless, five road camps operated continuously and graded 181 miles of new road, graveled forty-six miles and built three and one-half miles of retaining walls for highways in canyons. To the taxpayers, the cost of those roads would have been over one-half million dollars if built by free labor, the warden calculated. The participating counties in 1916-18 were Boulder, Larimer, Weld, Pueblo and Garfield.[49]

After World War I, the temporary decline in prison population caused Tynan to reduce the road camps from five to three (from an average of 792 in 1916 to 564 in 1920).[50] In a letter to Governor Oliver H. Shoup, the warden informed the governor of his strategy for camp reduction because he knew there would be a "fuss." He closed the Boulder camp because they had finished the Nederland road over a period of four years and dispatched those men to Larimer County where inmates were cutting an important road through the Continental Divide in Poudre Canyon. Secondly, he moved the Pueblo camp to Glenwood Springs because Pueblo "has gotten the most road work of anyplace." And the small camp at Weld County remained open.[51] Both the governor and the Board agreed with the warden's curtailment.

For some time, national sentiment had been rising against convict-labor. Increasingly, Colorado's appropriation bills for road work stipulated that the Highway Commission could use labor other than convict labor. Concerned about the future, Tynan complained that there was less demand for convict labor on public highways because

> ... the State Highway Commission has been so liberal
> with money that some of the Board have preferred to let
> contracts to private individuals ... even though we have
> been doing work with prisoners for 21% of the cost of
> contractor's prices.[52]

The warden suggested that the Board and the Governor "take this matter up vigorously with the Highway Commission" and the various County commissioners to insure work for the trustworthy inmates.

With a gain of over thirty-three percent in prison population by 1922, Tynan managed to keep three large camps working because of a better relationship with a new Highway Commission more committed to working prisoners. He disclosed:

> The present Board shows a marked contrast to former boards from the fact that, instead of endeavoring to drive the free labor of prisoners off the highways . . . it has worked hand in hand with this institution in a constructive way.[53]

Continuing to call attention to the inmate contribution, Tynan valued the inmate road work for the two years ending in 1922 at $400,000 if paid for in cash. While 181 convicts constructed dirt roads in Larimer, Weld and Montrose counties, the largest gang worked in Cañon City on Fremont County's first cement road; this extended for one and one-half miles in front of the prison and proved "that convict labor may be used for hard surfacing."[54] That successful hard-surfacing project encouraged the *Denver Post* to endorse an appropriation bill granting $500,000 for a 500 barrel cement plant. Figuring that the prison could produce cement for sixty cents a barrel instead of purchasing it for $2.70, the reporter projected a savings of $300,000 which would pay for the plant in two years. Concurrently, the state had conveniently purchased farm land which had plenty of cement rock.[55] However, the bill narrowly failed in the Twenty-Third General Assembly.

In his 1923 Inaugural Address, Governor William E. Sweet, alerted the public to the "surplus labor" problem by urging the legislature to reconsider the bill for a prison cement plant that would employ inmates and "save hundreds of thousands of dollars in the cost of road construction."[56] Unfortunately for that proposal, the largest cement plant in the state was Portland in Fremont County so the General Assembly continued to buy cement rather than set up a convict plant.

When the Prohibition law pushed the prison population upward in the 1920s, eight percent of the able-bodied were listed as idle in 1924 while road work occupied only 149 of the 881 convicts. Montrose, Larimer, Chaffee and Pueblo counties each had a camp, but the convicts had completed the Cerro Summit and Poncha Pass roads. Thus roadwork, quarry work, farm labor and institutional maintenance still did not meet all of the employment needs, so Tynan urged the legislature to consider the installation of a factory to manufacture some non-competitive articles.[57] Appropriating the capital to start a prison factory remained unacceptable to the legislators.

In one of his many newspaper interviews, Tynan continued to bemoan the "liquor law overflow" and publicly asked that the Highway Department utilize convicts on road work in 1925. After the last camp closed, surplus inmates were sleeping at the newly acquired canning factory and the hydro plant.[58] A few days later, the headline in the *Denver Post* read "Tynan Succeeds, gets a Highway Camp for 150." Adept in political maneuvers, Tynan opened one camp in Saguache and Gunnison counties, two in Fremont and Chaffee counties and stationed one in Clear

Creek County at Loveland Pass while a Pueblo camp rip-rapped the Arkansas River to protect the State Hospital property from flooding. So for a time 194 again moved out to camps.[59]

Despite his overt successes, political embattlement — the fate of all wardens — surrounded Tynan for over two years. In April of 1927, Warden Tynan resigned, and Governor William W. Adams appointed the Rocky Ford rancher, Boone Best. Effort and hope spring eternal as revealed by the headlines heralding Best's elevation: "New Warden Will Seek to Make Pen Self-Supporting."[60] But soon a car accident claimed Boone's life and Samuel J.Burris became the third of four wardens to serve in the 1927-28 biennium. Since Burris had temporarily taken a leave from his job as chief of the Rio Grande Railroad Special Agents, the governor appointed the prison's chief clerk, Francis E. Crawford, after he passed the civil service test.[61] Nonetheless, the 1927-8 biennium produced the largest cash earnings in the first seventy years of prison history — chiefly due to the expansive agricultural production.

Understandably the era of roadwork almost passed with Tynan. Only two road camps operated in 1928 — one at Texas Creek with thirty inmates and one in Jefferson County with twenty-six.[62] Granted that Tynan's initiative piloted the road camps, other forces entered into the demise of the work. Certainly, private contractors, politics and unemployment presented obstacles to the inmate road work, but so did technology. Just as technology had opened the door for better roads and the employment of inmates, it helped to close that avenue with the development of heavy road machines operated by large construction companies.

Description of the Honor Camp

Pictures of the camps remain, but first-hand accounts of life in those camps are enlightening. The following is Reporter George Creel's 1911 description:

> The road camp - a clean, orderly collection of white tents - dotted a great pine grove at the foot of the mountain. . . . trooping in from a day's work were murderers, train robbers, forgers . . . not a single man in stripes. Nowhere an armed guard.[63]

Most importantly, Colorado's sanitary camps did not resemble the infamous camps where guards watched over chain gangs clad in striped garments of shame or kept the prisoners locked in cages or chained together on cots at night.

Another first-hand account noted that a camp included thirty to sixty men with six men sharing a tent. Not lacking in sanitary facilities, the bathhouse contained a corrugated iron tub. The trusties boiled water pumped from the stream and ate better meals than when inside prison walls. Soon they lost their prison pallor while working outside in Colorado's clear air. In their free time, they fished or played baseball with the local ranchers and miners and often listened to phonographs.[64]

Describing the camps to the Good Roads Congress in 1911, Governor Shafroth explained that two superintendents guided them in their work, but at night a convict stood guard, chiefly to protect the camp from coyotes. The honor camp could operate in this manner because of two factors — good laws (sentence reduction for good behavior and the indeterminate sentence) and wise administration (careful selection of trusty convicts). Shafroth continued, "We have an excellent warden, a man both firm and wise, who knows his men thoroughly and is considered by them a friend." Other governors at the conference complained that it cost them more to guard the prisoners than to construct the roads by contract labor, but Shafroth argued that Colorado's incentive system of giving ten days for every thirty days of work as well as good conduct rewards reduced the escape rate and improved the work quality considerably.[65]

At another Good Roads Conference three years later, the Colorado State Highway Engineer detailed the operation of the honor camps. He emphasized that the County and State Road Fund (as distinguished from the Penitentiary Fund) provided the quarters and transportation of the convicts to the sites while the penitentiary furnished the clothing and food. Although the superintendent and foremen were in charge at the worksites, prison officials appointed them and maintained custody at all times. Indeed Colorado's system contrasted sharply with the prior report from the Virginia State Highway Engineer who explained that his state contracted convicts to private companies and worked them under armed guards.

Colorado's spokesman further clarified that they did not classify trusties on the basis of types of crimes committed as did Virginia, but on the character of the men; he said that "All classes of crimes have been represented by the convicts worked upon the roads." He further corroborated Governor Shafroth and other Coloradans that the granting of credits to shorten the term of incarceration was the incentive and defended the absence of armed guards with:

> If you use armed guards to restrain the prisoners from any attempt to escape, then why exact any promises from the men, but if you accept a promise from them, to the effect that they will not attempt to escape, then they should be trusted.[66]

Accordingly, "as a general rule, the night watchman is one of the prisoners," he stated. In sum, the discussion at the American Road Congress revealed that the other states, with the exception of New Mexico, could not implement an honor system successfully, and that others looked to Colorado for advice.

Many testimonials credit trust as the key in the living and work arrangements. From the first camp in 1908 until 1913, Tynan indicated that although 1800 individuals had worked from fifty to 300 miles distant from the prison, only one in one hundred violated his pledge not to escape — which "is far less than the desertions from the United States army or navy."[67] Sharing an example, Governor Shafroth related that an escapee wrote that he would return to the prison at a certain time because he was distressed that he had broken his word to the warden and actually returned at the appointed hour.[68] The *Denver Daily Times* recounted that forty prisoners accompanied by their foreman traveled by train and bus from a road camp to see a play at the Denver Broadway Theater. The reporter concluded, "Yes Warden Tynan and his system were on trial, and they stood the test."[69]

But outcomes differed. For example, a life-long bank robber, Henry Starr, praised Warden Tynan in his reprinted 1913 book for having trusted Starr enough to give him the job as night guard "with a horse, saddle and gun" (the latter must have been for the coyotes).[70] Despite a seven to twenty-five year sentence for robbery, Starr earned parole in four years. This testimonial, however, did not end successfully. Seemingly, he won an early release so that he could pursue his "profession" to his death in a shootout in Arkansas.[71] If in all cases, reformation of the criminal did not result from the honor camp, at least motivation for trust, better work and discipline prevailed. In the course of those years with the honor system, Tynan believed that the men tripled their work.[72]

Analysis of Road Work

In consideration of the results of the roadbuilding period, three major segments can be highlighted — the convicts, the prison administration and the public. Contemporary news features called attention to the "Mending of Broken Men," "Birthplace of Convict Honor Work," "A Colorado Prison Reformer", "Building Good Roads in Colorado" and various travelogs telling of campsites and new scenic drives for tourists. With this kind of publicity, obviously this was not a period of "locking the convicts behind the walls" or "out-of-sight" inmates working in prison factories. Perhaps the media indicated that again Colorado was capitalizing upon an economic asset, i.e., good roads would enhance the attractive climate and scenery and subsequently produce economic growth by attracting tourists. Or possibly the publicity revealed an effort to develop a prison program to aid the convict physically and mentally, improve dicipline, relieve the overcrowded facilities and shorten the sentences through good time work. Or did the media merely reflect public satisfaction by seeing the inmate at "hard labor"? Possibly a warden was boosting his reputation. All of these points bear further inspection.

Consider first the reformation of the convict. A feature in *Harper's Magazine* in 1913 projected that Tynan's road and farm work made it "possible to save the criminal and send him forth from a penitentiary with self-respect regained, and with a desire to be the friend of society instead of its enemy."[73] Certainly the convict-author Henry Starr, who lauded Tynan's trust in him, did not become a "mended man," and this case undoubtedly fit the pattern of many convicts. Information as to how many inmates actually became law-abiding upon their release seems unavailable, but some did respond to the honor and dignity of labor.

In his appraisal under the heading of "saving of his manhood," Tynan said that "the men are being paroled at the expiration of their terms healthy and without prison pallor, in a better condition to earn their livings and with the habit of industry acquired." Contending that they had learned various skills in scientific road building, construction and agriculture, Tynan reflected that the trusties had learned "to take no unfair advantage of square dealing and fair intent."[74] Affirming this assessment, a camp superintendent wrote that two men who had life sentences did not betray their trust when "They journeyed alone from their camps more than one hundred miles by stage and train to the State Capitol to appear before the Board of Pardons," and afterward returned to their work.[75]

A further plus was that the outdoor conditions on both the roads and farms promoted better health for the workers as confirmed by a comparison of the health and longevity records of Colorado prisoners with those of other states. While statistics indicate Colorado's rates of sickness and death were much lower, the fact also remained that the dry climate and comparatively sanitary prison had always been more healthful than most other institutions.[76]

In viewing the effects of roadwork on the public, ambivalence again appears as four different roles for the public emerge — as taxpayers, as users of the roads, as humanitarians responsible for their incarcerated brothers, as free laborers and as lawmakers. Sometimes, the particular group interests collided, necessitating expedient and practical compromises.

For most of the public, namely the taxpayers, opportunity to save dollars dominated. As a matter of fact, inmate labor became the ingredient making possible mountainous roads that counties and the state could not otherwise afford. Comparisons of cost between free labor and convict-built roads have proved that economic fact. Without the free labor, many of the roads would not have been built. The cooperation of the State Highway Engineers who designated routes and corrected surveys helped the county commissioners and prison administration to carry out the program at a savings to taxpayers. Nonetheless, one ingredient was missing — the convicts received no remuneration for the labor and produced no "cash earnings" for the penitentiary. The public, as humanitarians, then bore the tax burden of caring for their incarcerated brothers but, at the same time, received some dividends from better roads.

As for the public (farmers, miners, teamsters, travelers) who used the roads and highways, the utility of graded or cement roads proved incalculable. The newly-opened scenic roads attracted tourists who, in turn, sparked the building of resorts and hotels. Farmers could expand their markets with more roads, communities became less isolated, more children attended schools, Henry Ford sold more cars and railroads were no longer the only means of commuting.

Although it is impossible to compute the exact number of miles constructed by inmates, the mileage was extensive even if not quite the "2,000" claimed by Tynan.[77] The real point for appraisal, however, is that road building proliferated from when the inmates first began blasting out rock for roads. Proving the point of increased opportunities for free labor, Tynan boasted:

> The convict roads are being used as models; for they
> have shown the public what good roads should be like,
> and how they should be constructed, and they have
> increased the demand for good roads in the different
> counties, until today roads are being constructed, under
> the wise supervision of the Highway Commission, in
> nearly all of the sixty-three counties of the state, and
> there are perhaps fifty camps of free laborers doing road
> work in the state, where six years ago there were
> practically none.[78]

Clearly and importantly, convict road work actually opened the door for more jobs for free labor. To most minds, this public work seemed compatible with the philosophy that road labor provided "the least conflict" with the opportunity for honest citizens to earn a living. Generally union spokesmen agreed with Samuel Gompers that public work was the avenue for prisoners under state custody.

Ironically, this program was not without its critics. The era of Colorado's successful and unique road honor camps had come to a standstill by 1928 largely because of changing sentiment. What had been non-competitive for a time had indeed become so. When markets declined in the 1920s, farmers explored opportunities for their teams of horses and mules and noted competing convicts driving state teams. Private construction companies pressured for more jobs, and workers saw their wages being kept low by free convict labor. Experienced paroled convicts with an edge on know-how gained jobs from contractors calling forth the paradox of reforming the inmate but competing with free labor. Engineers lost jobs because the convicts did not have to compute the exact yardage of dirt removed nor utilize other engineering techniques.[79] Ambivalence in the process of solving social problems has always prevailed.

Changing sentiment also appeared among the lawmakers when Congress prohibited federal highway grants from being used with convict labor. In accordance with the national trends for restrictive legislation against convict labor, Colorado's Highway Commission and legislature also approached inmate labor with dimmer views. While Tynan had complained about the Commission giving the work to private contractors, others agreed with an editorial in an employer magazine, *Mines and Minerals*, which stated that the kind of work for convicts that won't interfere with free labor is to "crack stones in the prison" for use on the roads.[80] Coincidentally, that is how road work began in California and Delaware at the turn of the century — by crushing stone in stockades for the roads.

Certainly politics played a deciding role in hastening the end to a successful road period. When Governor-elect Edwin C. Johnson appointed a committee to investigate the entire prison operation in December, 1932, the committee faulted the county commissioners and highway commissioners for not continuing the road work which they believed to be the best employment for inmates. Citing various state laws as recent as 1931 which enabled those officials to employ convicts and which they ignored, the committee said:

> Many excuses are offered for this conduct of public
> officials in disregarding the plain intent of the legisla-
> ture, but back of and controlling all of them is politics.
> Each public official is jealous of the patronage which he
> controls and disregards the general welfare of the state.[81]

And lastly, how did the resignation of Warden Tynan affect the road work? Tynan had become almost synonymous with honor road camps which ended shortly after his departure. As with all wardens, controversy developed around him. This is especially the case when a long term official maintains a high profile. While the public relations of Tynan rated high with most of the media, sufficient questioning by disgruntled ex-employees and others caused Governor William Sweet to request an investigation by the National Society of Penal Administrators in 1924. Recall that Tynan was not a professional and did not attend the meetings of the American Prison Association even though his publicity and reports of his work appeared at their meetings through the efforts of others. The committee wrote that "he has won praise for his road work which is the only part the general public has heard or known about, ... and whether that confidence is justified is a matter entirely outside of this report."[82] But the next step for the committee was to demand Tynan's dismissal for alleged mismanagement and cruel treatment of inmates. Despite his nation-wide renown for selecting trusties, the report faulted his method as "arbitrary."[83] Bypassing the report, the Civil Service Commission refused to dismiss Tynan, and he prevailed for one more term. Perhaps a *Denver Post* reporter, who lauded Colorado's widely emulated road work and honor camps as "historic," appraised the warden's contribution best. He concluded that - "the working of the honor system to a large degree depends upon the character of the men employed as wardens."[84]

Aside from the immeasurable aspects of Colorado's honor road camps, some consensus exists about the importance of Colorado's innovation. Nearly every Good Roads Congress and American Prison Association discussed the topic of convict road and farm camps from 1910 on through the 1930s. Prison historian Blake McKelvey paid tribute to Colorado when he wrote, "Colorado"s success in developing honor camps on the roads in 1906 had prompted a dozen western states and several in the Northeast to organize similar camps within a decade."[85]

Another commentator suggested that "Many of the new reforms are the inspiration of individual wardens. There is the honor system of scenic road building conceived by Cleghorne and perfected by Tynan in Colorado."[86] A federal digest of convict labor laws in 1923 reveals that all states permitted prisoner employment on farms and road work outside of the walls, but only a few states attempted to implement the honor camps, and none succeeded so well as Colorado.[87] In prison labor literature, most reference to honor camp success highlights Colorado's efforts.

In the beginning, Colorado sought to emulate the eastern traditions of prison labor but later initiated its own successful contribution to the paradox of prison labor with it "honor" road work. An even broader assessment came from criminologist Joe Sullivan when he wrote: "The honor system in some form is necessary for the accomplishment of the only purpose of imprisonment — the reform and readjustment of the offender. He must be tried before released."[88] Even if only temporarily, Colorado contributed to the science of penology with its honor camp era.

NOTES - CHAPTER V

[1]E.Stagg Whitin, "Industrial Penology,"*Prison Labor*, (Philadelphia: American Academy of Pollitical and Social Science, 1913), p. 1.

[2]E. Stagg Whitin, "Making Roads Through Prison Labor." *The Review* (February, 1911), p.10.

[3]Sydney Wilmot, "Use of Convict Labor for Highway Construction in the North," *Proceedings of the Academy of Political Science in the City of New York IV* (New York: The Academy of Political Science, 1914), p. 250.

[4]"Convict Labor," *United States Department of Agriculture Bulletin #414*, (Washington: GPO, 1916) pp. 6-8.

[5]Wilmot, "Use of Convict Labor, p.250.

[6]Ibid., p. 243-4. There are tables of statistics showing the relation of illiteracy to areas with no roads.

[7]Governor B. Orman, "Biennial Message," *Laws Passed at Fourteenth General Assembly*, 1902, p. 32.

[8]*First Biennial Report of the Bureau of Labor Statistics of the State of Colorado, 1887-88* (Denver: Collier and Cleaveland, 1888), p. 417.

[9]*Cañon City Clipper*, April 4, 1899, 1:1.

[10]*Rocky Mountain News*, Jan. 19, 1896, 2:1. Hereafter RMN.

[11]*Denver Daily Times*, June 25, 1899, 4:4.

[12]Governor Charles S. Thomas, *Inaugural Address to the Twelfth General Assembly*, 1899. (pamphlet) p. 80.

[13]*Denver Daily Times*, August 2, 1898, 8:3.

[14]*Fremont County Record*, Feb. 18 and April 22, 1897, 2:1.

[15]*RMN*, Dec. 26, 1896 and Jan. 1, 1897, 5:1 and 1:3.

[16]*Laws Passed at Twelfth Session of the General Assembly*, 1899, (Denver: Smith-Brooks, 1899), approved April 22, 1899, pp. 120-1.

[17]John Chetelat, "Report of the Construction Superintendent on the State Wagon Road," Colorado State Archives, Denver, Box 26949, file folder 12 and 13. Letter to Governor Thomas, Dec. 31, 1899.

[18]Ibid., letter from Thomas to Board of Penitentiary Commissioners, June 1, 1901.

[19]Minutes of Board of Penitentiary Commissioners v. II, June 22, 1900, p. 291.

[20]Sixth Biennial Report of the State Board of Charities and Corrections ending Nov. 30, 1902 (Denver: Smith-Brooks, 1903), p. 84.

[21]Third Biennial Report of the State Board of Charities and Corrections ending Nov. 30, 1896, p. 10. In chapter I, I described the problems of Pennsylvania in this regard.

[22]Seventh Biennial Report of the State Board of Charities and Corrections ending Nov. 30, 1904, p. 98-9.

[23]Laws Passed at the Fifteenth Session of the General Assembly, (Denver: Smith-Brooks, 1905), April 11, 1905, p. 171.

[24]Minutes of Board of Penitentiary Commissioners II, June 8, 1905, p. 476.

[25]Cañon City Clipper, April 18, 1905, 1:4.

[26]Cañon City Record, October 12, 1905, 1:5. Many accounts use the figure of $6,400 as the cost, but they have confused it with the Royal Gorge road which cost that and is listed in the Warden's reports. Also see October 5, 1905, 1:4. An article in the same paper on June 11, 1932, describes the gateway to the newly-erected Skyline Drive. Civic leaders had obtained a sample of native stone from the governor of each state and placed the stones in the pillars to the gateway.

[27]Ibid., August, 8, 1981, 8:2. Also see Wilbur F. Stone, History of Colorado IV, (Chicago: S.J. Clarke, 1918), p. 820. In 1905, Cañon City had eight cars. In 1901, Dr. Frank L. Bartlett, renowned metallurgist, ordered the thirteenth Oldsmobile ever made. In the Minutes of the Canon City Chamber of Commerce for Jan. 2, 1917, the members were concerned about Denver's "appropriating" the name Skyline Drive for the Mt. Evans road, and sent protests. Minutes, Fremont History Room, Cañon City Library.

[28]Biennial Report of the Colorado State Penitentiary for 1905-6, (Denver : Smith-Brooks, 1906), p. 10-11. Hereafter called BR of CSP.

[29]*Colorado Revised Statutes, Sixteenth General Assembly*, (Denver: Smith-Brooks, 1908), p. 1378.

[30]*BR of CSP*, 1908, pp. 6-10.

[31]Ibid., pp. 11-12.

[32]Ibid.

[33]*Minutes of Board of Penitentiary Commissioners III*, Dec. 8, 1908, p. 75. Also see Feb. 16, 1909, p. 88.

[34]Ibid., Mar. 9, 1909, p. 89.

[35]*First Biennial Report of State Highway Commission of the State of Colorado*, 1910, (Denver: Smith-Brooks, 1910), p. 12. See also the *Second Biennial Report of State Highway Commission* , 1912, pp. 5-12 for an involved explanation of the financing dating back to territorial days and the internal improvement fund. Hereafter State Highway Rep. For the law see same on pp.80-83.

[36]*Session Laws, Sixteenth Session*, April 30, 1909, pp. 219-20, March 6a, 1909, p. 330.

[37]*RMN*, January 2, 1909, 2:4.

[38]Robert G. Athearn, *The Coloradans* (Albuquerque: University of New Mexico, 1976), p. 219.

[39]*BR of CSP*, 1910, p. 6.

[40]Ibid., pp. 6-9.

[41]William Gemmill, "Employment and Compensation of Prisoners," *Journal of Crime, Laws and Criminology 6*, 1916, p. 516.

[42]Ibid., p. 18.

[43]John F. Shafroth, "Roads and Pavements," *American City*, Sept., 1911, p. 223. Note pictures in appendix.

[44]*Colorado Springs Gazette*, May 13, 1911, 1:4-5.

[45]*BR of CSP*, 1912, p. 7. The exact figures were $46,805 to $270,285.

128

[46]Ibid., 1914, pp. 6-7.

[47]*State Highway Rep.*, 1914, pp. 12-13.

[48]*BR of CSP*, 1916, pp. 4-5.

[49]Ibid., 1918, p. 9.

[50]Ibid., 1920, p. 5. From 1871-1940, there were only five times when inmate population dropped - two slight declines in 1898 and 1900, one in 1934 and the two during World War I.

[51]*Minutes of Penitentiary Board IV*, letter from Tynan to Governor Shoup dated April 14, 1919 and letter from Shoup to Board, dated April 19, 1919.

[52]*BR of CSP*, 1920, pp. 5-6.

[53]Ibid., 1922, p. 6.

[54]Ibid, 1922, p. 7.

[55]*Denver Post*, April 1, 1921, 9:1.

[56]William E. Sweet, *Inaugural Address delivered to Twenty-Fourth General Assembly*, Jan. 9, 1923, p. 22.

[57]*BR of CSP*, 1924, pp. 15-6 and 45. Of the total, 82% were unemployed.

[58]*Denver Post*, Nov. 29, 1925, 1:4. Of the 968 average prison population, 162 were liquor law violators in 1925. Seea also Dec. 6, 1925, 8:1.

[59]*BR of CSP*, 1926, p.9.

[60]*RMN*, Feb. 2, 1927, 5:2.

[61]*Denver Post*, Dec. 1, 1927, 7:2.

[62]*BR of CSP*, 1928, p. 42.

[63]*Denver Daily News*, June 1, 1911, 4:2. Reporter Creel became President Wilson's wartime censorship czar.

[64]Eugene Bertrand, "Giving the Convict a Chance," a pamphlet found in the Colorado State Archives Box # 9871, no date.

[65]Shafroth, "Roads and Pavements," pp. 222-3.

[66]*Proceedings of the Fourth American Road Congress*, Atlanta, Georgia, November 9-14, 1914, p.276.

[67]Thomas J. Tynan, "Prison Labor on Public Roads," *Prison Labor* (Philadelphia: American Academy of Political and Social Science, 1913), p. 59.

[68]Shafroth, "Roads and Pavements," p. 223.

[69]*Denver Daily Times*, September 22, 1911, 2:4.

[70]Henry Starr, *Thrilling Events* (College Station, Texas: Creative Publishing Co., reprinted 1982 from original 1914), pp. 92-3.

[71]*Prison Record Book*, State Archives, p. 156. He was #7613 and 36 years old.

[72]Tynan, "Prison Labor," p. 59.

[73]Arthur Chapman, "A Colorado Prison Reformer: Tynan and His Convict Boys," *Harper's Weekly 57*, August 2, 1913, pp.18-23.

[74]Ibid., 1910, p. 9.

[75]Joseph H. Pratt, "Economics of Convict Labor in Road Construction," *North Carolina Geological and Economic Survey*, Chapel Hills, N.Car., Feb. 18, 1914, p. 15.

[76]Ibid., p. 13. The tables illustrate lower death rates in Colorado prison.

[77]To validate the number of miles, I searched for reports, but the Highway reports are not available after 1916.

[78]*BR of CSP*, 1914, p.9.

[79]Pratt, "Economics of Convict Labor," p. 4.

[80]John Mitchell, "The Wage Earner and the Prison Worker," *Prison Labor* (Philadelphia: American Academy of Political and Social Science, 1913), p. 16.

130

[81]*Report on Committee on Penal Reform*, Denver, January 16, 1933, p. 18.

[82]Paul Garrett and Austin MacCormick, ed., *Handbook of American Prisons, 1926* (New York: G. P. Putnam and Sons, 1926), p. 146.

[83]Ibid., p. 136.

[84]*Denver Post*, July 12, 1915, 1+:2.

[85]Blake McKelvey, *American Prisons, A History of Good Intentions* (Montclair, N.J.:Patterson Smith, 1977), p. 275.

[86]Corinne Bacon, compiled, *Prison Reform* (New York: H.W.Wilson Co., 1917), p. 220.

[87]"Convict Labor in 1923," *United States Bureau pf Labor Statistics* (Washington: GPO, 1925), pp. 4-23.

[88]Joe Sullivan, "Good Roads," *Journal of Crime, Law, and Criminology 5*, 1915, p. 783.

CHAPTER VI

WORKPLACES: AGRICULTURE, INDUSTRY AND CONSTRUCTION, 1900-1940

Idleness more than any other one thing
produces moral deterioration and crime.
Charles Henry Davis[1]

During the first four decades of the twentieth century, the Colorado State Penitentiary continued its search for options that could bring jobs, self-support, remuneration or vocational training to its inmates. Having described the remunerative nineteenth-century work and the road work, it is pertinent to focus on the two major areas of twentieth-century prison labor income — agriculture and industries.

Several points require consideration regarding those work categories. In contrast to the road work which produced no direct earnings, agriculture and industries became remunerative labor. Agriculture, in this case, refers not only to the production of food and livestock feed, but also to livestock production. The reference to "industries" applicable to this prison includes the prison shops which prepare or manufacture articles for sale or use. Realistically only a small proportion of the inmates worked in areas yielding direct income while most prisoners labored at over-assigned levels (assigning more than needed to avoid overt idleness) in maintenance, construction, quarry work and prison duty.

Agriculture - Farms, Livestock and Poultry

Recommending outdoor work as treatment for criminals, penologist H. R. Cooley, in a 1911 article, urged the establishment of farm labor as an appropriate environment for rehabilitating prisoners. As an example of successful farm experience, he described the Cleveland, Ohio, Correction Farm which comprised an estate of 2,000 acres set aside for an almshouse, a tuberculosis hospital, a municipal cemetery and the prison. For four years, 5,000 prisoners had labored there at diversified skills of building (quarrying and crushing stone, grading, road making, draining the land, clearing timber) and of tilling the soil to produce food for institutional needs. In performing those labors, Cooley stated that the inmates gained in various ways and developed a "common sentiment that it is a mean and cowardly thing to take a sneak from the farm."[2] Another successful example of farm work in the 1920s was Indiana's purchase of 1,602 acres of good land where the inmates not only tilled the soil, but also raised huge quantities of willows to provide an industrial basketry factory for those who could not be trusted outdoors.[3]

When Colorado's leaders located the prison on a small tract, they did not plan for a profitable farming operation. With a small prison garden and a few leased farms, they could not produce enough for their own needs. In fact, Warden E.H. Martin dispensed with farming leased lands and kept only the prison gardens in 1906 because of "the expense of guards, teams and equipment."[4] Instead, they had adapted inmate labor to their own rock resources. Continuing through the first decade of the twentieth century, lime and quarry sales amounted to 65.4 percent of the total cash earnings. But during the second decade, sales of prison lime and quarry products decreased to only 16.8 percent of the prison income. In the 1920s and 1930s, the natural resource earnings declined to a negligible amount; this resulted from restrictive laws against inmate production and also from the slow-down and closure of Colorado smelters. This did not mean that inmates no longer worked on the traditional rock quarries, but that their rock labor sustained only institutional building materials.

In another sense, Colorado itself had also changed. Part of what Stephen Long had termed the "Great American Desert" unfit for cultivation had been made to bloom, and, by 1890, agriculture replaced mining as the leading occupation. Back in 1880, the mining industry employed 29 percent of all Colorado wage earners while only 13 percent worked in agriculture. But by 1890, that had reversed; 10 percent worked in the mineral industry and 20 percent in agriculture.[5] Consider also that only 1,738 farms existed in Colorado in 1870, but by 1900, there were 24,700 farms.[6] On the other hand, Fremont County which hosted the prison was one of the eleven counties with the lowest amount of cultivated acreage and the lowest value of crops in Colorado.[7] Since agriculture had become important to Colorado's economy, then the question arises — did the prison adapt its labor to that pursuit? This study indicates that, despite the obstacles, it did adapt and produced some revenue. The following chart reflects this change by showing that agricultural sales supplanted quarry product sales from 1914 to 1940:

Cash Earnings of Farms, *Livestock and Provisions

Decade	Cash sales	Percentage	Total Earnings
1902-1910	$34,159	14.7%	$231,668
1912-1920	$182,019	69%	$263,646
1922-1930	$214,714	60.45%	$355,213
1932-1940	$159,696	53.75%	$297,104

*Livestock includes cattle, hogs, poultry and dairy products.[8]

Shortage of prison land hampered prison farming. During the first decade of the twentieth century, the Penitentiary Board had acquired some extra land to enlarge the limestone production, but overall the prison owned only about 37 acres in 1910. Leasing small farms and sharecropping had been the only option for prison agriculture before the legislature appropriated money for land purchase. In harmony with the sentiment for outdoor and farm work, the Commissioners began urging the state to purchase 1,200 acres of land for permanent farming, but nearby land had become expensive since the opening of the prison in 1871.[9] Yet a detailed study by the Bureau of Labor Statistics reported that over "thirty-one million dollars were sent out of Colorado in 1909 to buy agricultural products that should have been produced in the State."[10] Nevertheless, the same legislatures which authorized the above study delayed in providing opportunities for an economic solution to prison maintenance.

Although the legislature purchased no land during the second decade of the twentieth century, the penitentiary officials continued to increase the leased land. At that time, the prison entered into an era of profitable livestock and poultry raising. Between 1910-12, the prisoners produced 1,244 pigs which they sold to farmers throughout the state for fifteen dollars each at weaning if thoroughbred or three dollars each if common stock. Considering the poultry department one of the most satisfactory, Tynan reported the sale of 1,300 thoroughbred chickens and the consumption of 1,050 chickens with a stock of 868 on hand.[11] They also sold geese, turkeys and eggs. At Easter time, they sold 135 lambs, and the sheep department provided 8,000 pounds of mutton for prison food. Marketing hides added a small profit along with a larger investment for future years. All-in-all, scientific agricultural methods enhanced inmate skills, and the results of reformation pleased the warden who reported that the outdoor work had "raised the parole rate to an eighty percent level of success."[12]

The biennium ending in 1914 marked the first single period in which farm and animal husbandry exceeded the earnings of lime and quarry sales. Prison farmland truly expanded; new leased lands included 800 acres in Pueblo County and a large ranch of 8,000 acres between Colorado Springs and Cañon City in El Paso County with 500 acres under cultivation. The El Paso land proved an excellent bargain because the owner furnished free pasture land, all equipment and teams in return for one-half of the crop. Additionally, the prison leased a small ranch of 65 acres in Fremont County.

While many more inmates worked on "improvements" than on the farms, much of the construction directly aided the farm production. To store corn ensilage for the dairy, for example, they constructed stone silos — "the most substantial ever built in Colorado." Propagating garden plants and flowers became possible after the inmate "architect" designed two large greenhouses, called by Tynan "the most perfect houses ever constructed in the state" Other new enterprises presented diversified opportunities. Through the cooperation of Governor Teller Ammons and the State Game and Fish Commission, the inmates built "the most perfect pheasantries in the country" in the park across from the penitentiary and produced 700 young Mongolian pheasants. More fortunate than the prisoners, the pheasants were liberated in various valleys of the state where "they are thriving splendidly." When coal strikes made it impossible to obtain fuel, about twenty-three inmates utilized their skills to dig 2,854 tons at $1.12 each on a leased mine only one mile from the institution.[13] Even though the total cash earnings for 1913-14 were the lowest of any biennium in the twentieth century, diversified labor experiences enabled many convicts either to practice their skills or return to society with new ones.

When World War I elevated the demand for food, farm products accounted for 82.5 percent of the cash earnings for 1915-16. Again the Board enlarged farm leases to include one farm and one ranch containing 8,000 acres, one school section of 640 acres in Avondale near Pueblo, another farm of 700 acres and a seventy-acre ranch. In addition, they raised vegetables on about twenty acres of prison garden land. To increase production on the fertile Avondale land in Pueblo County, Warden Tynan asked for money to develop more irrigation by sinking wells and pumping with electricity. He also requested $5,000 for the purchase of two large automobile trucks to release ten horse teams for work on the farms.[14]

Not until 1916 did the warden or matron give a specific report on female inmate work, but the demand for agricultural products seemed to open field jobs for women prisoners also. The matron reported that thirty-three female inmates stayed busy with gardening, tending rabbits and chickens and in performing domestic chores. This farm work, the matron believed, caused most of them to "go out strong and resolute" after coming in "weak from the use of drugs or liquor."[15] As a point of clarification, not all of those thirty-three female convicts were Colorado wrongdoers because the Colorado prison received many of the federal female felons from west of the Mississippi. In tune with war patriotism, the matron reported in 1918 that, in addition to their prison chores, the women prisoners had voluntarily cut 10,000 yards of material for the Red Cross, knit 2,000 pairs of socks, and made 500 suits for ten-tear-old Belgian boys.[16]

War activities also inspired the male inmates whose numbers dropped from 792 in 1916 to 600 during the war years. They increased road construction as well as farm production and joined their free brothers in purchasing Liberty Bonds and War Saving Stamps. In 1917, the Board ordered the warden to distribute 1,000 pounds of beans to various charitable organizations. At this time, the inmates also produced sandstone fluxing which they sold to the Colorado Fuel and Iron Company in Pueblo for use in war materials.[17]

Demand for war-time food and higher sale prices more than doubled the total cash earnings, but the cost of maintenance increased as much as 19 to 132 percent on every necessary item including salaries for guards. Although profits accrued from leased lands, Warden Tynan suggested that profit would be greater on prison-owned lands; he lamented that only twenty acres of farm land belonged to the prison. At Avondale, this "richest of farmland," convicts had installed wells and pumps and leased 200 acre feet of water for $1,000 until the end of 1918.[18] But they could not irrigate the land at its higher elevations without buying 200 Bessemer Ditch water shares at $20,000, an obstacle they could not surmount. This highly valued acreage by itself yielded agricultural products selling for $48,820 or 62 percent of the total cash earnings for the 1917-18 term. Over and above the cash earnings, Avondale production added $42,486 worth of prison-consumed products and a $10,457 feed and livestock inventory.[19] Notably then, this section of land yielded $50,000 a year. During the fourth and final year of lease, the ranch products sold for $46,586 at a production cost of only $15,485.[20]

Unfortunately for the prison farm program, the State Land Board sold the 640-acre Avondale ranch for $100 an acre in 1919 at the urging of Pueblo investors. This action led to Warden Tynan's outburst appearing in the *Denver Post* with the caption "Tynan Denounces Land Shark Seeking to Grab Prison Land." Not reluctant to defend his turf, Tynan irately accused the legislature of acting as "political messengers" for Pueblo investor John Thatcher and associates. To the charges that the trusty convicts menaced the local residents, Tynan responded that inmate conduct was superior to that of the Avondale residents and that road gangs had lived in the Pueblo baseball park while receiving excellent conduct ratings from Puebloans. Defensively, Tynan charged that the investors actually began the rumors of convict misbehavior in order "to get Tynan" and to take possession of parcels of land. Further, he claimed that Thatcher reduced tenants on his land to a state of peonage by paying only six dollars a ton for their alfalfa when prison alfalfa sold for $25 a ton. Tynan's caustic arguments, however, did not win his battle to keep the Avondale farm. According to him, the State Land Board arbitrarily disposed of it against the "wishes of the Governor" and the prison board.[21] Since the inmates had made considerable improvements on the leased land, the Avondale buyers compensated the prison in the amount of $16,898 which the Board set aside for an initial payment on the purchase of farm land. Losing Avondale meant that from fifteen to forty inmates lost their farm jobs.

Ending this second decade, the auditor reported that the cost of daily maintenance per prisoner was ninety-three cents, but after subtracting the earnings, the actual cost to taxpayers was seventy-five cents. He complimented the Board and warden for maintaining inmates at a lower cost than four similar prisons — Illinois at $1.04, Kansas at $1.24, Nebraska at $1.69, Utah at $2.18.[22] Reducing costs had been Tynan's goal, as it had for all wardens. The daily expense of a Colorado inmate amounted to $1.53 when he had assumed office in 1908.[23]

During the 1920s, Colorado prison history again paralleled national history. First, the post-war decrease in the food demand resulted in lower farm prices. One example was prison hay which had sold for $25 a ton in 1919, but in 1924, "the prison sold it for $15 a ton to lower Arkansas Valley dealers who sent it to points in Texas."[24]

A second parallel concerned the havoc caused in attempting to enforce the Prohibition law. For the prison, it meant severe overcrowding; the 1922 bed count showed an increase of 300 inmates over the 1920 number. To a large extent, bootleggers boosted prison population; many were farmers whose farms failed to pay and who turned to the profitable production of illegal liquor. Practically, Tynan suggested, those men were not habitual criminals and should work on their own county roads rather than overcrowding the penitentiary.[25] Illustrating Tynan's belief that the liquor violators were not necessarily hardened criminals was a less famous John Brown who, when convicted in Glenwood Springs, delivered himself to the warden.[26] The local newspaper recorded the influx of prisoners as well as the violence of the Prohibition era and the Ku Klux Klan activity in Colorado during the twenties. Noteworthy enough to publish was the announcement on June 25, 1925, that the 13,000th "fish" entered the penitenitiary gates.[27]

A third analogy to national history was the debacle at the end of the 1920s. For the nation, it was the stock market crash, but for the prison, it was the bloodiest riot in its history; eight guards and ten inmates died in a rampage of destruction on October 3, 1929. Some historians connect Colorado's riot to the outbreak of riots that began in Joliet, Illinois, in 1918 and spread over a half dozen states in the next three years, followed by a second series beginning in Leavenworth in 1929 and sweeping through Auburn and Dannemora in New York to Cañon City. How much connection Colorado's riot had to the others is debatable. Actually the fact that the ring leader had a particular reputation for escape and daring as well as many inmate followers might have made the riot more singular. Investigators of Colorado's riot never mentioned outside influence, but blamed lax discipline, dining room facilities and other obstructions in the guarding procedures. On the national scale, historian Blake McKelvey also added that the relaxed discipline of the reformatory era following the breakdown of the strict Auburn system, the restlessness of idle inmates and the overcrowding and intermingling of all types of criminals caused the riots.[28]

Struggling to find remunerative farm products in the depressed farm markets of the 1920s, the prison turned to fruit growing which flourished in Cañon City's private sector. As early as 1897, Fremont County farmers nurtured over 2,000 acres of fruit orchards and supported three cooper firms making 50,000 barrels for their apples alone.[29] An unusually successful 1925 fruit and vegetable crop in Cañon City and a defunct canning factory resulted in the shipment of crops to canneries as far away as Crowley and Manzanola.[30] Seizing the opportunity, the Colorado Board of Corrections purchased from the bondholders of the closed Colorado Packing Corporation the "largest and best equipped canning factory in the State" in October, 1925 for $40,000.[31] Idle for two years, the reopened factory offered not only a market for local fruit growers but also about twenty to thirty jobs for the increasing prison population. Together with the factory purchase, the Board paid $30,000 for ninety acres of full bearing fruit trees, vines, berries and truck garden commodities. Contract financing for the project proved to be favorable with the payments coming from the earnings rather than the taxpayers; in four years of operation, it indeed paid for itself. Considering that the state had won a bargain, Tynan estimated the actual real estate value of the factory and ranch at $150,000. Furthermore, the warden claimed that the state-owned canning factory offered better prices to Cañon City farmers for their fruit than they could obtain elsewhere.[32]

After the resignation of Warden Tynan in 1926 and the two short stints of Boone Best and S. J. Burris, F.E. Crawford assumed control. His addition to the farm program was a four-year contract on 5,200 acres in Pueblo County known as "Broadacre." About 132 inmates lived and worked at the Broadacre farm and sold $21,000 worth of products in the first year of its operation.[33] Most of their crop was sugar beets, but they also raised grains and livestock. Still, the Board lamented that the prison was not self-sufficient in vegetables and meat.[34]

The distant farms offered easier access to escape for those not sufficiently wise to cooperate for "reduced time." In fact, two-thirds of all escapees left from farm sites, and most of the others left outside assignment areas (even three band members left their place of work in Hugo, Colorado one year). Because the newspapers, especially the local ones, diligently reported each escape, it behooved the wardens to minimize the escapes. Accordingly, they blamed the scattered work areas and distances from the "walled city." In addition to those living at Broadacre, another 146 prisoners labored on various parts of the 1600 acres in Fremont County. Nine trusties worked on construction of the Manufacturers' and Merchants' building at the State Fair Grounds in Pueblo, some cleaned Cañon City streets and alleys and a gang fought fires in San Isabel Forest. Although sixty escaped from those dispersed assignments, the warden reported that the net loss was nothing, "in other words, the number returned and located in other prisons offsets the number of escapes during the period."[35]

Many stories of the lost and found convicts exist, but one clarifies the manner in which forty-nine escapes in one biennium can equal "no loss." Robert Green, alias Thomas Walker, returned to the prison fourteen years after his escape when authorities in London discovered his false passport. During his many years away from Colorado, he had pursued a career as a distinguished continental lecturer and expert on the conditions in the Soviet Ukraine.[36] Overall, Warden Crawford considered that, of the 596 inmates he had designated as trusties, forty-nine escapes were a "small loss." For this small loss, Warden Crawford attributed the incentive action of the Board of Corrections in granting an additional five days of "good time" to farm workers.[37]

At the close of the third decade, how many of the 1,090 inmates worked at farming? Only about 400 or 36.7 percent of the total prison population farmed, and they produced about 60.5 percent of the actual cash earnings. Although the canning factory produced good profits and had paid for itself, its operation required only about twenty workers. Profits seemed not to be uppermost in Warden Crawford's mind in 1930 when he disclosed a profit on the Broadacre farm of "twenty to twenty-five thousand dollars," but added that the major importance of Broadacre concerned housing for 149 inmates.[38] Overcrowding has continued to be a perennial problem.

Just as national phenomena of the 1920s affected Colorado's prison, the Great Depression and the Hawes-Cooper Act in the 1930s limited the sale of convict-made products and altered the prison's directions for the final decade of this study. With national unemployment high, how could convict labor compete with free labor? Even before the Hawes-Cooper Act took effect in 1934, prison officials had to plan for the disposition of their products to other public institutions.

Aside from those problems, the aftermath of the 1929 riot resulted in political turmoil with investigations and attempts to place blame.[39] Again the administration endured an upheaval in wardens as it had after Tynans's resignation. Some of the Board of Corrections blamed the warden for the riot, so they filed charges with the State Civil Service Commission which resulted in Crawford's suspension. Governor William Adams then appointed the chief clerk of the prison, John P. Allen, as warden, but he died in August of 1932. Finally, the governor designated Boone Best's son, Deputy Warden Roy Best, to manage the prison.[40]

Much of Governor William Adams' *Inaugural Address* on January 13, 1931, pertained to the prison problem. Three of his five recommendations to correct the "inefficiency and low morale of the inmates and the employees" had to do with labor: provide employment, legislate for road work and adopt a broad farm policy. Regarding the latter, he specifically asked that permanent instead of seasonal housing be provided at the farms.[41] Responding to the 1929 prison riot and Governor Adams' appeal for prison farms, the Twenty-Eighth Session of the General Assembly in 1931 appropriated $25,000 for the initial installment on the purchase of farmland. As an emergency measure, the legislature appropriated another $25,000 for construction of barns, ranch buildings and housing for one hundred farm inmates and thirty-five dairy workers at the farm.[42]

Another motivation for the purchase of a farm in 1932 had been the failure to renew the lease on the Broadacre farm with the Ingersoll Investment Company of Pueblo. Indeed, the Broadacre farm was a serious loss. In only one year, its cash earnings equaled $33,337 while all other farm and livestock earnings for two years (1931-32) totaled only $12,760. Additionally, the amount of additional food raised at Broadacre and consumed at the prison amounted to $38,600.[43] Because the rioters had destroyed the license plate factory which should have added some earnings, the farm and livestock earnings had little competition for that biennium and, despite the obstacles, contributed 86 percent of the meager 1931-32 total.

At the same time, however, poor farm markets caused many to offer tracts of land for sale, making it feasible for the prison to choose one tract only four miles east of the penitentiary. Unlike the water problem at Broadacre, this 1,500 acre tract had excellent water rights. At a price of $60,000, this new state-owned "Ranch Number One" became the location of the dairy and many other farm operations. Another perspective to farm expansion during the Great Depression was that employment opportunities abounded at Ranch Number One with the building of a modern reinforced concrete dairy barn, ten corrals, a bunk house to accommodate 75 men, brooder houses, sheds, turkey shelters, a granary and wells for domestic water. Two other inmate activities at this well-chosen ranch were making adobe bricks and quarrying building stone for ranch structures and another dormitory for 86 workers.[44]

Although drought and low prices decreased earnings in the years of 1933-34, agriculture still contributed over one-half of the total earnings — albeit the lowest total since 1914. More meaningful than the drop in cash earnings was the 66 percent rise in prison population which placed a heavy demand on consumption needs. Consuming only $8,458 worth of its home-grown food, the prison spent $81,623 in the marketplace for food.

The emphasis on livestock production began to pay dividends; in 1936, turkeys, hogs, sheep and poultry added $17,517 to the cash earnings while the farms and gardens sold only $3,134 worth of produce. The 1936 frost which ruined the fruit crop contributed to the low yield.[45] Roy Best's short reports lacked details on the amount of prison-produced food consumed by inmates, so the total production of the farms is incalculable.

For the first time in 26 years, agriculture accounted for less than half (46.03 percent) of the total earnings in 1938. Of a total of 2,000 acres, only 400 were cultivated, and the remainder was hilly and rocky, suitable only for grazing. Prison population increased 16.18 percent during those two years, and Best said, "The two major obstacles to...efficient administration...are overcrowding and umemployment."[46] Ironically, on his "Distribution of Labor" chart, he claimed only three percent of the able-bodied were unemployed but obviously much of the assignment was seasonal and overstaffed. About 152 worked at farm and livestock production.

When Best received permission to make the final mortgage payment of $23,000 on Ranch Number One with a transfer of funds from "Industries" to "Land Purchase," handwriting on the wall indicated the dominance of agriculture in cash earnings had ended.[47] Agriculture had survived the Great Depression and provided healthy employment for many but would never again be the chief source of cash earnings. During the decade of the thirties and in the aftermath of Hawes-Cooper and state use laws, Warden Best eyed the prospects of prison industrialization as the means of supplying many institutional needs amd providing some vocational training.

Small Industries

While serving as warden during the first decade of the twentieth century, John Cleghorn understood the ambivalent problems besetting inmate industrial labor; he had inspected the contract labor system operating in eastern prison industries and decided that it was an improper means for Colorado. After considering the possibility of in-house manufacturing for the market, he deemed the capital outlay for machinery too expensive and the market too risky. Facing low earnings and an inmate unemployment rate of 23 percent in 1906, he suggested that legislation require public institutions to purchase their clothing, underwear and shoes from the prison. The extra demand would provide employment for many inmates within the walls. But Cleghorn was far ahead of his time in 1906.[48] Not until 1933 did Colorado adopt the state-use system which required institutions to purchase articles made by the prison.

Although Wardens Cleghorn and Tynan pursued the acceptable options of road and farm work, the quest continued for industries that could employ the many convicts unsuitable for trusties or outdoor work. Sometimes, however, a talented inmate provided job opportunities for others. One inmate mattress maker taught his cohorts how to manufacture 790 excelsior mattresses to replace the straw ticks; they even sold twenty-five to the reformatory in Buena Vista. "By utilizing the knowledge of the tinsmiths who are inmates," Tynan reported that they manufactured 596 night buckets and water pails at a cost of twenty-six cents each, a saving of $2.64 each.[49] Similar innovations occurred from time to time, but the first real industry began with the license plate factory in 1925.

Joining the trend to manufacture license plates in prisons (22 states were making them), the General Assembly appropriated $35,000 for the Board of Corrections to build a manufacturing plant.[50] An excellent stamping machine which could exert sixty to eighty tons of pressure was purchased from the Toledo Machine and Tool Company and located in the old boiler house. With sheet metal unavailable from the Colorado Fuel and Iron Company, the Board obtained it from an eastern state and hired a manager from Jackson, Michigan.[51] The first prison-made plates for 1926 were green with white letters and the next were black with white letters. In the first two years, only 31 inmates had work for about three months. The warden sought other markets but most prisons pursued the same business. Adding a road marker shop expanded their options and New Mexico became its first out-of-state customer.

With a profit of $19,579 in the first two years, the tag plant promised a remunerative future.[52] Although the profit grew to $37,000 for the increasing number of vehicles in 1927-29, the plant accommodated only 35 workers.[53] Unfortunately, disaster struck in October, 1929 when the rioters destroyed most of the plant. For the next four years, the inmates could not make the plates. When they resumed operation in the basement of building number four, the *Denver Post* proudly pointed out that while the state had paid 16.5 cents from a private contractor for the 1934 tags, the prison fabricated the 1935 tags for 11.6 cents.[54] With somewhat different accounting, Best reported that the license plates had only cost 6.4 cents to make. Regardless of the profit, inmate labor supplanted a private manufacturer in what has become a traditional prison industry and, as a result, offers no skill for the job market outside the "walls." Enlarging the industry with a separate road sign plant employed about twenty more inmates who made federal and state signs.[55]

Of course the canning factory, also considered an industry, continued profitably with an out-of-state market until the federal Hawes-Cooper law became effective in 1934 and subjected convict-made goods of foreign states to state restrictions. Later Colorado's state-use legislation helped to compensate for market losses by requiring other institutions to purchase from the prison. Between 1926 and 1940, gross sales of canned goods ranged from a high of $129,283 in the biennium ending in 1930 to a low of $34,356 for the years of 1933-34. The accounting system prevents an understanding of the exact profit, but, from the earnings, the Board paid for the factory in four years and accrued a profit of at least $12,000 per bienium. Additionally, the factory supplied much of the institutional canned food.

Together the canning factory and tag plant employed fewer than one hundred inmates. Other small industries enlarged employment opportunities by optimizing the many diverse skills represented by the inmates; further, they provided vocational training and some of the supplies for the institutions. Clarifying their own philosophy regarding diversification work, the Board said that they were "unanimous in the opinion that any single large industry is impractical because of the large capital investment required and the uncertainty of returns if all your eggs are in one basket."[56] Consequently, small shops set the pattern in the 1930s.

Although Best continued to strive for a separate industrial building, he began his shops by remodeling the storeroom (called Building Number Four) with appropriations from the 1933 General Assembly. The license plate plant occupied the basement; the main floor housed the carpenter and paint shops; the second floor contained the enlarged tailor and shoe shops.[57] Three years later, he convinced the legislature that the shops would pay for themselves and obtained appropriations for a new building which housed a canteen and curio shop employing eight inmates, a soap plant producing varied soaps and insecticides with 28 employees, a knitting plant for underwear and socks for 17 workers, a plumbing, metal and electric shop with 20 employees and a blacksmith shop with seventeen inmate workers.[58] Only four years later Best "urgently" requested $65,000 for another new industrial building because of overcrowded conditions and "the merits of this vocational training."[59]

During the decade of the thirties and in the aftermath of the Hawes-Cooper and state-use laws, Warden Best eyed prison industrialization as the means of supplying many institutional needs while providing some vocational training. But he cautioned that "The industries to be undertaken at this time should be selected with the approval of labor leaders and representatives of the manufacturers and job-bers."[60] In fact, the Colorado Federation of Labor had helped to enact legislation which required inmate production for state institutions and its subdivisions.[61] Following these guidelines, prison officials opened factories for mattresses and hooked rugs (to be sold in the curio shop), a slaughter house and then in 1937 installed two hydraulic metal stamp machines to make Colorado's tax tokens.[62] In 1939, four inmates made 5,500,000 tax tokens valued at $9,760. Formerly, the state had bought the tax tokens through contractors' bids, so this state-use probably caused some loss to a private manufacturer.[63]

From the intermittent newspaper accounts, the public became aware of the industrial output and obviously looked with favor on the news that prisoners were producing for themselves or the state. The *Denver Post* reported that the new knitting machine would enable the prisoners to produce 1,000 pairs of cotton socks per day for which they were paying 7.5 cents per pair from private vendors. With 6,000 people in Colorado institutions in 1934, that would be cost effective.[64]

One of the most public areas for inmate employment, and which surely matched the qualifications of some incoming convicts, was the thirty-memeber prison band. Aside from their summer Sunday concerts on the porch of the administration building, the band played at the 1925 Colorado State Fair in its first "outside" appearance to "applause and cheers." Other off-site concerts followed. Notably, Governor Edward C. Johnson invited the band to play at the 1935 National Education Association reception.[65]

Was there profit in the various industrial endeavors? Did they pay for themselves as Best had predicted? Only the 1938 report gives any concrete explanation. It listed the following sales for the years of 1937-1938:

> Licenses plates $157,360
> Road signs 17,931
> Sales tax tokens 8,973
> Soap products 30,139
> Knit goods 19,362
> Civilian Clothing 10,578
> Total Sales $244,344
>
> Plant Disbursements...............................$167,663
> Equipment 55,693
> Profit...$27,758 [66]

Undoubtedly these industries contributed to the institution, but the amount listed as an expenditure for "Clothing and Dry Goods" in the two years ending in 1940 was $75,708.[67] Obviously, the prison could not fulfill all of its needs. Other than Best's comments, that "the industries make possible the production of inmate wearing apparel and household needs at sub-market cost," the records do not clarify the amounts.

Defending his direction for inmate employment, Best said, "A progressive industrial program has ever been my paramount objective" as it provides an increased outlet for surplus labor.[68] Turning toward industry was also the basic trend in Colorado's private sector. Interestingly, the *Colorado Yearbook* reported that manufacturing surpassed agriculture in 1935 in value of products and numbers of those engaged in each even though Colorado ranked thirty-sixth among the states in value of manufacturing. And where else could the inmates work in the economically depressed times of the 1930s? In Fremont County as well as all of Colorado, there were WPA and PWA projects hiring unemployed coal miners, farmers and others. The unemployed were canning surplus food at community centers for relief distribution through the auspices of FERA. A transient camp existed on the outskirts of the prison. At the least, the industries provided work for inmates and caused the least complaint from the public sector. To bolster prison industries by putting teeth into the state-use plan, Colorado's General Assembly required institutions to purchase what the prison made at a cost of ten percent more than other vendors.[69]

When Roy Best, the youngest state prison warden in the nation, became president of the National Wardens' Association in Atlanta in 1935, the *Cañon City Daily Record* credited his management for making "Colorado State Penitentiary one of the few in the nation that is industrialized."[70] While the reporter's perception regarding industrialization might not have been wholly accurate, that was the necessary trend for remunerative inmate employment.

Non-Remunerative Construction

Just as he had calculated the worth of inmate road work at the free labor rate, Warden Tynan also performed those mathematical exercises for the prison plant construction. On this basis, for example, his 1910 report revealed that each inmate contributed seventy cents daily to the state.[71] This was his way to show that a prison could pay for itself. But the bottom line was that tax money contributed $250,000 in 1909-10 to the cost of incarceration. Further, to discuss the increased value of the institution in tandem with profits becomes a moot point — had there been no law-breaking inmates, there would have been no need for a prison. Yet there is more economic ambivalence. Some taxpayers become prison employees or vendors for which they receive state money in paychecks — a motivating factor in locating the institution. It is, therefore, relevant to describe the unremunerative inmate employment in construction.

A further relevant consideration is the great rise in inmate population with its added problems - a 39 percent increase from 1902 to 1940 and a 46 percent increase from 1920-1932 (this latter when Colorado's population climbed by only 10.2 percent).[72] Thus the problem of providing housing and jobs continually increased.

Much labor had transformed the original unenclosed cellhouse to the 1940 multi-structured facility hidden by high walls and guarded by the gate's electric eye and the towers' bullet proof glass. Even though construction returned no cash earnings, an inspection of the inventory value of the Colorado prison in 1871 reveals a $40,000 structure on donated land, but contrast that with 1940 when the *Colorado Yearbook* listed the value of all prison property at $2,159,174, and one must admit that inmate labor had contributed some value.

Inmates had built every structure with the exception of the first cellhouse and prepared much of the material such as rock and bricks while changing the limestone formation bordering the prison land on the West; a large portion of it had disappeared through sixty-nine years of continual quarrying. Instead, parts of that formation composed prison structures, houses, churches and business buildings in Cañon City, Cripple Creek and other parts of Colorado. Work on the "rock pile" proved more than punishment at "hard labor." Unquestionably, the natural resource proved to be the chief asset of the prison property. With a source of building material and the need to expand prison facilities, it is no surprise that the majority of inmates worked in some phase of construction. Biennium reports continually reveal assignments such as stone quarry gangs, spall gangs, dirt gangs, extra gangs, carpenters, blacksmiths, plumbers, dynamo plant, prison duty, wrecking gangs and cellhouse crews.

Twentieth-century construction in the first decade included cellhouse Number Four, a library, an ice house, more lime kilns, new roofs, a bakery and a hospital. Among much other repair work, they had screened all doors and windows which resulted in "not having one case of typhoid."[73] Counting women along with the sick and feebleminded, the wardens listed approximately 20 percent as unemployed during those years.

Much of the building during the second decade occurred on the leased farms. When they lost the Avondale farm, the improvements brought a sale price of

144

$16,898.[74] After razing the old prison wall, they prepared stone and erected a new wall. Not only did they build a two-story horse barn but a garage for their two new trucks. Employing another type of skill, they replaced the arc lights with new tungsten lights. But the overarching achievement entailed the construction of the three-story administration building replacing the thirty-five-year-old structure. One self-taught "architect" prisoner designed the 100 by 50 foot building and the inmates cut the stone, burned the lime for mortar, hauled the sand, excavated the fourteen foot basement, poured the concrete and, for $12,000, erected a "magnificent" and efficient building worth at least $70,000. Among other projects was the installation of steel toilets with pipes for running water to each cell; according to Tynan, this saved the cost of two buckets, forty minutes of the convict's time at bucket duty each day and promoted "absolute sanitation and decency."[75]

Performing the varied projects of expansion and maintenance in the 1920s required diverse talents and trained inmates in new skills. When the state purchased building lots adjacent to the prison, the prisoners erected a State Military Armory and laid the steam and electric lines from the prison grounds.[76] A bridge, concrete streets, a garage, a hydro electric plant and hospital expansion added variety to construction projects.

Following the 1929 riot, the mass destruction required extensive repair labor. Fires had damaged the dining room, offices, chapel, library, and Cellhouses One and Two. Cellhouse Three, where the hostage standoff had taken place, received approximately 2,000 rounds of ammunition and a dynamite blast. Necessarily, some inmates slept in army tents until they could replaster and repaint the cellhouses.[77] When the inmates completed the new Cellhouse Five by 1930, it had single cells for only 232 inmates, and so another new cellhouse was already needed. Having learned from the riot the importance of segregating inmates, they arranged for two separate dining rooms with a guard tower between them. Financed by $67,000 fire insurance benefit fund, this new central building also housed the deputy warden's office, barber shop, library, identification bureau and the chapel.[78]

Aside from the approximately 265 in agriculture, the lists of specific assignments for 1930 reveal an overall picture of the disbursement of prison labor. While construction occupied about 137 inmates in 1930, another 165 worked in the quarries, sand and lime areas. Repairs occupied 49, and 25 prisoners composed the sewer gang which installed a twenty-inch sewer pipe to carry the discharge from two twelve-inch mains to the Arkansas River. Customarily overstaffed were the areas of prison detail with 224, engineering with 32, wrecking and recycling gangs with 68 and 112 in commissary. The dispersion of 24 individuals off the grounds at various sites such as the state capitol or fair grounds often aroused critical questions as to favoritism or danger. With this distribution of labor, the warden calculated that only 3 percent of the able-bodied were unemployed.[79]

But consider the missing component that work for many was seasonal and erratic; as in most prisons, therefore, much more idleness existed than the figures indicate. The Committee on Penal Reform, appointed by the governor to investigate the post-riot conditions, reported that "the great necessity for giving employment has resulted in utilizing many more inmates than are required. . . . In some places they are so numerous that they fall over each other and actually impede the work."[80] Nevertheless, the decade of the twenties closed with few of the total inmates in remunerative jobs, but most of them employed at least part-time and some of them gaining useful skills.

An extraordinary amount of building occurred in the thirties. Among the larger projects were Cellhouse Six, an underground tunnel from the administration building to the central or dining room and the installation of a prison water system which lowered the cost of Cañon City water from eight cents to one and one-half cents per thousand gallons. Further work included painting, reroofing and installing the mandated gas chamber to replace the system of execution by hanging (the first victim was William Cody Kelly on June 22, 1934).[81] Twenty inmates began the two year program of building a separate women's prison on the outside of the east wall; this simple two-story concrete and stucco prison, however, did not resemble the pretentious women's prison which Sing Sing inmates had built a hundred years before.[82]

On the eve of World War II, 561 inmates, almost one-third of the prison population, worked in the quarries and the "dirt gangs" preparing materials for building, recycling and repairing. During the Depression days of high overall unemployment and high prison population, the wardens reported only one to three percent of able-bodied inmates "unemployed." At that time, fulfilling the institutional needs caused by expansion provided jobs.

The continuing stream of visitors who paid to tour the "walled city" observed new gates, a new deputy warden's house, more towers, a new industrial building with well- equipped shops and a new cellhouse - Number Seven - accommodating 512 single cells. As this new cellhouse opened in 1940, the population averaged 1,465, but the maximum capacity was only 1,378. Optimistically, Best wrote, "The building program which was enacted by the Thirty-first General Assembly [a five year plan and appropriation] will no doubt care for the impending congestion."[83] What the tourists did not see was the first territorial cellhouse because, in that same year, the wrecking gangs had removed it — the only structure not built by inmates.

Appropriately, this study ends at the threshold of World War II when Warden Roy Best, whose twenty-year tenure ending in 1952 proved to be the longest term of any warden, became the beneficiary of the only period in the prison's history when inmate population decreased and defense contracts temporarily eased the inmate labor problem.[84] In 1940, the federally-created Prison Industries Reorganization Administration issued a study of Colorado's prison in which it commended Colorado for being "among the more advanced states" in some aspects of its penal administration and "for the excellent combination of agricultural, industrial and maintenance activities giving employment to every available prisoner."[85] During its first seventy years, Colorado, profiting from earlier prison experiences, had made some innovative contributions to the problem of inmate labor, but the ambivalence of prison labor continues.

ENDNOTES - CHAPTER VI

[1]Charles Henry Davis, "Use of Convict Labor," *Proceedings of the Academy of Political Science IV, 1913-14* (New York: Columbia University, 1914), p. 241.

[2]H.R. Cooley, "Outdoor Treatment of Crime," *Outlook 97*, February 25, 1911, pp. 403-8.

[3]Fred E Haynes, *The American Prison System* (New York: McGraw-Hill Co., 1939), pp. 105-6.

[4]*Biennial Report of the Colorado State Penitentiary, 1906* (Denver: Smith:Brooks, 1906), p. 6. Hereafter cited as BR of CSP.

[5]Harry Seligson and George E. Bardwell, *Labor-Management Relations in Colorado* (Denver: Sage, 1961), p. 316.

[6]*Eighth Biennial Report of the Bureau of Labor Statistics, Colorado, 1901-02* (Denver: Smith-Brooks, 1902), p. 389.

[7]*Yearbook of the State of Colorado, 1929*, p. 62.

[8]I tabulated these percentages from the total cash earnings listed in each Warden's report from 1902-1940, added all the agricultural earnings for each decade and calculated the percentages.

[9]*BR of CSP, 1910*, pp. 4-5.

[10]*Bureau of Labor Statistics, Colorado, 1909-10*, p. 288.

[11]*BR of CSP*, 1912, pp. 17-18.

[12]Ibid., p. 5.

[13]Ibid., 1914, pp. 13-14 and p. 22.

[14]Ibid., 1916, pp. 5-6.

[15]Ibid., 1916, pp. 47-8.

[16]Ibid., 1918, pp. 13 and 53.

[17]*BR of CSP*, 1918, p. 13, 11.

[18]*Minutes of the Board of Penitentiary Commissioners*, v. III," 1918, pp. 531-2.

[19]*Fourteenth Biennial Report of Board of Charities and Corrections, 1917-18* (Denver: Eames Brothers, 1918), pp. 34-5.

[20]*BR of CSP*, 1920, p. 8.

[21]*Denver Post*, September 8, 1919, 9:2.

[22]*BR of CSP*, 1920, pp. 7-9.

[23]*Board of Charities and Corrections*, 1908, p. 187.

[24]*Cañon City Daily Record*, December 4, 1924, 1:4.

[25]*Rocky Mountain News*, Feb. 25, 1927, 5:2, In a retirement speech, Tynan denounced frequency of executive clemency and the giving of bribes for pardons; he also called the prison a "poor man's Prison" and scored the "present method of prohibition enforcement as an utter failure."

[26]*Cañon City Daily Record*, Feb. 13, 1926, 1:3.

[27]Ibid., June 25, 1925, 1:3.

[28]Blake McKelvey, *American Prisons, A History of Good Intentions* (Montclair, N.J.:Patterson Smith, 1977), pp. 294-5.

[29]J.A. Ricker, *Cañon City Illustrated*, (Denver, 1897), p. 3. pamphlet in Western History Collection, Denver Public Library.

[30]*Daily Record*, August 20, 1925, 1:8.

[31]*BR of CSP*, 1926, p. 12.

[32]Ibid, 1928, p. 10 and 1926, p. 13.

[33]Ibid., 1928, p. 7.

[34]*Minutes of the Board of Corrections*, IV, September 19, 1928, unnumbered.

[35]*BR of CSP*, 1928, pp. 7, 12 and 42.

[36]*Cañon City Daily Record*, August 3, 1935, 1:2.

[37]*BR of CSP*, 1928, p. 12.

[38]Ibid., 1930, p. 7.

[39]The riot has had much publicity because of the eight guards and ten inmates who died. Father O'Neil who attempted to end the riot by carrying the explosives across the yards also received publicity. Box # 15828 at the WHC at the Denver Public Library contains a pamphlet written by an inmate, R.M. Crane, "That Red October Day." "Report of the Governor's Special Committee to Investigate the State Pen" (Denver: Eames, Dec. 4, 1929), at the Denver Public Library gives the political reasons and judgements as to causes. The serious discipline applied afterward and the hiring of Colonel Patrick Hamrock, the main figure in the Ludlow coal incident, as deputy warden appears in *RMN*, Feb. 7, 1930, 1:3.

[40]*BR of CSP*, 1932, p. 5.

[41]*Inaugural Address of Governor William H. Adams before the Twenty-eighth General Assembly at Denver, Colorado*, January 13, 1931. (no page numbers)

[42]*BR of CSP*, 1932, pp. 18-9.

[43]Ibid., p. 34.

[44]Ibid., 1934, pp. 8 and 19.

[45]Ibid., 1936, p. 14.

[46]Ibid., 1938, pp. 3, 12 and 32.

[47]Ibid., 1940, p. 7.

[48]Ibid., 1906, p. 9.

[49]Ibid., 1912, pp. 16-7.

[50]*Laws Passed at the Twenty-Fifth Session of the General Assembly*, (Denver: Eames Bros., 1925), Approved April 22, 1925, Ch. 141, pp. 405-6.

[51]*Cañon City Daily Record*, Sept. 18, 1925, 1:2.

[52]*BR of CSP*, 1926, pp. 11-12 and 23.

[53]Ibid., 1928, pp. 12 and 42.

[54]*Denver Post*, December 2, 1934, sc.4, p. 8.

[55]*BR of CSP*, 1934, p. 3 and 1936, p.3.

[56]Ibid, 1932, p. 2.

[57]Ibid., 1934, pp. 3-4.

[58]Ibid., 1936, pp. 3-4. This building also housed the laundry, gym, dressing room and isolation cells.

[59]Ibid., 1940, p. 11.

[60]Ibid., 1932, p. 15.

[61]*"Report of Committee on Penal Reform to the Governor of the State of Colorado, January 16, 1933,"* p. 12.

[62]*BR of CSP*, 1938, p. 5.

[63]*Cañon City Record*, July 9, 1935, 4:2.

[64]*Denver Post*, Nov. 24, 1934, 4:2.

[65]*Cañon City Record*, Sept. 21, 1925, 3:2. Also, Sept. 24, 1925, 1:4. Also July 1, 1935, 1:8.

[66]*BR of CSP*, 1938, p. 13.

[67]Ibid., 1940, pp. 5 and 13.

[99]Ibid.

[69]*Session Laws, Twenty-ninth General Assembly*, 1933, p. 782.

[70]*Cañon City Daily Record*, October 30, 1935, 1:2.

[71]*BR of CSP*, 1910, pp. 8-9.

[72]Tolbert R. Ingram, *Yearbook of the State of Colorado, 1930*, p. 5.

[73]*BR of CSP*, 1910, p. 8.

[74]Ibid., 1920, p. 14.

[75]Ibid., 1914, pp. 20-24.

[76]Ibid., 1922, p. 7.

[77]Ibid., 1930, p. 6. See also *Pueblo Chieftan*, Sept. 30, 1956, 8c:1:5.

[78]*BR of CSP*, 1930, p. 8.

[79]Ibid., pp. 11 and 43.

[80]*Committee on Penal Reform*, p. 10.

[81]*BR of CSP*, 1934, p. 59. An interesting history of the gas chamber is in the *Denver Post*, May 16, 1971, clipping file of the Western History Collections, Denver Public Library.

[82]Ibid., 1934, p. 6. The prison was a two-story building with lower floor or basement used for laundry and kitchen, dining, and the main floor for thirty individual cells, offices, hospital rooms, showers. The front porch was a sun room. The building had a separate wall around it with the tower of east gate guarding it. Today it is the prison museum.

[83]Ibid., 1940, pp. 3 and 29.

[84]The year 1941 had the largest number of inmates, 1553, until 1957. Population decreased during the war years. The low year was 1945 with 1,035 inmates and then there was a gradual rise to 1957, and it has escalated ever since to over 9000 today.

[85]*The Prison Problem in Colorado, a Survey by the Prison Industries Reorganization Administration* (Washington, D.C.: GPO, September 30, 1940), p. 2. This study followed studies of 24 other state prisons.

CHAPTER VII
ANALYSIS

Philosophies of one age have become the
absurdities of the next.
Sir Willieam Osler[1]

While today's current news headlines and official concerns of the Department of Corrections mirror earlier days, one major exception is that few dare to think that a prisoner's labor might be profitable. Technological changes, burgeoning prison population, curbs on types of labor and emphasis on vocational training have relegated some practices to the past. So from this specific study of another historical time, what can be learned? Did old ways lay foundations for present problems?

Certainly this research, did not proceed from the assumption that findings might be specifically applicable to questions involving convict labor today, but the study should add a perspective to incarceration matters that are, or should be, of great public concern. Humbly, we recognize that the historian can contribute, if not by telling how things ought to be, then, at least, by explaining that they need not be the way they are. And in the words of the venerable student of crime and punishment, Cesare Beccaria, "If these monarchs, I say, suffer the old laws to subsist, it is because of the infinite difficulties involved in stripping from errors the venerated rust of many centuries."[2] Perhaps this historian's work will loosen the "venerated rust" and wiser leaders will strip the errors for future change.

In the final analysis, the incarceration process depends upon legislative policies. It is, therefore, imperative that lawmakers become better informed. A glimmer of hope that historical research could enlighten policy makers occurred when the editor of the *Pueblo Chieftan*, referred to a portion of this study in his commentary that lawmakers must define their prison industry objectives and obtain a balance between work programs and the economic consequences thereof.[3] Influenced by a multi-voiced and often uninformed public, the legislators make qualitative assumptions as to who should compose the prison population. Only after the prison becomes crowded, do they discuss the quantitative and physical aspects of incarceration and the problem of jobs for convicts.

A conspicuous example of a qualitative law is Colorado's 1984 increased sentencing law. Although the nation's average sentence is twenty-four months, Colorado's lawmakers have been lengthening sentences resulting in average terms of thirty-nine months (this excludes life sentences). This also translates into adding 200 new beds to the prison system for every month of extension and typifies the quantitative problem.[4] Reacting to prison problems in piecemeal fashion with crisis mentalities and without an explicit view of the past, legislators respond to the public mood of "lock 'em up" with little regard for the quantitive problems of cost (now at least $70 a day), housing and training programs.

152

Today's well-known problems create frequent media headlines resembling those of the past:

Prisons Short on Staff and Beds
New Prison Surge Saps Taxpayers
Prison Terms Milk Taxpayers
Crime Rate Unaffected by Longer Terms
Crisis Waiting to Explode
Dearth of Blacks in Authority[5]

Obstacles facing both eras which have received less publicity and attention are apathy and the lack of a public consensus on policy directions. By enhancing awareness to these areas, perhaps a historian's research can be most useful.

As we have seen, Colorado's early transplants based their prison system largely on heritage. In the beginning, Colorado copied the single cell plan until over-crowded conditions made it impossible. As in New York and elsewhere, the choice for a prison location resulted from political vote-trading, and the social therapy consisted of strict discipline with stripes, silence and lockstep. Moreover, Colorado adopted a similar administrative system consisting of a politically appointed warden and board of commissioners and also hoped that the mandate for "hard labor" would help pay the penitentiary costs. Even though most of those traditions had already become problematic by the time the Territorial Penitentiary opened in 1871, Colorado followed the pattern described by Colorado historian Robert Athearn as "responses to eastern advances and to the traditional western desire to keep abreast with that part of the nation,"[6]

In historian Athearn's opinion, Coloradans were "not innovative," but this research uncovered some unique labor experiences in the history of the Colorado State Penitentiary. In contrast to the manner in which most contract labor systems operated elsewhere, Colorado retained authority over its prisoners regardless of where they worked. When prison authorities could not introduce industry success-fully, they expediently found it profitable to quarry the lime and sandstone ridge forming their western periphery; the products supplied the young mining and building industry market. Later, they innovated the honor camp for road work and achieved renown for the most successful unarmed guarded outdoor work in the United States. Fortunately, Colorado's climate, sparse population and legal fiat against private exploitation of contract labor enhanced the opportunities for avoiding most of the inmate abuse taking place in older prisons.

But what are the legacies of the first seventy years of Colorado's prison experiences? Foremost is the building of structure after structure to enlarge the walled complex for the rapidly increasing population; that led to prison after prison until Colorado can count sixteen separate facilities (with more on the drawing board) holding 9,000 convicts in early 1993. Ironically, most people viewed incarceration as a method to deter crime, but contrary to the very first arguments for building a territorial prison, the structure did not stop violence or crime. In fact, all of the recorded lynchings which happened in Fremont County occurred after the prison opened and often adjacent to the edifice. As violence steadily increases today, incarceration seems to be no deterrence. Yet increasing incarceration is a legacy.

Concerned about recidivism rates, many wardens indicated that incarceration, harsh discipline and inmate labor did not always "reform" the convict. During early years, no records concerning a convict's incarceration in other states existed, but the prison registration book listed second and third Colorado prison terms for many. Even with mental and social counseling as well as more vocational opportunities for the inmates today, recidivism is still discouraging. A recent national study shows that 62.5 percent of released convicts had been rearrested in three years.[7] In Colorado in 1979, an ex-convict had a 20.9 percent chance of returning to prison in three years, but ten years later, the recidivism rate was 39.3 percent. Apparently the lesson to be learned from the past is that public opinion must decide if it wants to treat overcrowded prisons as a success or failure; if a success, keep building; if a failure, should not the legacy be discarded?

Another legacy being followed with great intensity is the selection of a penitentiary site for political reasons with no regard for the best interests of all concerned. From the beginning, Cañon City's great distance from the major centers of population and crime added expense and hardship for the inmates' families. Locating the prison almost within city limits permitted little institutional expansion, and the shortage of farm land inhibited the prison from growing its own food. Leasing and buying land distant from the institution required extra transportation of inmates, easier escapes and charges of favoritism in land transactions. After five decades, the state acquiesced to the Commissioners' requests and purchased prison land east of town where today seven newer prisons (Skyline, Centennial, Four-Mile, Fremont, Shadow Mountain, Pre-Release and the women's facility) sprawl across the area. In addition to farming and livestock activities, a dairy, a wild horse training center, a saw mill, a brick plant and other enterprises provide work for inmates.

Clearly one lesson from the past should be to choose a prison site with productive land to allow favorable outside inmate employment. Whether the two recent politically-located prisons (on Crowley County's sixty donated acres and on Limon's 320 acres) will offer any remunerative opportunites remain to be seen. Most likely that is a moot point unless the present policy directed toward inside diversified prison industries changes.[8] Only three years old, the Ordway and Limon prisons have developed different problems such as a shortage of trained personnel who will live in the isolated rural areas and an absence of minority (Hispanic and black) employees.

Consider a further legacy. Is the prison still a viable community option for a sagging town economy? Without a doubt, the Territorial Prison enhanced the economy of Cañon City from its inception. Even when three guards received only a $25 monthly salary and the warden a yearly stipend of $1000, the payroll brightened the community. Later in an 1893 description of "Colorado Enterprising Cities," the author verified the prison's contribution — "a payroll of $40,000 per annum is not to be despised."[9] Prosperity prevailed in 1954 when the local newspaper under the title of "Operation of Prison is Big Business" revealed that "It [the prison] is only exceeded by the Ideal Cement plant at Portland [in Fremont County] from the standpoint of yearly salaries and it is only exceeded by the Royal Gorge Bridge from the standpoint of a tourist attraction."[10] More recently, it has far surpassed Ideal Cement in payroll, and, whereas the prison no longer entertains tourists, the first women's cellhouse is now a museum charging fees for admittance. Currently, the Territorial Penitentiary alone generates a yearly payroll of over $7,000,000. With 264 employees at the Arkansas Valley Prison and 249 at the Limon facility, those payrolls boost the economically depressed, waterless prairie lands of Ordway and Limon to some extent, but there is a tendency for employees not to reside in those towns. Overall, the Colorado Corrections Department currently pays 3,040 state employees over $111,000,000.[11] Most assuredly, the answer is "yes" to the question, "does the prison pay?"

But to whom does the prison pay? In addition to the direct salaries paid to prison employees, the general economy benefits from added demand for service products; the local realtors and contractors market more houses for the employees; extra teachers for the children of prison personnel are needed; more social workers must service the neglected and displaced families of inmates and extra court personnel are required to handle the increasing caseloads. But it is the taxpayers who fund this operation, again causing a "Peter and Paul" condition. For many economic developers, the prison, like all government agencies, is seen as an industry which generates jobs. Recently, the Fremont County Economic Development director said that "The corrections industry is about the most stable industry you can court. We use the stability of the prison economy as a selling tool to prospective businessmen who are looking at locating here."[12] Thus while the prison is a taxpayer's nightmare, the expenditures diversify the economy.

How does society break the cycle of a policy with such a long heritage and economic importance for those who profit? Can we cut through that dilemma for a wiser use of tax money? Victor Hugo once said that to open a school was to close a prison. While this is not infallible thinking, ironically, current events in the "prison town" reverse the situation. When the private boys' Holy Cross Abbey school recently closed in Cañon City, it reopened as an employee training facility for the prison. Since Colorado State Penitentiary, following the lead of other states, reorganized as the "Corrections Department" with a phenomenal enrollment, should we consider the expenditures as educational investments and direct all policies toward that? Consider that the annual cost for a Colorado public school student averages around $5,000 but for a convict approximately $22,000 annually.

Since the effort to keep inmates employed is the major focus of this research, are there any lessons of merit transferrable from early inmate labor? Certainly, the honor road camps and other public works projects benefited both the public and the inmate. For a time, agencies of government and the public cooperated in permitting selected inmates to live and work responsibly outside the walls. At least some inmates learned skills and trustworthiness that prepared them for liberty. But again a change in economics ended the road building camps. The stifling fears of infringement on private enterprise and a rising period of unemployment diminished cooperation between government officials and interrupted what could have continued as a less costly method of punishment. Pursuing this example from the past with innovative planning and cooperation, inmate public work projects could begin again.

Gone also is the legacy for inmate construction which earlier afforded opportunity for matching convict skills or teaching them building skills when today they are not permitted to work on construction of the prison complex. Depleted too are the lime and sandstone supplies used in the construction. After the federal government built the first prison, the officials quickly converted miners, laborers and tradesmen to stonecutters and lime kiln operators. When the prisoners blasted out large areas of the hillside and leveled the land for structures composed of the displaced rock, they also changed the landscape. Today, the Environmental Protection Agency would restrict them from scarring the east side of the Hogback. Despite the hurdles, the success of construction work merits a second consideration.

By 1940, the old tradition of "making a prison pay for itself" had gradually given way to more tax support for teaching trades while avoiding public markets. The framework of this study articulated the influence of private business and labor in curtailing competition from convict labor. Of course, no one would deny to the unions and free enterprise their rights for protection from competition by an artificial society of wrongdoers. But the solution, and one still being sought, is to create a balanced relationship between restrictions on prison labor and their effect on society as a whole.

An example of labor gridlock occurred during the height of the Depression when the Cañon City Chamber of Commerce pleaded for inmate labor to prepare a back entrance road for tourist access to the Royal Gorge Bridge. When contactors protested the use of inmate labor, the plan died. Lacking sufficient funds for private construction, this labor waste impacted the tourist trade.[13] Another lost opportunity for inmate labor has been prison construction since its transferrence to private contractors has become a "bigger economic plum." Present day spokesmen claim that the inmates are "too clever to be trusted in building their own domiciles."[14]

The *deja vu* aspect of prison history regarding who is incarcerated also requires attention. Corroborating what historians learned about other state prisons, this study also reveals that, during times of economic depression, the prison population increased; moreover the inmate profile showed that the incarcerated were generally poor, young (the average age ranged from 26-32), and they were largely from other states. The foreign-born chiefly came from Europe until after 1920; thereafter, about 40 to 50 percent of the foreign born inmates came from Mexico. The occupational profile also discloses that almost half of the prisoners listed some trade, but there was no way to ascertain if they were employed at the time of conviction. Practically speaking, the variety of useful skills, ranging from "finger-print worker" to various types of machinist and contruction knowledge, must have made it convenient to perform the vast amount of prison expansion. Further profile study indicated that during the 1920s and 1930s, the violators of the Prohibition law often composed one-third of the population, impacting the facilities just as the drug law violators do today.

Although many states compensated their inmate labor to aid their dependent families, Colorado left no legacy for that. Many families of convicts became victims and depended on welfare payments. During the early years, there is one meager recorded incident when a convict made restitution for his crimes while incarcerated, and that was by requiring one escapee to pay for his apprehension in 1879, a total of $56.25. Recently, one legislator suggested that those who could afford to pay should pay for their incarceration. Can we not innovate various forms of restitution to lower the exhorbitant costs?

Another perspective on the cost escalation evolves from this study. In 1928, for example, there were 115 employees and 1,129 prisoners which reflects a ten percent ratio between inmates and employees. But consider today's situation with 9,000 prisoners and 3,040 employees. That translates into slightly over one employee for every three prisoners. Again, we ask the question — to whom does the prison pay? One final historical glance into the past is that at the end of this study in 1940, Colorado's state government had incarcerated one-tenth of one percent of its population, but in 1990, two and two-tenths of all Coloradans were state prisoners.

Reformers in the line of criminal justice have allowed their narrow sense of history to confine them to the period before penitentiaries when public tortures, the gallows and edicts of banishment dominated punishment; they continue with the perception that prison is a humane and practical reform. It behooves Coloradans to update their historical perceptions by looking at the past to plan for the future. Then, they might change the qualitative laws which have led to overcrowding the prisons. If it takes a crisis to open doors to change, now is the time to adopt less drastic measures of social control and initiate methods of punishment other than wholesale incarceration. Applicable to the future of punishment for felons is the statement of Eleanor Roosevelt after she viewed the fate of Hiroshima, "God grant to men greater wisdom in the future."

NOTES - CHAPTER VII

[1]Sir William Osler, *Boulder Daily Camera*, quoted by Christopher Brauchli, April 8, 1990, p. 6.

[2]Adam J. Hirsch, "From Pillory to Penitentiary," *The Michigan Law Review*, v.80: 1265.(mimeographed, no date).

[3]*Pueblo Chieftan*, Jan.21, 1988, 4A.

[4]*Denver Post,* Sept. 20, 1992, 1 and 12.

[5]Ibid., Sept. 21, 1992, 1 and 3.

[6]Robert G. Athearn, *The Coloradans*, (Albuquerque:University of New Mexico, 1976) p. 206.

[7]*Denver Post*, April 3, 1989, 3A:2.

[8]Telephone Interview, Elizabeth McDonough, Communications Officer, Department of Corrections, Colorado Springs, March 20, 1990.

[9]*Historical and Descriptive Review of Colorado Enterprising Cities*, Denver, 1893, Western History Collection, Denver Public Library, p. 53..

[10]*Cañon City Daily Record*, Mar. 20, 1954, 1:2.

[11]Interview, Dixie Reed, Office of Finance, Department of Corrections, October 15, 1992.

[12]*Cañon City Daily Record*, May 12, 1989, 8:2.

[13]"Minutes, Cañon City Chamber of Commerce", June, 1933, Colorado History Room, Cañon City Library.

[14]Telephone Interview, McDonough, Oct. 15, 1992.

APPENDIX

WARDENS OF THE STATE PENITENTIARY

Term	Warden
1871	Mark Shaffenburg, U.S.Marshal of Colorado
June 1871	Albert Walters, Acting adm. under Shaffenburg
June 1873	J.C. Reed
Feb. 1874	Anson Rudd (first Territorial Warden)
June 1874	David Prosser
Dec. 1875	Benjamin Allen
March 1877	M.N. Megrue (first appointed under State)
Dec. 1880	Willard B. Felton
1882-84	C.P. Hoyt
1884-86	R.A. Cameron
1886-88	C.P. Hoyt
1888-90	J.A. Lamping
1890-92	William A. Smith
1992-94	Frank A. McLister
1994-98	John Cleghorn
1998-1900	C.P. Hoyt (third term)
1900-02	E.H. Martin
1902-1909	John Cleghorn
1909-1927	Thomas J. Tynan
Feb.1927	Boone Best (killed in car accident)
Sept.1927	Samuel J. Burris (provisional appointee)
1927-31	F.E. Crawford
Oct.'31-32	John P. Allen (died August, 1932)
1932-1952	Roy Best

ESCAPES

Total escapes from beginning to 1940 1,048
Recaptured 764
Missing 284

COSTS

Cost per diem per capita	
1878	70 cents
1898	37 cents
1940	81 cents

*Compiled by author from Biennial Wardens' Reports.

160

CASH EARNINGS

Dates	Cash Earnings	Average Number of Inmates
1877-8	$7,920	146
1879-80	22,023	164
1881-2	59,787	251
1883-4	50,405	340
1885-6	70,067	356
1887-8	80,676	357
1889-90	53,836	477
1891-2	59,238	567
1893-4	36,724	608
1895-6	22,982	635
1897-8	16,378	606
1899-1900	26,935	549
1901-02	40,511	571
1903-4	34,374	660
1905-6	63,714	681
1907-8	54,943	651
1909-10	38,125	724
1911-12	33,144	768
1913-14	28,314	775
1915-16	39,373	792
1917-18	78,537	600
1919-20	84,278	564
1921-22	60,480	858
1923-34	51,481	881
1925-26	58,188	975
1927-28	116,844	1,049
1929-30	68,220	1,090
1931-32	53,552	1,225
1933-34	30,602	1,175
1935-36	47,148	1,205
1937-38	70,235	1,402
1939-40	95,568	1,465

	Appropriations	Maintenance
1877-78	$25,000	$58,348
1939-40	890,000	1,001,156

Emergencies, carry overs and cash earnings made up the deficits between the biennial general appropriation.

*Compiled by author from Biennial Wardens' Reports.

Occupational Chart

Year	White Collar Profession (%)	White Collar Semi- (%)	Laborers (%)	Farmers A (%)	Farmers *B (%)	Trades (%)	Miners (%)	Total
1875 - 76	4 (4)	12 (12)	24 (26)	8 (8)	8 (8)	33 (35.9)	11 (11.9)	92
1879 - 80	3 (1.3)	19 (8.4)	64 (28.3)	7 (3)	7 (3)	110 (48)	16 (7)	226
1885 - 86	6 (2)	23 (7.7)	69 (23)	11 (3)	22 (7)	146 (48.9)	20 (6.7)	298
1889 - 90	15 (2.6)	41 (7.2)	90 (15.9)	47 (8.3)	42 (7.4)	325 (57.5)	?	565
1895 - 96	6 (1)	27 (5)	106 (19.8)	42 (7.8)	35 (6.5)	280 (52.3)	39 (7.2)	535
1899 - 1900	8 (2)	21 (5.3)	75 (19.2)	27 (6.9)	16 (4)	207 (53)	35 (8.9)	390
1905 - 06	10 (2)	30 (6)	73 (14.6)	34 (6.8)	29 (5.8)	275 (55)	46 (9.2)	497
1909 - 10	17 (2.6)	33 (5.1)	108 (16.8)	45 (7)	35 (5.4)	365 (56.8)	40 (6.2)	643
1915 - 16	15 (2)	38 (5.1)	135 (18.3)	69 (9.3)	37 (5)	394 (53.6)	47 (6.4)	735
1919 - 20	9 (1.6)	47 (8.7)	76 (14)	86 (15.9)	8 (1.4)	285 (52.8)	29 (5.4)	540
1925 - 26	13 (1.3)	71 (7)	134 (13.2)	226 (22.3)	46 (4.5)	456 (45)	68 (6.7)	1014
1929 - 30	21 (1.9)	96 (9)	145 (13.6)	286 (26.8)	52 (4.9)	411 (38.6)	54 (5)	1065
1935 - 36	23 (2)	108 (9.7)	199 (17.9)	190 (17)	55 (4.9)	492 (44.2)	46 (4.1)	1113
1939 - 40	14 (1.2)	100 (8.8)	263 (23.2)	156 (13.8)	41 (3.6)	514 (45.4)	4.3 (3.8)	1131

*Compiled by author from Biennial Wardens' Reports.

SELECTED BIBLIOGRAPHY

ARCHIVAL SOURCES

UNIVERSITY OF COLORADO WESTERN HISTORY COLLECTION, BOULDER.

Byers, William, "Centennial State," Manuscript, Bancroft Collection, 1884.
Nichols, Dave. File Box, #1380.
Rogers, James Grafton. "The Mining District Governments of the West."
    Address delivered at the American Association of Law Libraries in Denver,
    June 28, 1935. (pamphlet.)
Stearns, Robert L. "Colorado: A Study in Frontier Sovereignty." Address given
    at the American Association of Law Libraries, Denver, June 26, 1935.
    (pamphlet.)
Taylor, Donna,"Memories from the Foot of the Royal Gorge," pamphlet file,
    Cañon City: Printing Class High School, 1969.

COLORADO HISTORICAL SOCIETY, DENVER.

Newspaper files.
Colorado History Room, Cañon City Public Library. Prison Files include
    newspaper clippings, interviews with pioneers on tapes, pictures of early
    area.
"Minutes, Cañon City Chamber of Commerce," Boxes,I,II,III. 1913-33.

COLORADO STATE ARCHIVES, DENVER, COLORADO.

Prisoner Record Book, Colorado State Penitentiary.
Governors' Correspondence, 1875-89, vol. I.Box #8919.
"Minutes of the Board of Penitentiary Commissioners," 4 vols. 1874-1930. Box
    19382 A-D.
Governor Waite files, Boxes #22692 and 22693.
Governor Thomas files, Box #26949. Letters from road superintendent,
    Chatelat. 1899. Penitentiary Reports and Miscellaneous Manuscripts of the
    first report of 1878. Contract between Catlin and Hoyt. Eugene Bertrand
    letter, boxes # 9870 and #9871.

ROCKY MOUNTAIN BRANCH OF NATIONAL ARCHIVES, DENVER.

Interior Department Territorial Papers, Colorado, 1861-88, "The Penitentiary
    at Cañon City." Microfilm #431
State Department Papers, Colorado Series, vols. 1-2, Dec. 28, 1859 - April 22,
    1874.

164

WESTERN HISTORY COLLECTION, DENVER PUBLIC LIBRARY.

Ricker, J.A., "Cañon City Illustrated." Denver, 1897. (pamphlet.)
"Historical and Descriptive Review of Colorado Enterprising Cities." Denver: John Lethem, 1893.(pamphlet.)
"The Story of the Arkansas Valley." Denver, 1919.(pamphlet.)
Wayne Patterson, former warden, 12 boxes of records and memorabilia. Not indexed.
Prison clippings file also includes souvenir booklet of 1955, "This is the Prison."
Woodson Hunter, "Cañon City" (pamphlet)
"Picturesque Cañon, Containing Illustrations in and around Cañon City." 1892. (pamphlet)

GOVERNMENT DOCUMENTS

Biennial Message of Governor Albert W. McIntire, 1895. pamphlet. Denver: Smith-Brooks, 1897.
Biennial Message of Governor James B. Orman and Inaugural Address of Governor James Peabody. pamphlet. Denver: Smith-Brooks, 1903.
Colorado Revised Statutes, Sixteenth General Assembly. Denver: Smith-Brooks, 1908.
Congressional Record, 70th Cong.,2nd sess., Hearings, April 3, 1928-Jan. 4, 1929. Washington: Government Printing Office, 1929.
Council Journal of the Legislative Assembly of the Territory of Colorado, 7th sess. Denver: Collier, 1868.
Council Journal of the Legislative Assembly of the Territory of Colorado, 8th sess. Denver: Byers, 1870.
General Laws of Colorado Territory Passed at the Eighth Session. Central City: Collier, 1870.
General Laws of Colorado Territory Passed at the Ninth Session. Central City: Collier, 1870.
General Laws of Colorado Territory Passed at the Tenth Session. "Report of Joint Committee of Council and House of Representatives of Colorado." Appendix. Central City: Register Printing House, 1874.
General Laws of Colorado Territory, Acts for Years 1870-76 and Laws Enacted at First General Assembly of Colorado. Denver: Tribune Stean Printing House, 1877.
Inaugural Address of His Excellency Honorable William H.Adams, Governor of Colorado Before the Twenty-eighth General Assembly at Denver, Colorado, January 13, 1931.(pamphlet.)
Inaugural Address of Governor Charles S. Thomas to the Twelfth General Assembly, 1899-90. (pamphlet.)
Laws Passed at the Fourth Session of the General Assembly of Colorado. Denver: The Times, 1883.

165

Laws Passed at the Sixth Session of the General Assembly of Colorado. Denver: Tribune, 1887.
Laws Passed at the Tenth Session of General Assembly of Colorado. Denver: Smith-Brooks, 1895.
Laws Passed at the Fifteenth Session of the General Assembly of Colorado. Denver: Smith-Brooks, 1905.
Laws Passed at the Sixteenth Session of General Assembly of Colorado. Denver: Smith-Brooks, 1907.
Laws Passed at the Twenty-Fifth General Assembly of Colorado. Denver: Eames Brothers, 1925.
Laws Passed at the Twenty-Sixth Session of the General Assembly of Colorado. Denver: Bradford-Robinson,1927.
Laws Passed at the Thirty-First Session of the General Assembly of Colorado. Denver: Bradford-Robinson,1937.
Laws Passed at the Twenty-Ninth General Assembly of Colorado. Denver: Bradford-Robinson, 1933.
Revised Statutes of Colorado, Seventh Session of the Legislative Assembly, 1867-68. Central City: Collier, 1868.
Statutes of the Population of the United States, Ninth Census. Washington, D.C., Government Printing Office, 1970.
United States Senate, 70th Cong. 1st sess., Hearings at Interstate Commerce Committee, Feb. 7, 8, 9, 17, 1928.
United States Bureau of Labor Statistics, "Laws Relating to Prison Labor in the U.S. as of July 1, 1933." Bulletin #596. Washington: Government Printing Office, 1933.
United States Congressional Globe, 35th Cong., 2nd sess. Washington, D.C.: John C. Rive, 1859.
United States Congressional Globe, 41st Cong., 3rd sess., Part III, Appendix. Washington: John C. Rive, 1871.
United States Congressional Globe, 42nd Cong., 3rd sess., Part III, Appendix. Washington: John C. Rives, 1873.
United States Department of Labor, Bureau of Labor Statistics, Bulletin #590. Washington: Government Printing Office, 1933.
United States Statutes at Large 14, December 1865-March 1867. George P. Sanger, ed. Boston: Little, Brown, 1868.

PUBLISHED REPORTS AND PROCEEDINGS

Biennial Reports of the Commissioners, Warden, and Physician, 1879-80. Denver: Tribune Publisher, 1881.
Biennial Reports of the Commissioners, Warden, and Physician, 1881-82. Denver: Times, 1883.
Biennial Report of the Commissioners, Warden, and Physician,1884-86 and 1887-88. Denver: Collier and Cleaveland.

Biennial Reports of the Commissioners and Warden. Denver: Smith-Brooks, 1889-90, 1891-92, 1893-04, 1895-06, 1897-98, 1899-1900.

Biennial Reports of the Colorado State Penitentiary. Denver: Smith-Brooks, 1901-02, 1903-04, 1905-06, 1907-08, 1909-10, 1911-12, 1913-14.

Biennial Reports of the Colorado State Penitentiary. Denver: Eames Brothers, 1915-16, 1917-18, 1919-20, 1921-22.

Biennial Reports of the Colorado Board of Corrections and Warden of the Colorado State Penitentiary. Denver: Bradford-Robinson, 1923-24, 1925-26, 1927-28,1929-38, 1931-32.

Biennial Reports of the Warden. Denver: Bradford-Robinson, 1933-34, 1935-36, 1937-38, 1939-40.

Biennial Report of Bureau of Labor Statistics of Colorado, 1901-02. Denver:Smith-Brooks, 1902.

Biennial Report of the State Board of Charities and Corrections of Colorado. Denver: Smith-Brooks Printing Company, 1892-1914.

Biennial Report of the State Board of Charities and Corrections of Colorado, 1917-18. Denver: Eames Bros., 1918.

Eighth Biennial Report of the Bureau of Labor Statistics of the State of Colorado, 1901-2. Denver: Smith-Brooks,1902.

First Biennial Report of the State Highway Commission of the State of Colorado, 1910. C.P. Allen, chairman. Denver: Smith-Brooks, 1910.

First Biennial Report of the Bureau of Labor Statistics of the State of Colorado, 1887-88. Denver: Collier and Cleaveland, 1888.

Fourth Biennial Report of the State Highway Commission Report of the State of Colorado, 1916. J. M. Kuykendall, chairman. Denver: Eames Bros., 1917.

Proceedings of the American Prison Association, 1929. New York: The Association, 1929.

Report of Committee on Penal Reform to the Governor of the State of Colorado, January 16, 1933. Denver: Clark Quick Printing Company, 1933.

Report of the Industrial Commission on Prison Labor, vol.III. Washington, D.C.: Government Printing Office, 1900.

Report on Convict Labor, United State Department of Agriculture Bulletin #414. Washington,D.C.: Government Printing Office, 1916.

Report of the Governor's Special Committee to Investigate the State Penitentiary. Denver: Eames Company, 1929.

Report of the Committee on Penal Reform to the governor of the State of Colorado. Denver: Clark, 1933.

Report on the Prisons and Reformatories of the United States and Canada made to the Legislature of New York, January, 1867. by E. C. Wines and W. A. Dwight. Albany: Van Benthuysen and Sons' Steam Printing House, 1867.

Second Annual Report of the Commissioner of Labor, 1886, Convict Labor. U.S. Department of Interior. Washington, D.C.: Government Printing Office, 1887.

Second Biennial Report of the State Highway Commission of the State of Colorado, 1912. C.P. Allen, chairman. Denver: Smith-Brooks, 1912.

Seventeenth Biennial Report, Colorado Bureau of Labor Statistics, 1919-20. James R. Noland, Labor Commissioner. Denver: Eames Bros., 1920.

Third Biennial Report of the State Highway Commission of the State of Colorado, 1914. J.M. Kuykendall, chairman. Denver: Smith-Brooks,1915.

Twentieth Annual Report of the Commissioner of Labor, 1905, Convict Labor. Department of Labor and Commerce. Washington, D.C.: Government Printing Office, 1906.

Twenty-First Biennial REport Colorado Bureau of Labor Statistics, 1927-28. Charles Armstrong, Labor Commissioner. Denver: Bradford-Robinson Company, 1928.

Twenty-Third Biennial Report, Colorado Bureau of Labor Statistics, 1932. Charles Armstrong, Labor Commissioner. Denver: Bradford-Robinson Company, 1932.

"Convict Labor in 1923," *United States Bureau of Labor Statistics.* Washington: Government Printing Office, 1923.

Yearbook of the State of Colorado. 1918 and 1930. Denver:Bradford-Robinson, 1918 and 1930.

Yearbook of the State of Colorado. 1920. Denver: Welch Haffner Printing, 1920.

UNPUBLISHED REPORTS AND THESES

Carey, James Lester, "A History of the Indiana Penitentiary System, 1821-1933." Ph. D. dissertation, Ball State University, 1966.

Flynn, Frank T. "The Federal Government and the Prison Labor Problem." Ph. D. dissertation, University of Chicago, 1949.

Gildemeister, Glen A. "Prison Labor and Convict Competition with Free Workers, 1848-98." Ph.D. dissertation, Northern Illinois University, 1977.

Hensel, Donald Wayne. "A History of the Colorado Constitution in the Nineteenth Century." Ph. D.dissertation, University of Colorado, 1957.

Johnson, Judith R."For Any Good At All, A Comparative Study of State Penitentiaries in Arizona, Nevada, New Mexico, Utah, 1900-1980." Ph. D. dissertation, University of New Mexico, 1987.

Norris, Robert L. "Prisons, Reformers, Penitentials, Publicists in France, England, and the United States,1774-1849." Ph. D. dissertation, American University, 1985.

Pratt, Joseph, "Economics of Convict Labor in Road Construction," *North Carolina Geological and Economic Survey*, Chapel Hills, N. Car., Feb. 18, 1914. (mimeographed.)

"Proceedings of the Fourth American Road Congress." Atlanta, Georgia, November 9-14, 1914.(mimeographed.)

"The Prison Problem in Colorado," A Survey by the Prison Industries Reorganization Administration. September,30, 1940. Washington, D.C.

Thomson, Georg, "The History of Penal Institutions in the Rocky Mountain West, 1846-1900." Ph. D. dissertaion, University of Colorado, 1965.

BOOKS

Athearn, Robert G. *The Coloradans*. Albuquerque: University of New Mexico, 1976).

Ayers, Edward L. *Vengeance and Justice, Crime and Punishment in the 19th Century American South*. New York: Oxford University Press, 1984.

Bacon, Corinne, compiled. *Prison Reform*. New York: H.W. Wilson and Company, 1917.

Bardwell, George and Seligson, Harry. *Labor-Management Relations in Colorado*. Denver: Sage, 1961.

Barnes, Harry Elmer. *The Evolution of Penology in Pennsylvania, a Study in Social History*. Montclair,New Jersey: Patterson Smith, 1968.

Barnes, Harry Elmer and Negley K. Teeters. *New Horizons in Criminology*. Englewood Cliffs, N. J.: Prentice-Hall, 1960.

Beaumont, G. de Beaumont and Tocqueville, A. de._*On the Penitentiary System in the United Statess and Its Applica-tion in France*. translated by Francis Lieber. Philadelphia, 1833.

Bennett, James V. Bennett. *I Chose Prison*. New York: Alfred Knopf, 1970.

Campbell, Rosemae Wells. *Fremont County, Colorado, 1830-1950*. Palmer Lake, Colorado: The Filter Press, 1972.

Commons, John R. Commons; Saposs, D.J.; Sumner, H.L.; Mittelman, E.B.; Hoagland, H.E.; Andrews, J.R. and Perlman S. *History of Labour in the United States* 2 vols. New York: The Macmillan Company, 1918.

Curti, Merle. *The Growth of American Thought*, Second Edition. New York: Harper and Brothers, 1951.

Foner, Philip S. ed. *Kate Richards O'Hare*. Baton Rouge: Louisiana State University Press, 1982.

Foucault, Michel. tr. by Alan Sheridan. *Discipline and Punish, The Birth of the Prison*. New York: Pantheon Books, 1977.

Hall, Frank. *History of the State of Colorado* 4 vols. Chicago: Blakely Printing Company, 1889.

Garrett, Paul W. and MacCormick, Austin H. editors, *Handbook of American Prisons and Reformatories, 1929*. New York: National Society of Penal Information, 1929.

Harrison, Fred. *Hell Holes and Hangings, an Informal History of Western Territorial Prisons, 1861-1912*. Clarendon, Texas: Clarendon Press, 1968.

Hawes, Joseph M., ed. *Law and Order in American History*. New York: MacMillian Company, 1960.

Hawkins, Gordon and Sherman, Michael. *Imprisonment in America, Choosing the Future*. Chicago: University of Chicago, 1981.

Haynes, Fred E. *The American Prison System*. New York: McGraw-Hill Company, 1939.

Knight, Harold V. *Working in Colorado*. Boulder: University of Colorado, 1971.

Lewis,David W. *From Newgate to Dannemora, The Rise of the Penitentiary in New York, 1796-1848*. Ithaca, New York: Cornell University, 1965.

Lewis, Orlando F. *The Development of American Prisons and Prison Customs, 1776-1845*. Albany: J.B.Lyon Company 1922.

Limerick, Patricia N. *The Legacy of Conquest, The Unbroken Past of the American West*. New York: W.W. Norton, 1987.

McKelvey, Blake. *American Prisons, A History of Good Intentions*. Montclair, New Jersey: Patterson Smith, 1977.

Maestro, Marcello. *Cesare Beccaria and the Origins of Penal Reform*. Philadelphia: Temple University Press, 1973.

Mitford, Jessica. *Kind and Unusual Punishment, The Prison Business*. New York: Alfred A. Knopf, 1973.

Paul, Rodman. *Mining Frontiers of the Far West,1848-1880*. Albuquerque: University of New Mexico, 1974.

Pomeroy, Earl S. *The Territories and the United States, 1861-1890*. Seattle: University of Washington Press, 1969.

Richardson, Albert D. *Beyond the Mississippi*. Hartford, Ct.: American Publisher, 1869.

Robinson, Louis N. *Should Prisoners Work?* Chicago: Winston Penn Company, 1931.

Rothman, David J. *The Discovery of the Asylum, Social Order and Disorder in the New Republic*. Boston: Little, Brown and Company, 1971.

Rusche, Georg and Kirchheimer, Otto. Punishment and Social Structure. New York: Russell and Russell, 1967.

Selected Literary and Political Papers and Addresses of Woodrow Wilson, 3 vols. New York: Grosset and Dunlap, 1921.

Shinn, Charles Howard, edited by Rodman Paul. *Mining Camps, a Study in American Frontier Government*. New York: Harper and Row, 1965.

Smiley, Jerome C. *Semi-Centennial History of the State of Colorado*. Chicago: Lewis Publishing Company, 1913.

Smith, Joan and Fried, William. *The Uses of the American Prison*. Lexington, Mass.: D.C. Heath, 1974.

Starr, Henry. *Thrilling Events*. reprint ed. College Station, Texas: Creative Publishing Company, 1982.

Stone, Wilbur F. ed. *History of Colorado* 4 vols. Denver:S.J.Clarke, 1918.

Sutherland, Edwin H., and Cressey Donald R. *Criminology*. Santa Barbara: University of California, 1966.

Walker, Donald R. *Penology for Profit, A History of the Texas Prison System, 1867-1912*. Lubbock, Texas: Texas A &M, 1987.

Walker, Samuel. *Popular Justice, A History of American Criminal Justice*. New York: Oxford University Press,1980.

ARTICLES IN JOURNALS AND MAGAZINES

Anderson, George L. The Cañon City or Arkansas Valley Claim Club,1860-62." *Colorado Magazine* 16, Nov.,1939, pp. 201-210.

Bennett, James V. "Prison Labor at the Crossroads." *Proceedings of the American Prison Association* (1934): pp. 245-9.

Chapman, Arthur. "A Colorado Prison Reformer: Tynan and His Convict Boys." *Harper's Weekly* 57, August 2, 1913, pp. 15-21.

Davis, David. "Movement to Abolish Capital Punishment." *American Historical Review* LXIII (October, 1957): 26-46.

Frey, John P. "Trade Union Attitude toward Labor." *Annals of the American Academy of Political and Social Science* 46 (March, 1913): pp. 136-40.

Gemmill, William. "Employment and Compensation of Prisoners" *Journal of Crime, Laws and Criminology* 6 (June, 1916): pp. 510-21.

Gill, Howard B. "The Prison Labor Problem." *Annals of the American Academy of Political and Social Science* CLVII. (September, 1931): pp.90-98.

Gompers, Samuel. "Convict Prison Labor." *American Federationist* 28, 1921, pp. 497-500.

Hiller, E.T. "Convict Labor." *Journal of Criminal Law and Criminology* 5 (July, 1914): pp. 241-269.

Hirsch, Adam J. "From Pillory to Penitentiary." *Michigan Law Review* 80. mimeographed and no date. pp. 80-1265.

Marshall, Thomas M. "Miner's Laws." *American Historical Review* 25 (April, 1920):428-439.

Murphy, Allen. "Penitentiary-Made Goods," *Colorado Manufacturer and Consumer*, February, 1927, pp. 10-11.

O'Hare, Kate R. "The World Tomorrow," *Nation* 8, May, 1925, pp. 37-8.

Perrigo, Lynn I. "Law and Order in Early Mining Camps. "*Mississippi Historical Review* 28 (June, 1941): 41-61.

Shafroth, John J. "Roads and Pavements." *American City*, September, 1911, pp. 221-24.

Tynan, Thomas J. "Prison Labor on Public Roads." *Prison Labor, American Academy of Political and Social Science* (1913): pp. 58-61.

Whitin, E. Stage. "Making Roads through Prison Labor." *The Review*, February, 1911, pp. 9-17.

Wilmot, Sydney. "Uses of Convict Labor for Highway Construction in the North." *Proceedings of the Academy of Political Science in the City of New York*IV (1913-14): pp.245-256.

INTERVIEWS

Booth, Hank. Cañon City, 1987.
Fisher, Cara, Cañon City, 1989.
MacDonough, Elizabeth, Colorado Springs, 5 March 1990.
McGoff, Mark. Colorado Springs, 3 November 1989
Patterson, Wayne. Cañon City, 1987, 1989, 3 March 1990.
Rey, John, Colorado Springs, 29 March 1990.
Wells, Rocky, Denver, 10 December 1989.
Wilson, Alex. Colorado Springs, 3 March 1988.

NEWSPAPERS

Cañon City Times, 1860-61.
Cañon City Clipper, 1887-89.
Cañon City Daily Record, 1883-1900 and 1921-1940.
Denver Daily Times, 1998-99.
Fremont County Record, 1894.
Rocky Mountain News, 1868-1940.
Denver Post, scattered from 1900-1940.